William Butler Yeats

Twayne's English Authors Series

Kinley E. Roby, Editor
Northeastern University

TEAS 328

WILLIAM BUTLER YEATS
(1865–1939)
Printed with the permission of
Morris Library, Southern Illinois
University at Carbondale

William Butler Yeats

By Richard F. Peterson

Southern Illinois University

Twayne Publishers • Boston

William Butler Yeats

Richard F. Peterson

Copyright © 1982
Twayne Publishers
A Division of G. K. Hall & Company
70 Lincoln Street
Boston, Massachusetts 02111

Printed on permanent/durable
acid-free paper and bound in
The United States of America.

Library of Congress Cataloging in
Publication Data

Peterson, Richard F.
    William Butler Yeats.

    (Twayne's English authors
series; TEAS 328)
    Bibliography: pp. 219–21
    Includes index.
    1. Yeats, W. B. (William
Butler), 1865–1939—
Criticism and interpretation.
I. Title. II. Series.
PR5907.P47   821'.8   81-7025
ISBN 0-8057-6815-7   AACR2

For Anne, Amy, and Stephen

Contents

About the Author

Richard F. Peterson is a professor of English at Southern Illinois University at Carbondale. He is the author of *Mary Lavin*, published for Twayne's English Authors Series in 1978. His writings on modern Irish writers, including Joyce, Yeats, and O'Casey, have appeared in *Modern Fiction Studies, Studies in Short Fiction,* the *James Joyce Quarterly, Eire-Ireland, The Journal of Irish Literature,* and *The Sean O'Casey Review.* He has given papers on Irish subjects at the International James Joyce Symposium, the Sean O'Casey Festival, and the Modern Language Association conference.

Professor Peterson has taught at Southern Illinois University since 1969. He has been recognized for his teaching excellence on several occasions by the Department of English and the College of Liberal Arts. In 1978, he received the Amoco Outstanding Teaching Award, the university's most prestigious teaching honor.

Preface

No introductory study needs to argue for the greatness of William Butler Yeats. His reputation as a master of the dramatic lyric is now clearly established. Today, many scholars, teachers, and common readers regard Yeats as the most important poet of the modern age, though he often seems a far less representative figure than Ezra Pound and T. S. Eliot. His choice of a visionary art places him more in the tradition of Dante, Milton, and Blake, while his poetic gift, his capacity to respond imaginatively to the emotional and intellectual rhythms of life, rivals that of Spenser, Shakespeare, and Keats.

The following study traces Yeats's development through the major phases of his life and career—his early search for dreaming wisdom, his difficult transition to a more vigorous and responsible poetry, his mature vision of the power of art and the imagination, and his final rage against old age and death. In each chapter, the individual poems, plays, and collections are discussed as a part of Yeats's deliberate effort to create a dramatic pattern out of the contraries that generate life. Throughout his career, Yeats wrote, revised, and arranged his poetry to create the impression of the artist moving inevitably toward a vision of reality. For Yeats, the poet stood at the center of the universe, and his search for symbol-making power and authority was the central drama of life and the essential subject matter of great art.

The study also attempts to represent the many critical views of Yeats that have developed over the years. The critical discussion of Yeats since his death in 1939 has been impressive and, since the centennial celebration in 1965 of Yeats's birth, almost overwhelming. The claims for Yeats's genius have greatly varied and generated their own conflicts and controversies both as to the nature of Yeats's talent and the meaning of individual poems, plays, and collections, but a tremendous amount of sensible and imaginative criticism has been done to identify the major themes and patterns of Yeats's art and the major influences on his career. Much of the basic work on Yeats's biography, his manuscripts and revisions, his aesthetics, his interest in myth, magic, politics, and philosophy, and his passion for life and art, has been summarized and commented upon in this study so that the reader will gain an introduction to both Yeats and his critics.

Years ago, while in graduate school, I was asked by a distinguished Joyce scholar to name the eponymous figure of the modern age. After looking up the word and discovering that it meant the figure who gives his name to an age, I avoided the obvious answer and selected William Butler Yeats. After writing this book, I realize that I am no wiser than I was over a decade ago. I still believe Yeats is the eponymous figure for modern literature, and my faith is even stronger after testing it in this study.

RICHARD F. PETERSON
Southern Illinois University

Acknowledgments

The selections in this book from "The Wanderings of Oisin," "The Song of the Happy Shepherd," "The Stolen Child," "The Lake Isle of Innisfree," "Who Goes with Fergus?," "He Hears the Cry of the Sedge," "He Thinks of His Past Greatness . . . ," "The Secret Rose," "He Wishes for the Cloths of Heaven," "He Tells of the Perfect Beauty," "Never Give All the Heart," and "To Ireland in the Coming Times" are reprinted with permission of Macmillan Publishing Co., Inc., from *Collected Poems* by William Butler Yeats, copyright 1906 by Macmillan Publishing Co., Inc., renewed 1934 by William Butler Yeats.

Selections from "Upon a House Shaken by Land Agitation," "No Second Troy," "The Mask," "King and No King," "All Things Can Tempt Me," and "The Cold Heaven" are reprinted with permission of Macmillan Publishing Co., Inc., from *Collected Poems* by William Butler Yeats, copyright 1912 by Macmillan Publishing Co., Inc., renewed 1940 by Bertha Georgie Yeats.

Selections from "September 1913," "To a Friend Whose Work Has Come to Nothing," "The Realists," and "Two Years Later" are reprinted with permission of Macmillan Publishing Co., Inc., from *Collected Poems* by William Butler Yeats, copyright 1916 by Macmillan Publishing Co., Inc., renewed 1944 by Bertha Georgie Yeats.

Selections from "Ego Dominus Tuus" are reprinted with permission of Macmillan Publishing Co., Inc., from *Collected Poems* by William Butler Yeats, copyright 1918 by Macmillan Publishing Co., renewed 1946 by Bertha Georgie Yeats.

Selections from "The Wild Swans at Coole," "In Memory of Major Robert Gregory," "Men Improve with the Years," and "The Phases of the Moon" are reprinted with permission of Macmillan Publishing Co., Inc., from *Collected Poems* by William Butler

Acknowledgments

from *Essays and Introductions* by William Butler Yeats (copyright Mrs. W. B. Yeats, 1961), *Explorations* by William Butler Yeats (copyright Mrs. W. B. Yeats, 1962), *Mythologies* by William Butler Yeats (copyright Mrs. W. B. Yeats, 1959), *The Variorum Edition of the Plays of W. B. Yeats*, edited by Russell K. Alspach (copyright Russell K. Alspach and Bertha Georgie Yeats, 1966; copyright Macmillan & Co., Ltd. 1965), and *The Letters of W. B. Yeats*, edited by Allan Wade (copyright 1953, 1954 by Anne Butler Yeats).

A. P. Watt, Ltd. has granted permission for the reprinted material from *Autobiographies* by William Butler Yeats (London: Macmillan, 1955), *Collected Plays* by William Butler Yeats (London: Macmillan, 1952), *A Vision* by William Butler Yeats (London: Macmillan, 1962), and *Memoirs*, transcribed and edited by Denis Donoghue (London: Macmillan, 1972).

I am grateful to many Yeats scholars—Richard Ellmann, T. R. Henn, Thomas Parkinson, and others—who have done so much to clarify Yeats's life, thought, and work, but I owe a special debt to Richard F. Finneran for his help and encouragement. I also want to thank my colleagues in the Department of English at Southern Illinois University—Manuel Schonhorn and David Vieth for their informative discussions of the eighteenth century and James Benziger for allowing me to study his unpublished writing on Blake's contraries—and Alan Cohn, the Humanities Librarian, for his constant assistance in locating material essential for this study. My special gratitude goes to the distinguished scholar of modern literature, Harry T. Moore, who recommended me to the editors of the Twayne Series and generously provided support for my work. I also wish to express my thanks to Pauline Duke—for her dedicated work in preparing the manuscript.

Chronology

1865   Yeats born June 13 at 5 Sandymount Avenue, Dublin. In the next several years, the Yeats family moves back and forth between Ireland and England.

1877   After a few years of private schooling by his father, Yeats is sent to Godolphin School, Hammersmith, England for his first formal education.

1881–   Yeats family moves from Bedford Park to Howth, just north
1882   of Dublin. Yeats enrolls at Erasmus Smith High School, Dublin.

1885   Yeats and a group of friends form the Dublin Hermetic Society. Attends meetings at the Contemporary Club, where he meets John O'Leary. First poems published in *Dublin University Review*.

1887   After Yeats's family returns to London, mother suffers a stroke. Yeats meets Madame Blavatsky and joins her London lodge of the Theosophical Society by the following year.

1888   Increases his activity as poet and literary editor, critic, and reviewer.

1889   January 30, meets and falls in love with Maud Gonne. *The Wanderings of Oisin and Other Poems* is published. Begins collaboration with Edwin Ellis on a study of Blake.

1890   March 7, initiated into the Order of the Golden Dawn. Resigns under pressure from the Theosophical Society later in the year. Yeats and Ernest Rhys form the Rhymers' Club in London.

1891   Makes first of several proposals of marriage to Maud Gonne and is refused. *John Sherman and Dhoya.* Plans are formed for an Irish Literary Society in London.

1892   With O'Leary's help, forms the National Literary Society in Dublin, but he is soon caught up in a futile struggle with

Gavan Duffy for leadership. *The Countess Kathleen and Various Legends and Lyrics.*

1893 *The Celtic Twilight* and the three volume *The Works of William Blake.*

1894 Meets Olivia Shakespear. *The Land of Heart's Desire* is performed in London. Yeats makes his first trip to Paris and sees *Axel* with Maud Gonne.

1895 *Poems.*

1896 Moves to Woburn Buildings and begins a brief affair with Olivia Shakespear. Travels with Arthur Symons to the West of Ireland, where he meets Lady Gregory. Forms plans for a Castle of the Heroes and meets John Synge at the end of the year.

1897 Spends first summer at Coole Park. *The Secret Rose.*

1898 Takes an active role in Wolfe Tone centennial. Meets with Lady Gregory and Edward Martyn to form an Irish Literary Theatre.

1899 May 8, *The Countess Cathleen* is performed with Martyn's *The Heather Field* in the Antient Concert Rooms, Dublin. *The Wind Among the Reeds.*

1900 Death of Yeats's mother. *The Shadowy Waters.*

1903 Devastated by Maud Gonne's marriage to John MacBride, Yeats travels to America for a successful lecture tour. *In the Seven Woods* is published as the first book of Dun Emer Press.

1904 December 27, the Abbey opens with *On Baile's Strand, Cathleen Ni Houlihan* and Lady Gregory's *Spreading the News.*

1906 *Poems.* The Abbey performs Yeats's *Deirdre.*

1907 Defends Synge's *The Playboy of the Western World* after Abbey riots. Tours Northern Italy with Lady Gregory and her son Robert. Death of O'Leary. Yeats's father leaves for America.

1908 Eight volumes of *Collected Works.*

1909 Death of Synge. First meeting with Ezra Pound.

1910 Annie Horniman withdraws financial support from Abbey.

Receives annual grant of 150 pounds from English Civil List. Death of George Pollexfen. *The Green Helmet and Other Poems.*

1911 Meets Georgie Hyde-Lees for the first time.

1913 Yeats and Pound spend first of three successive winters together at Stone Cottage, Sussex.

1914 Travels with Maud Gonne to Mirabeau, France, to investigate reports of a bleeding oleograph of Christ. *Responsibilities.*

1915 Death of Hugh Lane on the *Lusitania.* His collection of impressionist paintings, intended for Dublin, remains in London.

1916 April 24, Easter Rising, less than three weeks after private performance of *At the Hawk's Well* in London. Writes "Easter 1916" and, later in the year, purchases Ballylee, a ruined Norman tower in the West of Ireland.

1917 Proposes to Georgie Hyde-Lees after being rejected by Maud Gonne and her daughter Iseult. She accepts and the marriage takes place in London on October 20.

1918 Yeats and his wife supervise restoration of Ballylee. *Per Amica Silentia Lunae.*

1919 February 26, Anne Butler Yeats born. Expanded edition of *The Wild Swans at Coole.*

1920 Yeats and his wife travel to America for lecture tour.

1921 August 22, Michael Butler Yeats born. *Michael Robartes and the Dancer* and *Four Plays for Dancers.*

1922 Beginning of Irish civil war. Death of Yeats's father. Yeats buys house at 82 Merrion Square, Dublin. Becomes member of Irish Senate at the end of the year.

1923 Named winner of the Nobel Prize in literature at year's end.

1924– After periodical bouts of poor health, Yeats travels with his
1925 wife to the Mediterranean.

1926 The first edition of *A Vision*, dated 1925, appears in January. *The Plough and the Stars* causes riots at the Abbey.

1927 Becomes seriously ill during stay in Seville.

1928 Poor health continues. Yeats family moves to flat at 42

Fitzwilliam Square. Yeats ends his Senate term and travels to Rapallo at the end of the year. *The Tower*.

1929   Spends last summer at Thoor Ballylee. Suffers another relapse and returns to Rapallo where his illness is diagnosed as Malta fever.

1930   November, *The Words Upon the Window-Pane* performed at Abbey.

1931   Receives honorary degree from Oxford. Spends much of year at Coole Park.

1932   Death of Lady Gregory. Yeats family moves to Riversdale in Rathfarnham. After inauguration of Irish Academy of Letters, Yeats leaves for last American tour.

1933   Becomes briefly infatuated with O'Duffy's Blue Shirts. *The Winding Stair*.

1934   Undergoes Steinach operation for sexual rejuvenation. *Wheels and Butterflies*.

1935   July, death of George Russell. Travels to Majorca at end of year to help Shri Purohit Swami with translation of *Upanishads*. *A Full Moon in March*.

1936   Seriously ill again, Yeats travels again to Majorca but leaves in June after Margot Ruddock scandal and stays with Dorothy Wellesley in England before returning to Dublin.

1937   Second edition of *A Vision*. Writes essay for *On the Boiler* and does four poetry programs for BBC.

1938   Death of Olivia Shakespear. *Purgatory* performed at the Abbey. *New Poems*. By December Yeats and his wife are at Cape Martin.

1939   Health worsens. After a period of pain and breathlessness, Yeats dies on January 28. Buried at Roquebrune.

1948   Yeats's body is brought back to Ireland and buried in the ancestral churchyard at Drumcliff.

Chapter One

From Sligo to Byzantium: A Poet's Life

In "The Choice," a poem originally written as the penultimate stanza of "Coole Park and Ballylee, 1931," William Butler Yeats wrote: "The intellect of man is forced to choose/Perfection of the life, or of the work."[1] Having made the latter choice, Yeats believed that he had spent his life, as it advanced through the difficult stages of youth, ambition, maturity, and old age, perfecting his art. The poet seeking fulfillment in his life was like a fly struggling in marmalade; the poet seeking perfection in his verse hoped to create an image that was to be a vision of his life.

While keeping faith throughout his lifetime in the idea of the visionary power of art, Yeats did not escape, though he tried in his youth, the realization that the poet's blind, stupified heart and tattered coat of experience gave him the materials for his poetry, and that in verse-making the poet discovered the patterns of his emotions and created a form for his life. When his friends complained about Yeats's continual and sometimes drastic revisions of his poems, a practice that Sean O'Faolain called a kind of forgery, Yeats responded by writing:

> The friends that have it I do wrong
> When ever I remake a song,
> Should know what issue is at stake:
> It is myself that I remake.[2]

The last line, like the Byzantium poems, clearly expresses the supremacy of art, but it also reveals that the poet's journey to By-

19

zantium, the holy city of imagination, is made "Astraddle on the dolphin's mire and blood."

Country of the Young

William Butler Yeats was born on Tuesday, June 13, 1865, at Georgeville, a small house at 5 Sandymount Avenue, Dublin. Yeats's father, John Butler Yeats, had been a law student at the King's Inn since 1862 and was elected to the prestigious position of auditor of the Debating Society shortly before the birth of his first child. His career in law appeared destined for great success, and the strong health of his son, after his wife Susan had nearly died of diphtheria during their honeymoon, seemed a good omen for the future welfare of the Yeats family.

The marriage between John Butler Yeats of Dublin and Susan Pollexfen of Sligo on September 10, 1863, had brought together a number of diverse and even opposed qualities of personality and family background. The Yeats family had distinguished ties with the Anglo-Irish Ascendancy. Mary Butler Yeats, the poet's great-great-grandmother, was a direct descendant of the Ormonde Butlers, a family of great wealth and tradition, even though she married Benjamin Yeats, a Dublin wholesale dealer in linens. The poet's great-grandmother, Jane Taylor Yeats, was connected by family with the Castle Ascendancy, while his grandmother, Jane Grace Corbet Yeats, was a descendant of John Armstrong, one of Marlborough's generals. John Butler Yeats's decision to study law had actually broken with another tradition of the Yeats family. His father, William Butler Yeats, was rector of the Church of Ireland and held a curacy in the parish of Tullyish, County Down. His father's father, John Butler Yeats, had been the parson of Drumcliff parish in County Sligo. Indeed, when the Pollexfens attended Susan's wedding, they could feel proud that she was marrying "an authentic Irish landlord, a descendant of the Ormonde Butlers, of respected Irish clergymen, and men of power in the Castle, who was moreover a rising star in the King's Inn and well connected throughout Dublin."[3]

The Pollexfens, a respected Cornish and Devonshire family, had become Sligo people through marriage with the Middletons, a shipowner and merchant family. William Pollexfen, a lover of ships and the sea, had visited his cousin Elizabeth, the widow of William Middleton, and stayed on in Sligo to merge his business interests with the Middletons and eventually to marry Elizabeth's daughter. Susan Pollexfen Yeats was William Pollexfen's eldest daughter and inherited his emotional, brooding nature, his contempt for intellectual matters, and his firm Protestant belief in getting on in the world. Her marriage, in spite of its promising future at the time of William Butler Yeats's birth, was to bring her great unhappiness and sorrow, but it at least gave to her first son a broad, diverse, and impressive heritage, "a mixture of Anglo-Irish old and new, of Cornish and Devon gentry, smugglers, sea-captains, merchants, Castle officials, clergymen, soldiers."[4]

While writing "Reveries over Childhood and Youth," Yeats discovered, as he approached his fiftieth year, that his memories of his early life were fragmentary, isolated, yet curiously contemporaneous. Images of an Irish window and a wall covered with cracked or falling plaster, a London window at Fitzroy Road, a mastless toy boat at Sligo were still as real as the unreasonable misery remembered from his childhood. Yeats's explanation for his early unhappiness was his loneliness, an outcome of his natural shyness and awkwardness, and his fear of the imposing figure of his grandfather, William Pollexfen. Yet his early confusion and melancholy were also reflected in the images from Dublin, London, and Sligo summoned forth at the beginning of Yeats's planned autobiography.

Yeats's childhood misery had as much to do with his father's imposing personality and sporadic career as any inner turmoil or harsh encounter with his brooding grandfather. Admitted to the bar in January, 1866, John Butler Yeats could not adjust to the legal profession and by July, 1867, had set up a residence at 23 Fitzroy Road in London to pursue a career in art. The immediate effect of his decision was to force the family to leave Ireland for an uncertain period of time. Once it became clear, however, that life with father as a struggling artist meant relying on the dwin-

dling rent money from property owned by John Butler Yeats and
occasional loans from relatives, the family had to shift between
residences in London and Dublin and extended holiday visits to
Merville, the big eighteenth-century country house of the Pollexfens in Sligo.

In July, 1872, after a period of emotional anxiety and financial
uncertainty, Susan Yeats and the children left Fitzroy Road to
spend the next two years at Merville,[5] while John Butler Yeats
tried to establish himself in London as a professional artist. During
this period, Willie, as he was called by his family, fearful of his
serious-minded uncles and aunts, found some comfort and excitement by listening to the fairy stories told by family servants and
exploring the legendary landscape of Sligo with its mysterious
burial mounds and dolmens on Knocknarea and Ben Bulben. In
the midst of his family's shifting fortunes and residences, Willie
turned to Sligo, associated in his mind with romance, superstition,
and magic, as an emotional and spiritual touchstone.

Yeats's first impressions of his father in "Reveries over Childhood and Youth" are associated with his memories of his early
education. When John Butler Yeats returned to Sligo only to hear
the sing-song rhyme his eldest child had been taught during his
first day at dame school, he quickly decided to take Willie's education, including the task of teaching him to read, into his own
hands. Though the lessons did not go well, Yeats's father now became the dominant intellectual influence on his life, and, even
through periods of emotional and spiritual rebellion, would remain
so throughout the poet's youth and young manhood. When the
Yeats family returned to London in October, 1874, to live at 14
Edith Villas, West Kensington (North End at the time), John
Butler Yeats, while struggling with his own life and career, continued his private schooling of Willie by alternately humiliating his
son during the day and rewarding him in the evening with readings
from Chaucer, Shakespeare, and Scott. In early 1877, Willie finally
was sent off for his first formal education at the Godolphin School
on Iffley Road in Hammersmith, an experience that increased his

feelings of loneliness and longing for Sligo and reinforced his developing nervousness and shyness. Immediately sensing his difference in temperament, he also became aware that he was an Irish lad in a school of English boys proud of their heritage of Cressy and Agincourt.

Willie's record at school was disappointing even by modest standards. He did well in the classics but was ranked in the bottom half of his class in modern languages, English, and mathematics. His conduct was good, according to the master's report, but the school itself was "an obscene, bullying place."[6] While Willie was enduring the indignities of the Godolphin School, the family's spirits were lifted by a move in the spring of 1879 to 8 Woodstock Road in Bedford Park, a place intended for painters, writers, and others associated with the arts. They now lived "in a house like those they had seen in pictures and even met people dressed like people in the story-books."[7] Romantic excitement had reentered Willie's life, and even his fortunes at Godolphin improved when the headmaster began to emphasize science in the curriculum.

Unfortunately, John Butler Yeats's financial problems were mounting and by the end of 1881 he had to move his family to Balscadden Cottage in Howth, just north of Dublin, while he rented a Dublin studio near Stephen's Green. Six months later the family moved again to Island View in Howth where they stayed for the next two years. Following his father's instructions, Willie enrolled himself at Erasmus Smith High School on Harcourt Street. Though he encountered no bullying, he discovered that there was little activity at school beyond his classroom work. While still fascinated by natural history, he struggled through his studies, which were constantly disrupted by his father, and soon developed a reputation as a queer and erratic student. To his classmates, he seemed aloof and even mildly repellent in his manners and speech.

In the summer and fall of 1882, William Butler Yeats's childhood fantasies and his schoolboy interest in Darwin and Huxley gave way to sexual awakening, first love, and poetry. The awakening of sex, the "great event of a boy's life," came upon Yeats like "the bursting of a shell."[8] Though he still carried his specimen net with him as he explored the ground of Howth Castle, Yeats, tortured by his guilt-ridden sexual desires and the vividness of his dreams, now began "to play at being a sage, a magician or a poet."[9] In his imaginings, he became Manfred, Prince Athanase, and Alastor; and when he thought of women, he transformed them into the creations of his favorite poets.

While dreaming of becoming the solitary hero of romance, Yeats met a distant cousin Laura Armstrong. Given to periods of emotional instability, she was three years older than Cousin Willie, but he quickly fell in love. Though she was engaged to a solicitor, Yeats flirted with her through letters in which she took the name "Vivien" to his "Clarin." The relationship ended when Laura Armstrong married her solicitor in September, 1884, but before it had Yeats had written his first poetry and plays, "Time and the Witch Vivien" and "The Island of Statues," both of which have egotistical and reckless heroines.

In early 1884, the Yeats family moved again from Howth, which was dearly loved by Susan Yeats, to a flat at 10 Ashfield Terrace in Terenure, south of Dublin. Now finished with high school, Yeats, unwilling and, considering his academic shortcomings, probably unable to continue the family tradition at Trinity, enrolled at the Metropolitan School of Art, where he stayed from May, 1884, to April, 1886. At art school, he met George Russell, later to take the name AE, and discovered that his new friend shared and encouraged his belief in magic, dreams, and visions. On June 16, 1885, Yeats and a group of friends that included Russell and Charles Johnston formed the Dublin Hermetic Society for the study of European magic and Eastern philosophy. Under the influence of A. P. Sinnett's *The Occult World* and *Esoteric Buddhism* and the teachings of the Brahmin Mohini Chatterjee, Yeats turned to theosophy, while proposing to the Hermetic Society that "whatever the great poets had affirmed in their finest moments was the nearest we could come to an authoritative religion, and that their mythology, their spirits of water and wind, were but literal truth."[10]

In 1885, Yeats also took his first step into Irish politics by attending the Dublin meetings of Charles Hubert Oldham's Contemporary Club. There he met the Fenian leader John O'Leary, who had just returned to Ireland after spending five years in an English prison and fifteen in political exile. From his Contemporary Club debates with the great orator John F. Taylor and from O'Leary's conversations and books, Yeats found new confidence in himself and new materials for his art. He especially admired O'Leary's condemnation of senseless violence and his belief in the importance of Irish culture and the need to free it from English influence. It was also through his association with the Contemporary Club that Yeats, approaching the age of twenty, became a published poet. Yeats submitted two poems, "Song of the Faeries" and "Voices" (later called "The Cloak, the Boat and the Shoes"), to the *Dublin University Review*, a journal recently started by Oldham and his friends, and had them accepted for the March, 1885, number. Yeats's poetry, including the verse plays "The Island of Statues" and "Mosada," also appeared in five other numbers of the *Dublin University Review* in 1885 and in seven more in 1886.

Oldham was also responsible for introducing Yeats to Katharine Tynan, a young woman already with a reputation as a poet. Yeats wrote to her frequently over the next several years, mostly about his personal and physical woes and his various literary projects, but he never seemed quite sure about his feelings toward her. He was pleased, however, to have her encouragement along with the support of O'Leary and even of Edward Dowden, the Trinity professor and friend of John Butler Yeats. Through O'Leary's help, he also began to write for *The Boston Pilot*, a Catholic weekly, and *The Providence Sunday Journal* on a variety of Irish subjects and writers. By the end of 1886, Yeats felt confident enough to write reviews in Irish journals that attacked Dowden's conservative critical views, which Yeats believed had belittled Irish writers in the name of English literature. In a review of Samuel Ferguson's poetry, he proclaimed his own belief in an Irish literature that reflected a "world of selfless passion in which heroic deeds are possible and heroic poetry credible."[11]

Cathleen Ni Houlihan

Yeats gave the years from 1887 to 1891 a special significance in his autobiographical writings. "Four Years" begins with the family's return to London in 1887 after spending the last five and a half years in Ireland. They first lived in a small house at 58 Eardley Crescent in South Kensington, where Susan Yeats, dispirited by the move, suffered a stroke. After his wife's second stroke, John Butler Yeats moved the family in early 1888 to Bedford Park again, this time at 3 Blenheim Road. It was to be the last home for Susan Yeats, who remained an invalid until her death in 1900.

William Butler Yeats wanted to help the family by finding some steady work in journalism. When his father discouraged him, he wrote the fantastical short story *Dhoya* and the autobiographical novella *John Sherman*, both eventually published in 1891. Yeats also reviewed a number of Irish books during this period and edited some Irish books of his own, including *Fairy and Folk Tales of the Irish Peasantry*, published in 1888, and *Representative Irish Tales*, which appeared in 1891. With the help of O'Leary, he found enough subscribers for an edition of his own poems, published as *The Wanderings of Oisin and Other Poems* in 1889. As he attracted some attention as a poet, Yeats also met several key literary figures in London, including Oscar Wilde, George Bernard Shaw, William Morris, and W. E. Henley. While not agreeing with Morris's socialism, Yeats attended the Sunday evening meetings at Kelmscott House because he liked Morris's spontaneity. He also published poems for several years in Henley's *Scots Observer*, eventually to become the *National Observer*, even though he could not agree with Henley's imperialist politics.

At the beginning of 1889, while struggling through the first steps of a literary career, Yeats also began the greatest emotional adventure of his life. In the early 1880s, he thought himself in love with Laura Armstrong and later, probably in 1888, had half-heartedly proposed to Katharine Tynan and been turned down. On January 30, 1889, however, Yeats finally met and fell in love with the woman whose physical presence corresponded to his vision of the highest beauty. On that fateful day, Maud Gonne, armed with an introduction from O'Leary, arrived at Bedford Park ostensibly to meet John Butler Yeats, but her eye was for the young poet. Some twenty years after that first meeting, Yeats wrote that Maud Gonne's entry into his life was like the sounding of a Burmese gong: "I had never thought to see in a living woman so great beauty. It belonged to famous pictures, to poetry, to some legendary past."[12]

The years of the great emotional troubling in Yeats's life ran parallel with the period of turbulent and tragic political actions in Ireland. The distinguished Irish patriot John O'Leary had arranged Maud Gonne's first meeting with Yeats, and the Irish struggle for freedom from English rule provided the common drama, the shared vision, and often the source of conflict between Ireland's most beautiful woman and the young man destined to become Ireland's greatest poet. By 1889, Yeats, believing in the idea of Unity of Culture for Ireland, had already argued against nationalists eager to exploit Irish art for the sake of political propaganda. Maud Gonne, however, did not entirely share Yeats's enthusiasm for Gaelic Revivals or Celtic Twilights. She had embraced Irish nationalism and political activism in the same year Yeats attended his first meetings at the Contemporary Club. Already successful in her work in the West of Ireland for the Land League, Maud Gonne in 1889 was looking for "some memorable action for final consummation of her youth."[13]

Yeats quickly intensified his public efforts for cultural unity in the wild hope that he could win Maud Gonne's heart through heroic action. Ignoring the warnings of O'Leary and others, he began a variety of cultural projects for the sake of his beloved. Yeats's first step, however, was to write an Irish play that Maud Gonne could act in Dublin. By 1891, he read to her an unfinished draft of *The Countess Cathleen*, the play that he saw as the symbol song of her burdened life. In the summer of the same year, Yeats became so upset by her unexplained spells of unhappiness that he made the first of several proposals of marriage. What Yeats did not know, however, was that marriage was impossible because of Maud Gonne's secret life in Paris, where, since 1887, she had been the mistress of Lucien Millevoye, an ardent Boulangist, and, in early 1891, had given birth to her first child. Later in the year after rejecting the proposal, she wrote to Yeats from Paris about her "adopted" child Georges, who was now near death. When she returned to Ireland on October 11, 1891, she carried her own private grief because of her child's death, while coincidentally attending Ireland's public shame and sorrow—on the same mailboat bringing her back to Dublin was the coffin bearing the body of the fallen Irish leader Charles Stewart Parnell.

While writing the lyrics of frustrated love that were collected in 1892 for *The Countess Kathleen and Various Legends and Lyrics*, Yeats turned to the idea of literary societies in the hope of further attracting Maud Gonne's attention and approval. In the last week of December, 1891, Yeats and T. W. Rolleston formed the plans for an Irish Literary Society in London to publicize the idea of Irish culture. In May, 1892, Yeats, with the strong support of O'Leary, founded the National Literary Society in Dublin to attract those who had become disenchanted with Irish politics since the defeat and death of Parnell. Yeats planned to convince various factions and key personalities that politically divided Dublin could become the intellectual capital of Ireland, while sending Maud Gonne about the Irish countryside to form new branches of the society.

The Irish Literary Society and the National Literary Society, the latter instrumental in the founding of Douglas Hyde's Gaelic League, were not Yeats's first ventures into literary clubs or organizations. In early 1890, he and Ernest Rhys were mainly responsible for forming the Rhymers' Club in London. The group, which included at one time such accomplished poets as Lionel Johnson, Yeats's closest friend and adviser among the Rhymers, Arthur Symons, and Ernest Dowson, met at the Cheshire Cheese to read and discuss each other's verse. Though his association with the Rhymers appealed to his youthful aestheticism and drew him to Blake, Rossetti, and Pater, Yeats now was seeking an Irish voice for his poetry. By late 1891, the Irish Literary Society was meeting in the quarters of the Rhymers' Club, which Yeats believed all along should be dominated by the Celtic vision.

While Yeats hoped to win Maud Gonne's heart through his cultural projects, he also dreamed of capturing her soul through his occult arts. Shortly after his family's return to London, Yeats met Madame Blavatsky and by 1888 had joined the Theosophical Society's Esoteric Section, an inner circle dedicated to the study of magic. While Yeats resigned from the Society in late 1890 because he had written an article critical of *Lucifer*, its official organ, he had been initiated earlier in the year on March 7, 1890, into the Isis-Urania Temple of the Order of the Golden Dawn, a secret society organized by MacGregor Mathers and William Wynn Westcott for the study of speculative and practical theurgy. On November 16, 1891, Yeats, who took the name of Demon Est Deus Inversus for the Order, could well have believed that his dream of perfect love was nearly at hand when Maud Gonne was also initiated into the Golden Dawn.

Whatever Yeats might have dreamed for Maud Gonne and Ireland, he soon suffered a major disappointment that, coupled with his serious eye trouble, nervous exhaustion, continuing money woes, and sexual frustration, caused a great deal of bitterness in his life. His troubles began in 1892 when he decided to battle Rolleston and Charles Gavan Duffy, one of the founders of the *Nation* in 1842, for the leadership of the National Literary Society. The object of contention was a projected series of Irish books to be published and circulated among Young Ireland societies. Though Yeats originated the idea, Duffy took control of the project and insisted, according to Yeats, on the publication of "works of political associates or of friends long dead."[14] Though Yeats worked out a compromise to insure the publication of the work of Douglas Hyde and Standish O'Grady, his attacks on the patriot Duffy, a symbol in Yeats's mind of the political exploitation of Irish literature, polarized his position and alienated him from several influential nationalistic leaders.

Yeats did have better success publishing some of his own work.

The Celtic Twilight, a collection of commentaries and stories about Irish folklore, appeared in 1893, as did *The Works of William Blake*, which marked the completion of an elaborate study Yeats had undertaken in collaboration with his father's friend Edwin Ellis in 1889. In February, 1894, Yeats, encouraged by his publications, made his first trip to Paris, where he stayed with Mathers and his wife, the sister of Henri Bergson. Arthur Symons, who had urged Yeats to make the trip, joined him after a few days and took him to see the symbolist poet Verlaine. Yeats also saw a production of Villiers de L'Isle Adam's *Axel* with Maud Gonne, and before leaving he proposed to her only to be rejected again.

Maud Gonne's refusal notwithstanding, Yeats's relationship with women dramatically changed in the next few years. In London, Florence Farr, a close friend of Yeats since 1890, had persuaded a wealthy Englishwoman named Annie Horniman to subsidize a season of plays, which began in late March, 1894, with Yeats's *The Land of Heart's Desire* and John Todhunter's *A Comedy of Sighs*, the latter replaced, after a few performances, by Shaw's *Arms and the Man*. Yeats had originally written his play with Florence Farr's verse-speaking talent in mind, and he saw in its successful performance the possibility of a new artistic movement in the theatre to counter the influence of Ibsen's realism. With a new dramatic movement in mind, he began rewriting *The Countess Cathleen* and started an entirely new work that he called *The Shadowy Waters*.

In early 1894, Yeats also met Lionel Johnson's cousin, Mrs. Olivia Shakespear, the "Diana Vernon" of his autobiographical writings. The friendship soon became intimate and by late 1895 Yeats had moved from Bedford Park to Symon's flat in the Temple where he had hoped to consummate the affair. After moving again, this time into some rooms at Woburn Buildings in March, 1896, Yeats finally overcame his nervousness and entered his first sexual relationship even though his obsessive love for Maud Gonne brought the affair to an end after about a year. While his first experience with sex gave him "many days of happiness,"[15] Yeats denied himself any further sexual relationships for the next several years, while he continued his quest for Maud Gonne's love.

Shortly after his move to Woburn Buildings, Yeats traveled with Symons to the West of Ireland, where he and Symons stayed with the playwright Edward Martyn at Tulira Castle in Galway. George Moore, Martyn's cousin, joined the party and Lady Augusta Gregory, a neighbor of Martyn, stopped by and invited Yeats and Symons to dine at Coole Park. Lady Gregory was fascinated by Yeats and decided to help his work by bringing some order and security into his life. In November, 1897, after spending the first of many summers with Lady Gregory, he wrote to her that no one "has ever shown me such kindness. Everybody tells me how well I am looking, and I am better than I have been for years in truth. The days at Coole passed like a dream, a dream of peace."[16] At the end of 1896, Yeats returned to Paris, and, while staying at the Hotel Corneille, met John Synge. Once Yeats convinced Synge to give up his ambition of becoming a literary critic, to return to Ireland and the Aran Islands and discover a voice for a life that lacked dramatic expression,[17] the cast was in place for the beginning of the Irish National Theatre. Martyn and Moore, Florence Farr and Synge, Annie Horniman and especially Lady Gregory, all would play key roles in the shaping of a new direction in Yeats's life, a direction destined to bring a greater energy and sense of reality to his art.

Yeats's first meetings with Lady Gregory and Synge did not, however, instantly change his life or his dreams. He went to Paris in late 1896 to gather occult material for his autobiographical novel *The Speckled Bird*, and to enlist Mathers's help in preparing the rituals for a Castle of the Heroes, an order of Celtic mysteries, to be located at Castle Rock in Lough Key. On a more public front, Yeats became involved, for Maud Gonne's sake, in the protests against the celebration of Queen Victoria's Jubilee, even though he was appalled by the violence of the Dublin riots. He also took on the presidency of the English Committee of the Wolfe Tone Memorial Association in the hope that the mass procession held

in August, 1898, would unite all the factions in Irish politics.
The Wolfe Tone centennial brought no political unity, however,
and Yeats turned away from politics to literary matters. Though
Maud Gonne disagreed with his decision, she was still willing to
accept a spiritual marriage with Yeats after finally telling him about
her secret life in Paris and her three-year-old daughter Iseult.

Frustrated in love but still hoping for Unity of Culture, Yeats
turned to his dream of an Irish Literary Theatre, which took on a
definite shape in the summer of 1898 at a meeting between Yeats,
Martyn, and Lady Gregory. They decided to collect money to rent
a Dublin Theatre for a performance of Martyn's *The Heather
Field* and Yeats's *The Countess Cathleen*. Yeats wrote out a mani-
festo, stating their intent "to have performed in Dublin, in the
spring of every year certain Celtic and Irish plays" for what they
hoped to be "an uncorrupted and imaginative audience trained to
listen by its passion for oratory."[18] After failing to secure a theatre,
the group rented the Antient Concert Rooms in Dublin. Surviving
a brief controversy over charges of anti-Catholicism against Yeats's
play, they staged *The Countess Cathleen* and *The Heather Field*
on May 8, 1899.

The century ended for Yeats with new ambitions growing and
old dreams fading. His dreams of a unified Irish culture were now
limited to his work for the Irish theatre. At the end of 1899, he
picked up his work on *The Shadowy Waters* once again and began
a collaboration with George Moore on a play for the Irish Literary
Theatre on Diarmuid and Grania. With the publication in 1899 of
The Wind Among the Reeds and the appearance of the second
edition of *Poems*, the twilight phase of Yeats's career was at an end.
In *Poems*, first published in 1895, he had retained only selected
lyrics from his earlier volumes, thereby reaching what Joseph Hone
describes as "unalterable decisions as to what he would preserve of
his earliest verse."[19] Maud Gonne had now turned to political
agitation against English recruitment of young Irishmen for the
Boer War, and, critical of Yeats's work for a national theatre, turned
down yet another proposal of marriage. Even the Golden Dawn
reached a crisis state by early 1900 when Mathers tried to seize

control of the Isis-Urania Temple and had to be suspended by its members. Saddest of all for Yeats, however, was the death of his mother on January 3, 1900. She had been ill for so long that her death brought no visible change in Yeats's life, but it did herald the beginning of perhaps its most difficult period.

Adam's Curse

There were several promising events in Yeats's life in the early 1900s, including his lectures with Florence Farr on the art of the psaltery, the formation of the Dun Emer Press, and his first meeting with John Quinn, the American lawyer and patron of Irish arts. Devised by Arnold Dolmetsch, the psaltery, when paired with Florence Farr's lovely speaking voice, gave Yeats the opportunity to experiment with the lyrical voice of his poetry. The Dun Emer Press, eventually to become the Cuala Press, was run by Yeats's sisters Lily and Lolly, who published their brother's *In the Seven Woods* in 1903 as their first book. Out of his meeting with Quinn came plans for Yeats's first trip to America, a lecture tour which lasted from November, 1903 to March, 1904. Even more promising was Yeats's work for an Irish national theatre. By 1902, the Irish Literary Theatre had become the Irish National Dramatic Company as Yeats joined forces with an amateur acting company headed by Frank and William Fay. Though Yeats made the decision partly because of his growing differences with Moore, he also recognized that the Fays, with their fine speaking voices and simple stage movements, were perfectly suited to his idea of the theatre. The merger also eliminated a major criticism of the dramatic movement, that its Irish plays were being performed by English actors.

The company started with performances in April, 1902, of Russell's *Deirdre* and Yeats's *Cathleen Ni Houlihan* with Maud Gonne in the title role. Encouraged by the success of the productions, the company declared itself the Irish National Theatre Society with Yeats as its president. Now virtually in control of things, Yeats turned to the task of writing plays for the society. His letters of 1902–1903 mention repeatedly his work on *The Hour-*

Glass, A Pot of Broth, Where There Is Nothing, On Baile's Strand, and *The King's Threshold.* By January, 1903, even Lady Gregory, his fellow spirit in the dramatic movement, expressed her fears that he was forsaking his poetic genius. Yeats wrote back, however, that he "was never so full of new thoughts for verse, though all thoughts quite unlike the old ones. My work has got far more masculine. It has more salt in it."[20]

The test for Yeats's new aggressive pose came early in 1903. Though Maud Gonne had accepted the idea of a spiritual marriage, she still found political agitation far more meaningful than Yeats's Castle of Heroes or Irish National Theatre. Shortly after meeting John MacBride, an ardent nationalist and a hero who fought against England in the Boer War, she agreed to marry him. Yeats received word of the marriage, which took place on February 21, 1903, just before delivering a lecture. The shock was so great that afterward he remembered nothing of what he had said to his audience. At thirty-seven, Yeats had taken on new ambitions and conflicts, but the dream that had sustained him for the last fourteen years was suddenly gone.

Yeats's trip to America in November helped to settle things in his mind, and no doubt the enthusiastic response to his lectures and the 646 pounds profit from the tour also soothed his ego. Greeted with the heartening news on his return that Maud Gonne's marriage was failing because of MacBride's drinking, Yeats plunged once again into the affairs of the National Theatre. Annie Horniman, whose interest in the theatre was her own hopeless love for Yeats, had agreed to subsidize Yeats's society by taking the old Mechanics Institute, a part of which had been used as a morgue, on Abbey Street and having it converted into a theatre. The Abbey, as the new theatre was called, opened on December 27, 1904, with Yeats's *On Baile's Strand* and *Cathleen Ni Houlihan* and Lady Gregory's *Spreading the News.* By the fall of 1905, Yeats, with the backing of Lady Gregory and Annie Horniman, decided that the Abbey should become a limited liability company so that control of the theatre could be in the hands of a few officers. After much bickering the vote went in Yeats's favor and the control of the

Abbey was turned over to three directors: Yeats, Synge, and Lady Gregory.

In 1906, Bullen published *Poems*, which contained Yeats's major verse from 1895 to 1905, but Yeats's attention was still directed toward the Abbey. In early 1906, Yeats faced an open rebellion by those who felt that the Fays' idea of a people's theatre had been replaced by the directors' idea of a poetic theatre for the privileged few. The dissident actors and actresses resigned in May, but Yeats, undaunted in his work, spent the summer at Coole writing his poetic tragedy *Deirdre*, which was produced at the Abbey on November 24, 1906. The Abbey's greatest controversy began on January 16, 1907, when the audience rioted during the first night performance of Synge's *The Playboy of the Western World*. Synge had been a controversial writer, but his *Playboy*, with its mention of Irish women in their shifts and its outrageous treatment of peasant life in the West of Ireland, was too much for the Dublin audience to bear. Though Yeats was in Scotland, he quickly returned and at a debate held at the Abbey he attacked the narrow-mindedness of the rioters. More than ever he felt the gap between his vision of Ireland and what his father called the Land of Plaster Saints.

Yeats's contempt for the Dublin crowd and his growing adulation of the Anglo-Irish traditions associated with Coole Park were reinforced by the tour of Northern Italy he took with Lady Gregory and her son Robert in April, 1907. After visiting Florence, Milan, Urbino, Ferrara, and Ravenna, he identified himself even more with the aristocratic life. During this period Yeats also renewed his spiritual marriage with Maud Gonne, now that she had separated from MacBride. There is even the likelihood that Yeats became Maud Gonne's lover for a brief time during a visit to Coleville, her house in Normandy, in late 1907 or early 1908,[21] but the relationship, through her insistence, quickly returned to the spiritual plane. Since Maud Gonne's marriage, Yeats had consoled himself in affairs with Olivia Shakespear, Florence Farr, and Mabel Dickinson, a London masseuse. He had also alienated himself from John Quinn, who charged that Yeats had tried to seduce his mistress Dorothy Coates. While Yeats claimed his innocence in this case, he found himself in greater difficulties, according to Norman Jeffares, when he falsely believed that "an unmarried woman" with whom he was having an affair was pregnant.[22] He escaped this crisis as well, but the number of affairs reflected Yeats's reversal of the ascetic life of his earlier years with Maud Gonne, renewed spiritual marriage notwithstanding.

While Yeats pursued passion and precision, he had to face the further loss of old ties and even more trouble with the Abbey. John O'Leary, Yeats's personification of romantic Ireland, died in early 1907, and later in the year Yeats's father went to America where he stayed until his death in 1922. Yeats also mourned the deaths of Synge and George Pollexfen. Synge's death on March 24, 1909, deeply depressed Yeats and seemed a tragic blow against his struggle with the Abbey's enemies. His uncle's death a year later further isolated Yeats by bringing an end to his close ties with Sligo. Estrangement was also the key word in Yeats's work with the Abbey. The Fays openly split with the Abbey during an American tour in 1908 and formed their own theatrical company. Two years later Annie Horniman withdrew her financial support from the Abbey when Yeats refused to fire Lennox Robinson for keeping the Abbey open on the day after the death of King Edward VII. Her departure left Yeats and Lady Gregory in firm control of Abbey affairs.

Yeats's antagonism for Dublin's public officials and press was also intensified during this period when the Dublin Corporation resisted Hugh Lane's offer to donate his priceless collection of impressionistic paintings to the Irish people if a suitable place was found or constructed in Dublin for their showing. By 1913, the corporation voted to reject the gift and forced Lane, who was Lady Gregory's nephew, to remove his paintings to London. Yeats's bitterness at this latest blow to his vision of Unity of Culture was reflected in the lyrics of The Green Helmet and Other Poems (1910) and Responsibilities (1914). In several of the poems, Yeats expressed his now fierce hatred for Ireland's Catholic middle class and his pride in joining with those "honour bred" for higher things.

Another influence on Yeats's work during this period was his friendship with Ezra Pound, whose aesthetic of the concrete, precise image reinforced Yeats's own interest in the dramatic lyric. They first met in 1909, and by 1913 knew each other well enough to spend the first of three successive winters together at Stone Cottage in Sussex, where Pound acted as Yeats's secretary. Yeats's increased activity in writing poetry after several years of exhausting labor at the Abbey was matched by a new fascination with spiritualism. While attending séances at the home of a medium, he encountered the ghost of Leo Africanus, an Italian geographer, traveler, and poet. Yeats wrote letters to his attendant spirit, then wrote the replies while under the spell of Africanus. Maud Gonne, as in the past, shared Yeats's psychic interests, and in 1914 the two traveled with Everard Feilding, the president of the Society for Psychical Research, to investigate reports in Mirabeau, France, of an oleograph of Christ that had begun to bleed. Impressed if not convinced, Yeats wrote a report of the miracle but did not publish it.

Yeats also turned to the ghosts from his own past during this period. His acceptance of an annual grant of 150 pounds from the English Civil List in 1910 and his interest, never actualized, in replacing Edward Dowden as professor of literature at Trinity were part of a process of reconciliation with his Anglo-Irish heritage that eventually led to his decision in 1914 to write "Reveries over Childhood and Youth." His autobiographical writing also reflected Yeats's desire to come to terms with his father's influence and to treat him now as an intellectual equal. Yeats's identification with the Protestant Ascendancy and his hatred for the Dublin crowd intensified in 1915 with news of the tragic death of Hugh Lane, who had gone down with the *Lusitania*. Lane's death meant that his paintings would stay in London, at least for the rest of Yeats's life, because a codecil in Lane's will returning the paintings to Dublin, once a suitable place was prepared for them, had not been witnessed. Yeats even flirted with knighthood at the end of the year, but turned it down because he did not want his enemies saying that he had forsaken Ireland for a ribbon.

At the beginning of 1916, Yeats was occupied with preparations for a performance of *At the Hawk's Well*, his first play in six years and the first of several to be written in the form of the Japanese Noh play. When the poetic drama was performed in Lady Cunard's drawing room on April 2, 1916, Yeats had no idea that other preparations were taking place in Ireland for an event that would have a profound impact on Ireland's national consciousness. On April 24, 1916, the Monday after Easter, a band of Irish patriots commanded by Padraic Pearse seized several buildings in Dublin. From their central location at the General Post Office, the armed volunteers declared the independence of the Irish Republic and resisted the English forces in several days of fierce fighting. When the struggle ended after an English gunboat had shelled the center of Dublin, the English military authorities quickly executed the surviving leaders.

At first, Yeats had ambivalent feelings about the Easter Rising, but the brutal executions changed things utterly. He had no idea that any political action could move him so deeply and, though he felt despondent about the future, he was determined to return to Ireland "to live, to begin building again."[23] While his first significant act was to write the powerful political poem "Easter 1916," Yeats, later in the year, purchased Ballylee, a ruined fourteenth-century Norman tower in the West of Ireland, which he hoped, after reconstruction, would become his future home. His greatest concern, however, was the effect of the execution of John Mac-Bride, who joined the Rising immediately after the fighting began, on his future relationship with Maud Gonne. Learning of her despondency, he went to her in Normandy and proposed once again. When she refused, Yeats returned to Coole Park for the summer to finish the essays for *Per Amica Silentia Lunae*, but in August, 1917, he returned to Normandy this time to ask Iseult to marry him. After being rejected, Yeats, determined now to marry and return to Ireland, wrote to Lady Gregory that he was going to propose to Georgie Hyde-Lees, a twenty-four-year-old Englishwoman he had first met in 1911 and had sponsored for initiation into the Golden Dawn in 1914. George, as Yeats called her, accepted the proposal,

and on October 20, 1917, the marriage took place at the Harrow
Road registrar office in London.

Solomon and Sheba

Though Georgie Hyde-Lees won Yeats by default, she was an
attractive, intelligent woman who had a keen interest in her husband's work, especially his occult studies. When Yeats became depressed in the first days of the marriage, she turned to automatic
writing to distract her husband from thinking about Maud Gonne
and her daughter. At first, she faked a few sentences to assure him
that he had made the right decision in marrying her, but she quickly
discovered to her husband's great excitement and her own amaze-
ment that the words and sentences were being formed by someone
beyond her conscious control. The unknown writer took his theme
from Yeats's theory of the mask in *Per Amica Silentia Lunae* and
built up an elaborate classification of personalities and history based
on the phases of the moon. Over the next several years, Yeats
worked the classification into his great philosophical work *A Vision*,
which first appeared in 1926, even though Yeats's story of his wife's
automatic writing was not included until the publication of the
second edition in 1937.

Yeats's marriage also brought a greater sense of continuity to his
life than he had ever known before. In England, the Yeatses moved
out of Woburn Buildings, where Yeats had stayed since 1896, and
settled at Broad Street in Oxford where they could entertain old
friends like Robert Bridges, John Masefield, and Sturge Moore,
while Yeats studied at the Bodleian. In Ireland, they stayed at Lady
Gregory's Ballinamantane House in Gort, while supervising the
renovation of what Yeats now called Thoor Ballylee. They also
rented Maud Gonne's house at Stephen's Green for their visits to
Dublin, but trouble occurred when Maud Gonne, forbidden legal
entry under England's Defense of the Realm Act, smuggled herself
into Ireland and turned up at Stephen's Green while the Yeatses
were staying there. Yeats refused to allow her to stay, however, be-

cause George Yeats was suffering from influenza and inflammation of the lungs and badly needed rest and quiet. In spite of the hysterical scene, Yeats held firm and proved to Maud Gonne and himself that his loyalty was to his young wife.

On February 26, 1919, George Yeats gave birth to a daughter, Anne Butler Yeats, at a nursing home on Upper Fitzwilliam Street. At the age of fifty-three, Yeats had become a father. No longer did he need to ask his old fathers to pardon him because he had nothing but his poetry to prove his blood. In January, 1920, the Yeatses traveled to America for a lecture tour to finance a new roof for Ballylee and to give John Butler Yeats a chance to meet and approve of his daughter-in-law. After first returning to Oxford, Yeats went to Dublin in September to supervise Cuala's preparation of *Michael Robartes and the Dancer*, which was published in 1921. This slim volume of verse together with the publication of the expanded Macmillan edition of *The Wild Swans at Coole* in 1919, *Four Plays for Dancers* in 1921, and "The Trembling of the Veil," the second phase of *Autobiographies*, in 1922 reflected Yeats's response to the dramatic events of the past few years, especially his marriage, the political violence in Ireland, and the deaths during the War of Hugh Lane and Lady Gregory's son, Robert, killed in air action over Italy.

With the violence increasing in Ireland, the Yeatses spent most of 1921 in England, where, on August 22, 1921, George Yeats gave birth to a son, Michael Butler Yeats. While Yeats had serious misgivings about returning to Ireland because of the questionable Treaty signed with England in 1921 creating an Irish Free State under the conditions of partition of Northern Ireland and allegiance to the King, George Yeats went to Dublin and found a Georgian house at 82 Merrion Square. Just before purchasing the house, however, Yeats received word that his father had died on February 3, 1922. The death left a void because Yeats had for so long accepted his father's ideas as an influence on his work. He wrote to Olivia Shakespear: "I find it hard to realise my father's death, he has so long been a mind to me, that mind seems to me still thinking and writing."[24]

The next several years brought Yeats his greatest public recognition, yet also forced him to rage against ill-health and old age. In 1922, as Ireland headed into a civil war between the Free State and the Republican party, Yeats decided to support the new government, first as a delegate to the Irish Race Congress in Paris. At the end of the year, primarily because of Oliver Gogarty's influence and his past membership in the Irish Republican Brotherhood, Yeats was appointed a member of the first Irish Senate. While detaching himself from the violence that continued until June, 1923, Yeats plotted to have the Abbey adopted officially as the Irish State Theatre and took an active role in forming an Irish Academy of Letters, writing a new copyright act, striking a new Irish coinage, and bringing about improvements in education.

In December, 1922, Yeats finally received an honorary degree from Trinity College, and, at the end of 1923, he was named the winner of the Nobel Prize. In his lecture to the Swedish Royal Academy, Yeats acknowledged Synge and Lady Gregory as the two who would have been the most pleased to stand beside him as he received his medal and diploma. Upon his return to Dublin, Yeats had a brief fling as the anonymous sponsor of *To-Morrow*, a radical literary journal, but his main concern was completing *A Vision*, which, while dated 1925, finally appeared in January, 1926. In the Senate, he aligned himself, much to Maud Gonne's regret, with the Jameson group of Protestant conservatives. In a June 11, 1925, speech against a bill denying the right to file for divorce, he clearly identified himself with the Protestant minority and the past glory of eighteenth-century Ireland: "We against whom you have done this thing are no petty people. We are one of the great stocks of Europe. We are the people of Burke; we are the people of Grattan; we are the people of Swift, the people of Emmet, the people of Parnell."[25]

Yeats's most nagging problem during this period of political, philosophical, and literary excitement was his poor health. He had always suffered from serious eye trouble and periodical bouts of colds and influenza, but by the end of 1924 high blood pressure, hearing difficulties, and an increasing weight problem forced him, under doctor's orders, to slow down for a while. George Yeats took him to Sicily and then on to Capri and Rome. On his return, however, Yeats plunged into philosophy to strengthen his system in *A Vision*. His letters from this period mention Whitehead, Plotinus, Spengler, Croce, Wyndham Lewis, Plato, and Hegel. Yeats also returned to writing the most complex and challenging verse of his career. Alternating between vision and bitterness, his poems celebrated intellect and passion, cursed old age, and brought poetry to the threshold of philosophy and religion.

In late 1927, Yeats, already troubled by the assassination of his close friend Kevin O'Higgins, the Irish minister of justice, came down with an exhausting cold which developed into congestion of the lungs. After recovering from high fever and delirium, he went to Spain for a rest. At Seville, however, he suffered from haemorrhages of the lung and after ten days was taken to Cannes, where he survived two serious bouts of influenza. He was again told by doctors that his condition was the result of overwork and was warned to avoid stressful climates and public affairs. The Yeatses moved on to Rapallo in February, 1928, to visit the Pounds and to plan a life-style more in keeping with the advice of Yeats's doctors. Now hoping to spend their winters in Rapallo, they returned to Dublin to dispose of their Georgian house for a flat at 42 Fitzwilliam Square.

In several ways, 1928 marked the beginning of the final phase of Yeats's life and career. *The Tower*, his most widely acclaimed volume of poetry, was published early in the year, and in July Yeats, approaching the end of his Senate term, gave his final speech, actually a brief statement expressing his Ascendancy view that it was more important to appoint able men to government than to elect representatives of the people. While Yeats was relieved that his work in the Senate was finished, he wrote to Olivia Shakespear that "the Abbey is the one work I cannot wholly abandon."[26] Over the years, he had kept his directorship so that he could judge the plays submitted to the Abbey, while occasionally offering a play of his own. During the 1920s, the Abbey, much to Yeats's regret, had turned to realism with its performances of Sean O'Casey's plays.

Reluctant at first to accept O'Casey, Yeats reacted to the riots at the performance of *The Plough and the Stars* in 1926 by proclaiming O'Casey's genius the equal of Synge's. Unfortunately, in early 1928, Yeats committed a serious blunder by advising Lady Gregory and Robinson to reject O'Casey's experimental drama *The Silver Tassie*. His action caused a major split between the Abbey and its most successful playwright and proved a great embarrassment when O'Casey made the rejection a public issue by publishing Yeats's letters on the matter. The bitter controversy was not resolved until 1935 when, after a reconciliation between Yeats and O'Casey, the *Tassie* was performed at the Abbey.

Yeats traveled to Rapallo for the winter months of 1928–1929, where he discovered a greater ease and happiness in writing verse than he had ever felt before. Always a painfully slow worker, he wondered if the new poems were as good as those written in bitterness and frustration. He also worked on a new introduction to *A Vision* in which he finally revealed that his wife's automatic writing was the chief source for his system. Upon his return to Ireland, Yeats spent a calm summer in Dublin with brief trips to Coole Park and Thoor Ballylee, but the trip to Ballylee was his last because the dampness of the tower was now a threat to his health. In late 1929, Yeats suffered another relapse while in London; when he finally reached Rapallo, he collapsed with what was diagnosed as Malta fever.

As he slowly recovered his fragile health, Yeats studied Swift with great intensity, and on his return to Ireland in the summer of 1930 he finished his Swift play *The Words Upon the Window-Pane*, which was performed at the Abbey in November. After a brief visit to England, including a day at Boar's Hill to celebrate the thirtieth anniversary of his friendship with John Masefield, Yeats returned to Dublin, where he spent the winter revising his poetry for a complete edition planned by Macmillan. In May, Yeats received an honorary degree from Oxford, but he was more concerned in 1931 with the rapidly deteriorating health of Lady Gregory. Except for brief trips to Dublin on Abbey business, he spent most of 1931 and the winter and spring of 1932 at Coole Park.

When Lady Gregory died on May 22, 1932, Yeats felt the deep loss
of a generous and intimate friend, and he also knew that her death
meant the end of his life at Coole Park, the country estate that had
long been the physical image for his belief in the value of a nation's
traditions and cultural life. Deprived of Coole Park and Thoor
Ballylee, Yeats moved in July to his new residence at Riversdale in
Rathfarnham, knowing his "lease for but thirteen years" would "see
me out of life."[27]

Yeats, however, still had miles to go before moving out of life.
In September, he saw his dream of an Irish Academy of Letters
become a reality. In late October, he left on his last American tour
to gather funds to support the Irish Academy's efforts to give annual
prizes for achievement by Irish writers. On his return to Ireland in
early 1933, he found letters praising *Words for Music Perhaps*,
which had appeared in November, and by the middle of the year
had become infatuated with the Fascist opposition to de Valera's
government. After meeting Eoin O'Duffy, the leader of the Blue
Shirts, he wrote three marching songs for the movement. Though
he soon became disenchanted with O'Duffy and altered the songs
so that they could not be marched to, Yeats obviously felt a stirring
in the blood for some heroic action to bring about "the despotic
rule of the educated classes."[28]

For the past few years, in spite of serious health problems, Yeats's
blood had also been stirred by passion. He eagerly read D. H.
Lawrence's novels and found *Lady Chatterley's Lover* sensational.
His verse, much of which appeared in the 1933 publication of *The
Winding Stair*, raged against old age and celebrated passionate
love. In May, 1934, he acted upon his desire to remake himself
physically by undergoing the Steinach operation for sexual rejuvenation. Experiencing a burst of renewed energy, he sought out
new relationships with attractive and creative younger women like
Lady Dorothy Wellesley, Ethel Mannin, and Margot Ruddock.
Yeats had also renewed his spiritual activities through his friendship
with Shri Purohit Swami and created Ribh, a new persona for his
passionate, yet metaphysical poetry. In between writing the verses
for "Supernatural Songs" and preparing *Wheels and Butterflies*, a

volume of plays, and "Dramatis Personae," the continuation of his *Autobiographies*, Yeats also managed a trip to Rapallo in June and an autumn visit to Rome to speak on the theatre to the Alessandro Volta Foundation.

While Yeats wavered between bouts of excitability and ill-health, friends and public officials prepared for the poet's seventieth birthday celebration, which passed with the expected flood of letters, public honors, and generous gifts. Yeats, however, saw the occasion as a time to consider what he knew would be his last verse.[29] In July, his thoughts about his final songs were made even more poignant by the death of George Russell, one of his oldest friends and last ties to his youth. By the end of 1935, Yeats decided to spend the winter in Majorca to help Shri Purohit Swami with a translation of the *Upanishads*, while he made the selections for a new edition of the *Oxford Book of Modern Verse*. In January, 1936, however, he became seriously ill again and had to spend the next few months convalescing. Though Yeats's movement was restricted, two controversies found their way to him. In April, he refused to nominate the Jewish poet Ossietsky for the Nobel Prize, even though Ernst Toller had hoped that Yeats's nomination might free Ossietsky from a Nazi concentration camp. A month later, Margot Ruddock, one of Yeats's female intimates, turned up at Majorca and created a minor scandal with her bizarre behavior. When Yeats returned to England in June, he ducked reporters by staying at Dorothy Wellesley's home in Sussex before moving on to Riversdale.

Yeats spent his time at Riversdale writing verse and completing *The Herne's Egg*, which he believed was his strangest and wildest play. In October, he felt strong enough to return to England briefly for two B.B.C. broadcasts on modern poetry. Ignoring his own good advice, he turned again to politics by writing ballads in defense of Parnell and Roger Casement, the poem on the latter bringing praise from the de Valera government. After a disastrous attempt to broadcast from the Abbey, he returned to London in March, 1937, for two poetry programs and completed two more in June and September. At Riversdale, he finished the proof sheets for a new edition of *A Vision*, published later in the year, while learning that an American committee, headed by Patrick McCartan, had provided a fund to ease Yeats's financial concerns for the rest of his life. He wrote more verse for *New Poems*, published in 1938, and by the end of the year had started a major essay for what he hoped would be an occasional publication called *On the Boiler* for his most violent ideas on race and government.

Yeats's political attraction for Fascism, his call for selective breeding, and his refusal to support Ossietsky, matters of great distress for Yeats scholars, were unpleasant extensions in Yeats's last years of his belief in an heroic ideal and his support of an elitist class of intellectuals, artists, and nobility. While Yeats's rightist politics were similar to Eliot's and his public actions were never as extreme as Pound's, his ideas nevertheless represent an unfortunate, if not sinister aspect of Yeats's mind. That his thoughts were most extreme during periods of ill-health and public frustration and disappointment and that they were uttered during the pre-Holocaust years tempers but hardly changes their character.

Yeats spent the first months of 1938, the last full year of his life, at Mentone, in the company of Edith Shackleton Heald, his latest female intimate, where he was later joined by George Yeats. He returned to Riversdale and in August entertained his old friend Maud Gonne. On August 10, he made his last public appearance at the Abbey for the opening performance of *Purgatory*. In October, just before leaving for the Riviera, Yeats learned of the death of another old intimate, Olivia Shakespear, for more than forty years the emotional center of his life in London. He wrote to Dorothy Wellesley, "For the moment I cannot bear the thought of London. I will find her memory everywhere."[30]

By December, Yeats and his wife were settled at the Hotel Idéal Séjour in Cape Martin to wait out another winter. To those of his friends gathered there, Yeats appeared in good spirits and recovered in health as he worked on *The Death of Cuchulain*. By January, however, Yeats's health worsened and he knew that he did not have long to live. After another bout of pain and breathlessness, Yeats died in the afternoon of January 28, 1939. He was buried at the cemetery in Roquebrune, where the body remained until September, 1948, when it was brought back to Ireland. George Yeats had decided to return her husband's remains to the ancestral churchyard at Drumcliff shortly after his death, but the war had delayed her plans. When the boat bearing Yeats's body entered Galway Bay, it was met by the poet's family and a group of government officials, including Sean MacBride, Maud Gonne's son. Yeats was finally laid to rest in his beloved Sligo, under a stone that bears the famous epitaph he had written for himself: "Cast a cold eye/On life, on death/Horseman, pass by!" (*CP*, 344). He could now fulfill his youthful pledge never to leave the land of his ancestors.

Chapter Two

The Lure of Dreaming Wisdom: The Early Poems

In June, 1932, while he was busy correcting proofs for the first edition of the Macmillan edition of the *Collected Poems*, Yeats wrote to Olivia Shakespear that he was astonished because he had said "the same thing in so many different ways."[1] From *The Wanderings of Oisin* to his most recent verse, Yeats recognized that the great theme of his poetry had been the clash between Oisin and Patrick, the swordsman repudiating the saint, "but not without vacillation."[2]

Yeats's comments, written at a time when he was recovering from the loss of Lady Gregory, are a remarkable summary of his poetic career. In his early verse and its pale world of conventional emotions, he had managed to find his theme in the conflict between wisdom and power and the ambivalent relationship between belief and desire. The dramatization of opposites and the vacillation between extremes engendered the rhythm and rhyme of Yeats's early verse, setting it in motion toward the unifying vision of his mature art. Yeats's letter, however, also reveals his awareness that his individual lyrics could be properly appreciated only through a continuous reading of the entire body of his work. Early in his career, he had made the deliberate decision to discard his weakest verse and revise and arrange the surviving poems into a definite pattern. Once he began his revisions, he continued the process throughout the rest of his career. At the time of his death, he was still changing his verse as he worked on the proofs for the definitive edition.

No poet ever worked as hard as Yeats at making and remaking

his art to fit a final vision of himself as poet. Astonishment notwith-standing, Yeats saw clearly in the last decade of his life that in his early years of frustrated passion, uncertain ambition, and painful self-discovery, he had found a theme and, after a long and exhaust-ing development of style that required revision as well as creative energy, had brought that theme to a state of perfection. To discover the source of that perfection, however, meant journeying back to pearl-pale Niamh and wandering Oisin, back even to the Arcadian shepherds and Indian lovers expressive of his first poetic sentiments.

The Wanderings of Oisin (1889)

Just before his death, while revising his verse for the definitive edition, Yeats wanted to make an important change in the arrange-ment of the individual poems. Several years before, on the advice of Harold Macmillan, he had agreed to the placement of his "longer narrative and dramatic pieces" at the end of the 1933 volume of *Collected Poems*, thereby effectively dividing his verse into Lyrical and Narrative sections.[3] For the definitive edition, however, Yeats decided to return his long poems to the chronological arrangement of his lyrical poetry.

The most dramatic outcome of Yeats's decision was the position-ing of *The Wanderings of Oisin* at the beginning of his verse. Yeats wanted his final edition to begin with the long narrative poem that was his first major effort to write on an Irish subject. Begun in 1886. when Yeats came under O'Leary's influence, *The Wander-ings of Oisin* has the highly decorative language and deliberate meter and rhyme of Pre-Raphaelite art, but its subject matter re-flects Yeats's romantic hope at the time of becoming the leader of "a school of Irish poetry—founded on Irish myth and history" and his practical realization that his chance of success was greater writ-ing Irish verse because it "helps originality and makes one's verses sincere, and gives one less numerous competitors."[4]

Knowing little Gaelic, Yeats borrowed the general idea of the ad-ventures of Oisin, the warrior-son of Finn, from the translation of Michael Comyn's eighteenth-century poem and the Middle Irish

dialogues of Saint Patrick and Oisin. Yeats, however, expanded
Oisin's journey to the land of the Tuatha de Danaan to three separate wanderings among the Immortals and enclosed the narrative
within Oisin's defiant meeting with Patrick. He also gave each adventure its own metrical pattern and its own special meaning. Told
retrospectively by Oisin, the wanderings begin in book 1 when
Niamh, the daughter of the Celtic god Aengus, chooses Oisin,
whose fame as warrior and storyteller has been recorded by the
immortal poets, to be her mate in Danaan land:

> Where men have heaped no burial-mounds,
> And the days pass by like a wayward tune,
> Where broken faith has never been known,
> And the blushes of first love never have flown....
>
> (CP, 353)

Resisting the pleas of his warrior comrades, Oisin rides with
Niamh to the first immortal island, where he is taken to the hall of
Aengus by a band of singing youths. After hearing Aengus sing
that "joy is God and God is joy," Oisin joins the youths in their
immortal dance. At the end of one hundred years, he finds a "dead
warrior's broken lance," a relic from his heroic life, and decides to
ride out again with Niamh in search of further adventure. Book 1
ends with the lovers departing the island of eternal song and dance,
while the Immortals sing forebodingly of the contrast between the
joy of ever-living youth and the sorrow of old age.

In book 2, Oisin and Niamh ride to the Isle of Many Fears,
where they enter a great door marred by the blows of warring giants
and gods. Hearing a fluttering sigh, they discover a mysterious lady
chained to two ancient eagles. Freeing her from her chains and
vowing to kill her enemy, Oisin, his "king-remembering" soul
aroused, fights a demon who keeps changing shapes during the
epic struggle. After one hundred years of victorious fighting, feast-
ing, and renewed challenges, Oisin discovers a beech-bough, another reminder of his mortal life, and rides forth again with Niamh.
Book 2 ends as Niamh murmurs that they are now going to the

Island of Forgetfulness since the Islands of Dancing and Victory have lost their power; but when Oisin asks which of these is the Island of Content, she sorrowfully replies that none know.

Book 3 begins with Oisin and Niamh's discovery on the last immortal island of a slumbering band of giants with bird claws and feathered ears. Their chief, awakened by the lovers, waves a bell-branch in the air, and its soft music lulls Oisin and Niamh into a deep sleep. After a hundred years Oisin is awakened by a fallen starling and decides to return to the heroic world of the Fenians. Warned by Niamh not to touch the earth if he has hopes of returning to her, Oisin returns to the world of mortals, only to discover that a feeble Christianity has taken the place of the Fenians and their worship of pagan gods. After mockingly tossing a bag of sand too heavy for common laborers, Oisin falls to the earth and suddenly, stricken by his three-hundred-year adventure, becomes an old man. The poem ends with Patrick telling the aged warrior to pray for his soul, but Oisin cries out in defiance:

> I throw down the chain of small stones! when life in
>   my body has ceased,
> I will go to Caoilte, and Conan, and Bran, Sceolan,
>   Lomair,
> And dwell in the house of the Fenians, be they in
>   flames or at feast.
>
>   (CP, 381)

Commentators over the years have judged *The Wanderings of Oisin* as far too derivative, ornamental, and uneven, but they have also accepted the poem as the first coherent production of Yeats's poetic career and the first indication, made clearer over the years through revision, that he was beginning to hammer his thoughts into unity. Balachandra Rajan finds craft in the poem but no insight, Peter Ure careful design but no depth, and Richard Ellmann a sureness of symbol but a highly colored style and uneven narrative.[5] Louis MacNeice, a harsh critic of Yeats's early poetry, thinks the poem ruined by romantic clichés and vulgar romantic rhythms.[6]

T. R. Henn also sees little more than Pre-Raphaelite formula, "sentimentality, occasional clumsiness of technique and a private symbolism."[7] John Unterecker is one of the few satisfied readers of the poem, pointing out its shifts in meter from book to book, its unified imagery of bird and tree, and its deliberately ambiguous symbolism.[8] Equally pleased, Harold Bloom thinks *The Wanderings of Oisin* a wonderful reflection of the romantic tradition, while Thomas R. Whitaker admires the poem's sense of history, which he sees as a foreshadowing of *A Vision*.[9]

Yeats, as indicated earlier, also commented on the poem from time to time. In a letter written in 1888, while he was correcting proofs, Yeats told Katharine Tynan that only the last book satisfied him, the rest being too shadowy, too full of cloud and foam. Yeats also wrote that in the second book, which had more inspiration than art, he had buried several private symbols: "The romance is for my readers. They must not even know there is a symbol anywhere. They will not find out. If they did, it would spoil the art. Yet the whole poem is full of symbols—if it be full of aught but clouds."[10]

Ignoring this warning, Yeats's critics have plunged into the foam and come up with some extravagant symbolic claims ranging from Ellmann's interpretation that the three books correspond to Yeats's life at Sligo, London, and Howth to the Freudian view of Oisin's battle with his demon as more Oedipal than epic.[11] While Yeats may have given the spur to all this symbol hunting, he also gave some sound advice on the reading of *The Wanderings of Oisin* in another letter to Katharine Tynan, written in early 1889. Feeling that his poem would need an interpreter, he wrote that the three books correspond to "three incompatible things which man is always seeking—infinite feeling, infinite battle, infinite repose—hence the three islands."[12] This comment, supplemented by Yeats's final judgment of the poem as representing the eternal conflict between swordsman and saint, still offers the most sensible guide for interpretation.

During his periodical revisions to improve the diction and meter of "The Wanderings of Oisin," Yeats preserved a three-part structure that reflects the emotional phases of adolescence, adulthood, and old age. Within this narrative balance between spontaneous joy, heroic assertiveness, and final calm, Yeats portrayed the eternal conflicts of action and dream, time and eternity, desire and belief. Finally, in Oisin's failure to find content among the Immortals and his return to a world now devoid of heroic action, Yeats projected the risk for those who follow the call of the imaginative life. This poetic dramatization of the imagination caught between eternal conflicts quickly became the dominant theme of Yeats's art. Believing that Irish legend would give him the "gloved hand" to reach out to the universe and that symbolic writing would give him the power to forge universal images, Yeats dramatized the dreams and self-doubts of the artist-hero in Oisin, Fergus, Aedh, Hanrahan, and Michael Robartes, whose actions, at times, seemed heroic, at other times, curiously evasive.[13]

Crossways (1889)

For the 1895 edition of *Poems*, Yeats selected fourteen ballads and lyrics from *The Wanderings of Oisin and Other Poems* and added "The Ballad of Father O'Hart" and "The Ballad of the Fox-hunter," written at the same time but not published with the poems in the 1889 volume. In his preface for *Poems*, Yeats wrote that he had placed this verse, which had been revised and rearranged, "in a section named *Crossways*, because in them he had tried many pathways."[14]

While *Crossways* is a representative sampling of what Yeats cared to preserve of his earliest poetry, it is certainly not an extensive one. Consigned to oblivion were dramatic poems like "Time and the Witch Vivien," "Mosada," "The Seeker," and "The Island of Statues," except for two of its songs, along with thirteen lyrics published in 1889. Preserved were fourteen lyrics that, with the two additional Irish ballads, Yeats hoped would create a clear impression of his subject matter and his mood when he was writing in the 1880s. Indeed, Yeats never removed or added another poem after the first appearance of *Crossways* as a section or separate book of the 1895 *Poems*. Whereas *The Wanderings of Oisin*, greatly revised for the 1895 volume, represented a critical moment of decision in Yeats's early career, *Crossways* was to reflect the uncertainties that preceded that decision.

Because of the limited mood and artificial style of *Crossways*, even after revisions removing archaisms and inversions, it is difficult to claim this first section of Yeats's collected works as one of his sacred books. Hugh Kenner has argued convincingly that Yeats, more architect than decorator, "didn't accumulate poems, he wrote books." Kenner's view is that Yeats, in opposition to the chronological arrangement of collected verse, "placed the *oeuvre*, the deliberate artistic Testament, a division of the new Sacred Book of the Arts of which, Mr. Pound has recalled, he used to talk."[15] Even Kenner, however, does not recommend the architectural approach until the publication of *Responsibilities* in 1914. Highly stylized, the poetry in *Crossways* is so much like the work of a decorator that Ellmann has compared it to "a Morris tapestry, static, statuesque, and exalted."[16]

Granted that Yeats's Pre-Raphaelite manner is the distinctive characteristic of *Crossways*, this does not mean that it has no architectural balance to justify calling it a book, even if its affectations disqualify it as a testament to Yeats's greatness. The sixteen *Crossways* poems are evenly divided into two groups of eight poems on Arcadian or Indian subjects and eight poems on Irish subjects. The first group begins with the pastoral "The Song of the Happy Shepherd," followed by its counterpoint, "The Sad Shepherd." "The Cloak, the Boat, and the Shoes" picks up the theme of sorrow, which extends through the two Indian poems, "Anashuya and Vijaya" and "The Indian upon God," on human frailty. A third Indian poem, "The Indian to His Love," turns to the subject of perfect love, but "The Falling of the Leaves" and "Ephemera" act as counterpoints with their themes of waning love and passion.

"The Madness of King Goll," the best poem, after drastic revision, in *Crossways*, opens the Irish group of poems with the theme, encased in Irish myth, of the calming, transforming powers of art and is followed appropriately by the bewitching "The Stolen Child" and its ambivalent summons to fairyland. "To an Isle in the Water" parallels "The Indian to His Love" with its precious vision of blissful love, and it, too, precedes two poems, "Down by the Salley Gardens" and "The Meditation of the Old Fisherman" on lost love and joy. The Irish group ends with three conventional ballads on Irish characters united by their stoicism but ranging from the kindly Father O'Hart, to the misbegotten Moll Magee, and finally to the aristocratic Foxhunter.

"The Song of the Happy Shepherd" sets the mood for *Crossways* with its sad pronouncement to the "sick children of the world" that the old Arcadian world of dreaming joy is dead. The shepherd of the poem, however, is happy because he believes that "Words alone are certain good" and that no truth exists "Saving in thine own heart." His advice is to

> Go gather by the humming sea
> Some twisted, echo-harbouring shell,
> And to its lips thy story tell,
> And they thy comforters will be,
> Rewording in melodious guile
> Thy fretful words a little while,
> Til they shall singing fade in ruth
> And die a pearly brotherhood. . . .
>
> (CP, 8)

After this opening song celebrating the comforting and trans-forming powers of art, the remaining lyrics and ballads establish the pathways theme by revealing the failure of love, passion, or sorrow to offer direction without the poet's song to weave them into melodious guile.[17] "The Sad Shepherd," for example, shows that sorrow in itself can pervert the poet's song into "inarticulate moan," while some of the later poems warn of the dangers of the heart's passion. "The Madness of King Goll" and "The Stolen Child" reveal the poet's dilemma in *Crossways* in even more striking terms. Capable of driving war from his land, King Goll cannot drive out the fire within his own mind. Only when he finds a tympan—a harp in the original verse—and plays a song of "some inhuman misery" does he find a relief from his own madness. While King

Goll's fate, after the instrument breaks, is to hear forever the distracting flutter of "the beech leaves old," the poem clearly illustrates the inadequacy of mortal triumphs to satisfy the imagination, yet the dangers of a vision not unified by art. The fate of King Goll, even more than the song of the Happy Shepherd, suggests that art and only art can ease a heart burdened by passion and control an imagination driven wild by visions.

"The Stolen Child," perhaps the best known poem in *Crossways*, demonstrates Yeats's early vacillation within the traditional Irish folk tale of the fairies stealing small children:

> Come away, O human child!
> To the waters and the wild
> With a faery, hand in hand,
> For the world's more full of weeping
>   than you can understand.

>   (*CP*, 18)

Much of the poem, like its refrain, appears on the side of fairyland with its gaiety and dancing, but, though the world is full of weeping, there is also something disturbing about the "unquiet dreams"—"evil dreams" in the original version—that the fairies inflict upon living things. And when the bewitched child is finally taken away, the entire mood of the poem shifts because of the imagery of calm and peace associated with the natural world the child is leaving behind.

"The Stolen Child" ends on a note that clearly sounds Yeats's dilemma in his earliest verse, at least as Yeats perceived it in 1895. Though obviously fascinated by the world of magic and dreams, he hesitated at the crossways, fearful of losing his way if he took the path to fairyland, yet equally afraid of his own strong emotions. Though it is difficult to argue with Robert Beum's statement that Yeats's early verse is "full of vaguely poignant moods, vague thought and imagery, unexamined archaism and inverted word order, and fashionable melancholy,"[18] it is not difficult to see that of all the paths projected by his earliest verse only art—"Words alone are certain good"—attracted him during a time of confusing emotions and dreams and saved him from the extremes of inarticulate moans and the mad songs of his "most secret spirit."

The Rose (1893)

The Rose, like *Crossways*, first appeared as a heading for Yeats's earliest verse in the 1895 *Poems*. For *The Rose* section, Yeats selected all but three of the poems from *The Countess Kathleen and Various Legends and Lyrics*, published in 1892. In 1925, Yeats wrote that he noticed "upon reading these poems for the first time for several years that the quality symbolised as The Rose differs from the Intellectual Beauty of Shelley and of Spenser in that I have imagined it as suffering with man and not as something pursued and seen from afar."[19] Yeats's own perception, years later, of his *Rose* poems of the early 1890s was that they were less remote and more in harmony with human feeling than the *Crossways* poems of the 1880s. Whether Yeats was right in his appreciation or merely looking through rose-colored glasses, the poems at least reflect a wider range of interest and emotion, more capable of bringing about a unity of dream and desire.

Rejecting the Neoplatonic rose of beauty, Yeats sought in the 1890s a symbolic rose to hide in its folds his intense study of the occult, his growing interest in Irish nationalism, and his adoration of Maud Gonne. While the occult and Irish nationalism represented the extremes of Yeats's subject matter, his love for Maud Gonne personalized the emotions of his lyrics, especially the sense of sorrow and frustration so common in his early verse. Attracted by the pathway of art in *Crossways*, he now wanted to avoid the poetry of *l'art pour l'art* by imagining a rose of many meanings and by taking "the only pathway whereon he can hope to see with his own eyes the Eternal Rose of Beauty and of Peace."[20]

Though few critics go so far as Bloom, who sees *The Rose* as "a major critical advance,"[21] most agree that the poems show greater control and confidence than those in *Crossways*. The collection is still haunted by Morris and Rossetti, but several poems are important expressions of Yeats's early poetic art. Unterecker has pointed out the architectural balance that qualifies *The Rose* as a book.[22] After "To the Rose upon the Rood of Time" opens the collection with the poet's expression of his "rosy ambition" to sing of the spiritual, natural, and personal, "Fergus and the Druid" and "Cuchulain's Fight with the Sea" appear as Yeats's "first important contributions to that Unity of Culture which he hoped to impose on Ireland by making her familiar with her legends."[23] These poems of heroic legend are followed by three Rose poems on beauty, peace, and mortal conflict and sadness and three poems, including "The Lake Isle of Innisfree," offering peace to those steadfast in their contemplation of the Eternal. The next five poems, beginning with "The Pity of Love" and including "When You Are Old," were written originally for Maud Gonne and attempt to personalize the poet's vision of the rose. "The Countess Cathleen in Paradise" and "Who Goes with Fergus?," both songs from *The Countess Cathleen,* return to the world of Irish mythology and anticipate the conflict between eternal dream and bitter reality in the five poems beginning with "The Man Who Dreamed of Faeryland" and ending with one of Yeats's personal favorites, "The Two Trees." *The Rose* then concludes with "To Some I Have Talked with by the Fire" and "To Ireland in the Coming Times," expressions of Yeats's faith in his "fitful Danaan rhymes" and his desire to be counted in the company of the Irish poets, Davis, Mangan, and Ferguson.

"To the Rose upon the Rood of Time" sets the pattern and the mood of *The Rose* with its evocation of the "Red Rose, proud Rose, sad Rose" to inspire the poet as he sings "the ancient ways." Yeats, free of Arcadian shepherds and Indian lovers, now seeks his images of beauty and wisdom in Irish mythology, thereby justifying his claim at the end of *The Rose* that he is an Irish poet. The opening poem, however, also reveals the poet's personal concern that his lofty vision will deny him the common things and lead him "to chaunt a tongue men do not know." Here again is the theme of "The Stolen Child," the vacillation in the midst of the poetic quest because of the fear of retreating irrevocably into the obscurity of arcane and ancient ways. Clearly his sympathies are with the world of magic and myth, but the poet is also mindful of the elemental creatures because he wants to sing as a poet of the people and bring about the Unity of Culture suggested in the Rosicrucian symbol of the mystical rose that blooms on the cross of time.

The conflict between dream and reality also appears in several other key poems in *The Rose*. In "Fergus and the Druid," Fergus gives up his throne to Conchubar for the Druid's "little bag of dreams," but when he, now removed from the mortal world, sees the miraculous stages of reincarnation, he realizes that he has "grown nothing, knowing all." While Yeats's revisions of the poem more clearly defined the role of the Druid by making Fergus more aware of his presence, there is still no doubt that the Druid with his ancient appearance and echoing questions is little more than an extension and foreshadowing of Fergus's desire for "dreaming wisdom" and his discovery of the "great webs of sorrow" that cling to those who foolishly forsake the common things.

The conflict is presented from the opposite perspective in "The Man Who Dreamed of Faeryland" and "The Two Trees." In the first poem, the man goes through four stages of his life that Unterecker believes "could stand as epigraphs for the chapters of Yeats's biography."[24] Each stage, however, whether it be the tenderness of love, the prudence of money-making, the anger of vengeance, or the coldness of the grave, fails to satisfy because of the eternal lure of fairyland. Even though Yeats's revisions changed the nature of the man's vision of fairyland so that, as Thomas Parkinson points out, it "has a closer relation to ordinary experience than does the presentation of the hero's temporal life,"[25] the poem still remains a testament to the higher demands of dream. Peace is only possible for Yeats's dreamer if he forsakes his mortal concerns for a visionary state beyond time.

"The Two Trees," a personal favorite of Yeats and Maud Gonne, takes up the same theme in its plea that the beloved gaze into her own heart rather than the bitter glass of outward reflection. What she will discover with her inward gaze is the holy tree of peace, joy, and inspiration rather than the "fatal image" of the "Broken boughs and blackened leaves" of unrest, barrenness, and cruelty.

"The Two Trees," with its rich evocation of the double-natured Kabbalistic Tree of Life and the scriptural and Blakean Tree of Life and Tree of Knowledge, is one of Yeats's most striking examples of his preference for dreaming wisdom over action and ambition.[26] Only when the poet learns to sing "a wizard song" that defies time and enchants his beloved can peace and perfect joy be found and brooding sadness be forgotten.

In several of Yeats's love poems, the appeal of an enchanted life or an existence beyond time takes the curious form of the poet's desire to see his beloved in old age or even in the grave. In "When You are Old," founded upon Ronsard's "Quand Vous Serez Bien Vieille," the beloved finds comfort and love only in the poet's verses she reads in her old age. In "A Dream of Death," a poem that greatly amused Maud Gonne, the beloved is buried in an obscure grave, her beauty forgotten until the poet carves her epitaph. This fascination with old age and death, perhaps anticipated in Oisin's fate and the waning passion of a few of the *Crossways* lyrics, is an odd feature of Yeats's early poetry, but understandable in a young poet seeking an escape from his own frustrated passions. Paradox aside, the Maud Gonne poems fit the pattern in *The Rose* of the quest for Eternal Peace and Beauty, though they have little of that sense of vacillation or conflict evident when the haunting odor of rose-breath or the troubling vision of fairyland is in the air.

In "The Lake Isle of Innisfree" and "Who Goes with Fergus?," two of the most popular of Yeats's early poems, there is no vacillation at all along the pathway of the Eternal Rose. The Innisfree poem, influenced by a reading of *Walden*, was conceived during a bout of homesickness for Sligo when Yeats, walking along Fleet Street, "heard a little tinkle of water and saw a fountain in a shop-window which balanced a little ball upon its jet, and began to remember lake water."[27] Though Yeats disliked the poem in his later years because of its nagging popularity, he also believed that, plagued by archaism and inversion, it was still his "first lyric with anything in its rhythm of my own music."[28] "The Lake Isle of Innisfree," moving with a biblical tempo, evokes out of "the deep heart's core" an isolated dream world of harmony, order, and peace in opposition to "pavements grey." Tightly controlled by its careful repetition of key words and phrases, the poem also offers a vision of a world free of need where time itself is mastered:

> And I shall have some peace there, for peace comes
>   dropping slow,
> Dropping from the veils of the morning to where the
>   cricket sings;
> There midnight's all a glimmer, and noon a purple glow,
> And evening full of the linnet's wings.
>
>   (CP, 39)

This sense of control, suggested by the rearrangement of the four times of day, is even more strongly dramatized in "Who Goes with Fergus?" where Fergus is the master of the four elements:

> For Fergus rules the brazen cars,
> And rules the shadows of the wood,
> And the white breast of the dim sea
> And all dishevelled wandering stars.
>
>   (CP, 43)

With its energetic tempo and provocative imagery, "Who Goes With Fergus?," a favorite of James Joyce, who sang the song at his mother's deathbed, offers to young man and maid an alternative to brooding on "love's bitter mystery" in Fergus's world of eternal dance and joy. Whether through what Ellmann calls an emphatic symbol like the dance or cooperative symbols like the four elements,[29] the poem also presents an aesthetic joy in its imaginative evocation of a state of perfect beauty. The poet, like Fergus, also has right mastery over natural things, but his power and wisdom comes from the imagination, which, like the legendary magic wand, transforms the elements into images of eternity.

The Rose poems actually represent, after the false starts of *Cross-ways*, Yeats's first tentative steps toward a role comparable to the magician's. While the elemental creatures danced about his table to a Druid tune, Yeats, still handicapped by conventional poetic

diction, sought to shape song into ritual and to take upon himself
the responsibilities of magus of the eternal imagination. The dangers
of obscurity remained but the pathway and mission seemed clear.
In "The Autumn of the Body," Yeats declared that the arts were
"about to take upon their shoulders the burdens that have fallen
from the shoulders of priests, and to lead us back upon our journey
by filling our thoughts with the essences of things, and not with
things."[30] *The Rose*, even with its expressed fear of chanting in an
unknown tongue and its vacillation between dream and desire, remains a testament to Yeats's recognition of the magical vocation of
art. The invisible rose-breath was changing into the vaporous odor
of the censer.

The Wind Among the Reeds (1899)

The Wind Among the Reeds is the first section of the poems in
Yeats's definitive edition that appeared originally as a separate book.
The collection was first published in 1899 and contained elaborate
notes prepared by Yeats to clear up what he believed was a reckless
obscurity in the mystical symbolism of the poems. For the first
volume of the 1908 *Collected Works*, Yeats shortened or omitted
some of the notes for *The Wind Among the Reeds*, changed the
titles of many of the poems to eliminate the personae of Aedh, Hanrahan, and Michael Robartes, and added an introductory note to
explain his original explanations:

When I wrote these poems I had so meditated over the images that
came to me in writing "Ballads and Lyrics," "The Rose," and "The
Wanderings of Oisin" and other images from Irish folk-lore, that they
had become true symbols. I had sometimes when awake, but more
often in sleep, moments of vision, a state very unlike dreaming, when
these images took upon themselves what seemed an independent life
and became a part of a mystic language, which seemed always as
if it would bring me some strange revelation. Being troubled at what
was thought a reckless obscurity, I tried to explain myself in lengthy
notes, into which I put all the little learning I had, and more wilful
phantasy than I now think admirable, though what is most mystical

still seems to me the most true. I quote in what follows the better or the more necessary passages.[31]

Readers encountering *The Wind Among the Reeds* for the first time after weaving their way through *Crossways* and *The Rose* will have little trouble accepting the commonly held view that this section represents the culmination of Yeats's dream-burdened poetry. They may, however, have difficulty accepting another common assumption by several Yeats commentators that the poems are easy to read, especially after encountering the everlasting Voices, the unappeasable host, the Boar without bristles, the Shadowy Horses, the Polar Dragon, the Valley of the Black Pig, and other Celtic and occult imagery. Ellmann's judgment of *The Wind Among the Reeds* as a poetic quicksand "where one sinks down and down without finding bottom" is extreme, but Rajan's view that it "is a more variegated collection than the remarks of some of its critics suggest" makes more sense than the notion that the poems represent little more than Yeats's last romantic swoon.[32]

The most obvious theme in *The Wind Among the Reeds* is the poet's unfulfilled desire for the beloved and his knowledge, gained from arcane sources, that

> Until the axle break
> That keeps the stars in their round,
> And hands hurl in the deep
> The banners of East and West,
> And the girdle of light is unbound,
> Your breast will not lie by the breast
> Of your beloved in sleep.
>
> (CP, 65)

The theme of denied passion, then, is intensified by the poet's apocalyptic vision of the end of the world. The critical knowledge that the unattainable beloved is Maud Gonne and that the *fin de monde* vision fits nicely into the *fin de siècle* mood of the 1890s also heightens the theme, but the range and complexity of *The Wind Among the Reeds* is primarily the result of the shifting personae in the poems and the dramatic conflict between the real and the transcendental experiences of love. The poet assumes several roles and discovers, thanks primarily to Yeats's affair with Olivia Shakespear, both vision and passion in his pursuit of the beloved—even if passion, being time-bound, is doomed to fade.

Allen Grossman sees *The Wind Among the Reeds* as Yeats's first sacred book in its discovery of poetic knowledge and contends that the book's richness is to be found within a structure based on "the temporal sequence in which the poems it collects were produced."[33] For Grossman, the first twelve poems have the variegated style of 1892–1894, the second thirteen, dominated by surrogate voices, cluster around 1896, the year when most were published in *The Savoy*, while the last twelve, reflecting a more intellectual interest in symbolism, were written in 1897 or after for the most part. This approach, based on the original 1899 arrangement of the poems, is supported at least by the fact that Yeats made only one change in the order of *The Wind Among the Reeds* for other editions, moving "The Fiddler of Dooney" from eleventh place in Grossman's first section to its present position as the last poem in the collection.

The personae Yeats used for the 1899 publication offers another key, now submerged because of the 1908 title changes, to arranging the poems in *The Wind Among the Reeds* into a meaningful design.[34] Yeats's original note offers some information on his personae, but his cryptic explanation is more for the adept than the common reader:

I have used them in this book more as principles of the mind than as actual personages. It is probable that only students of the magical tradition will understand me when I say that "Michael Robartes" is fire reflected in water, and that Hanrahan is fire blown by the wind, and that Aedh, whose name is not merely the Irish form of Hugh, but the Irish for fire, is fire burning by itself. To put it in a different way, Hanrahan is the simplicity of an imagination too changeable to gather permanent possessions, or the adoration of the shepherds; and Michael Robartes is the pride of the imagination brooding upon the greatness of its possessions, or the adoration of the Magi; while Aedh is the myrrh and frankincense that the imagination offers continually before all that it loves.[35]

Since Yeats associates fire with imagination—"a fire was in my head"—Aedh, Michael Robartes, and Hanrahan represent diverse forms of the imagination and a possible hierarchy of poetic postures. Hanrahan, originally the title character of "He Reproves the Curlew," "Maid Quiet," and "The Lover Speaks to the Hearers of His Songs in Coming Days," is the least successful of Yeats's personae because his imagination is distracted—"fire blown by wind"—by both the physical and occult. In "Red Hanrahan," the opening tale in *Stories of Red Hanrahan*, he is condemned to wander the countryside because his imagination, which lures him away from his responsibility to his sweetheart Mary Lavelle, fails him when he is brought by the Sidhe to Echtge, daughter of the Silver Hand. This vacillation between worlds, already expressed as a poetic concern in *Crossways* and *The Rose*, haunts the Hanrahan poems and several other lyrics including the two Mongan poems, now entitled "He Mourns for the Change That Has Come upon Him and His Beloved, and Longs for the End of the World" and "He Thinks of His Past Greatness When a Part of the Constellations of Heaven." In the Hanrahan poems, the wind symbolizes a disturbance—"There is enough evil in the crying of wind"—that awakens both passions and dreams—"words that called up the lightning / Are hurtling through my heart"—dooming the poet to a state of limbo between eternal beauty and mortal love—"Amid the hovering, piteous, penitential throng." The speaker in the Mongan poems, like the Fergus of "Fergus and the Druid," is caught by "Time and Birth and Change" and, haunted by "amorous cries," longs for the end of the world—"the Boar without bristles"—and the consummation of his love:

> Knowing one, out of all things, alone, that his head
> May not lie on the breast nor his lips on the hair
> Of the woman that he loves, until he dies.

(CP, 71)

If Hanrahan is the distracted artist tormented by both the Sidhe and his own passions, Michael Robartes, as "fire reflected in water" or "pride of the imagination," represents the adept artist, the role Yeats chiefly pursues in *The Wind Among the Reeds*. The magus is the key figure in the Michael Robartes poems, now entitled "He Bids His Beloved Be at Peace," "He Remembers Forgotten Beauty," and "The Lover Asks Forgiveness Because of His Many Moods," and several other poems, including the introductory pieces, "The Hosting of the Sidhe" and "The Everlasting Voices," and the popular "The Song of Wandering Aengus" and "The Cap and Bells." In the last two poems, Aengus and the Jester, lured themselves by beauty, win the beloved through magical songs and shapes and anticipate a life beyond time where souls and hearts are joined and lovers pluck the "silver apples of the moon, / The golden apples of the sun." In a Yeats short story, "Rosa Alchemica," Robartes, described as "something between a debauchee, a saint, and a peasant," is the chief adept of the Order of the Alchemical Rose. Even though he is stoned to death by ignorant fishermen, Robartes knows that divine powers

appear in beautiful shapes, which are but, as it were, shapes trembling out of existence, folding up into a timeless ecstasy, drifting with half-shut eyes into a sleepy stillness. The bodiless souls who descended into these forms were what men called the moods; and worked all great changes in the world; for just as the magician or the artist could call them when he would, so they could call out of the mind of the magician or the artist, or if they were demons, out of the mind of the mad or the ignoble, what shape they would, and through its voice and its gestures pour themselves out upon the world.[36]

The master of the Everlasting Moods, Michael Robartes, resisting the "Horses of Disaster" he hears in his own heart, transmutes the mortal beauty of the beloved into "the loveliness / That has long faded from the world" and appeals to her to summon forth, by crumbling the rose in her hair, the "Winds, older than changing of night and day." Like Aengus and the Jester, Robartes lures the beloved to "a more dream-heavy land, / A more dream-heavy hour than this." Like the speaker in "The Secret Rose," he is the magus preparing himself and his followers for the moment of divine revelation:

> The hour of thy great wind of love and hate.
> When shall the stars be blown about the sky,
> Like the sparks blown out of a smithy, and die?
> Surely thine hour has come, thy great wind blows,
> Far-off, most secret, and inviolate Rose?
>
> (CP, 67)

Between the extremes of artist as magus and artist as victim, Yeats places Aedh, who represents "fire burning by itself" or the imagination offering up rare gifts "before all that it loves." Aedh as gift-bearing artist is clearly evident in the first and last of the ten poems that had his name in their title for the 1899 collection. In "The Lover Tells of the Rose in His Heart," Aedh, now the lover, wants to take "All things uncomely and broken, all things worn out and old" and "build them anew" into the image of the beloved "that blossoms a rose in the deeps of my heart." In "He Wishes for the Cloths of Heaven," the lover, clearly not a Michael Robartes in possession of "heaven's embroidered cloths," offers the beloved only those things which purely belong to him:

> I would spread the cloths under your feet;
> But I, being poor, have only my dreams;
> I have spread my dreams under your feet;
> Tread softly because you tread on my dreams.
>
> (CP, 70)

In the other eight poems—"The Lover Mourns for the Loss of Love," "He Gives His Beloved Certain Rhymes," "He Tells of a Valley Full of Lovers," "He Tells of the Perfect Beauty," "He Hears the Cry of the Sedge," "He Thinks of Those Who Have Spoken Evil of His Beloved," "The Poet Pleads with the Elemental Powers," and "He Wishes His Beloved Were Dead"—Aedh becomes the poet inspired by the image of the beloved created out of his love and imagination, seeking "To build a perfect beauty in rhyme." Unlike Michael Robartes, who masters time and passion by summoning forth images out of *Spiritus Mundi*, Aedh must fail in his mission because as a poet he has only his "poor rhymes" to measure against his image of Ideal Beauty. The Aedh poems, however, by focusing on the poet attempting to draw together common things and the Elemental Powers, dramatizes the dreams and conflicts of a poet, neither magus nor madman, who cannot surrender to passion because of the image in his heart of the beloved, yet cannot reach a state of perfect bliss because of the limitations of his craft:

> And therefore my heart will bow, when dew
> Is dropping sleep, until God burn time,
> Before the unlabouring stars and you.

> (CP, 64)

Critics have judged *The Wind Among the Reeds* in various ways by Ellmann as poetic quicksand, by F. R. Leavis as a remarkable achievement, and by Edmund Wilson as a reflection of the *fin de siècle* writer's desire "to live apart from the common life and live only in the imagination."[37] Oddly enough, the judgments of Ellmann, Leavis, and Wilson are all correct, depending on which voice, Hanrahan's, Michael Robartes's, or Aedh's, sings in the critic's ear. In other words, *The Wind Among the Reeds* finally represents Yeats's attempt to find the role he should assume in pursuing the mission brooded upon in *Crossways* and envisioned in *The Rose*. Victim, magus, or artist of the beautiful, Yeats makes no absolute choice, but Aedh, the Irish word for fire, does represent Yeats's growing sense of vocation, which for John Crowe Ransom saved Yeats from total obscurity.[38] In *The Wind Among the Reeds*, Hanrahan and Michael Robartes reflect the extremes of art distracted or exploited by magic. Aedh, on the other hand, becomes the voice of the poet who recognizes that his own heart and imagination will provide the drama of his art. With mission and goal now taking clearer shape, Yeats, tentatively declaring the Druid powers of his own imagination while anxiously looking over his shoulder for the Sidhe, now needed the firmer stride to reach his goal of a perfect work of art.

Chapter Three

The Fascination of What's Difficult: Transitional Poems and Plays

In the 1900s, Yeats used a new vocabulary in his letters and essays to describe the kind of verse he now hoped to write. Seeking to express the definite and precise vision of the ancients, he wanted to get more masculine energy, more salt into his work. His early lyrics, stories, and essays were too burdened by the vague desire for the remote world of dreams. To AE, Yeats wrote in 1904 that the "region of shadows is full of false images of the spirit and the body."[1] Rejecting "sentimental sadness" and "womanish introspection," he now called for "no emotions, however abstract, in which there is not an athletic joy."[2]

Critics have offered two basic reasons for Yeats's decision to escape the shadowy regions of his early poetry and write the more concrete, energetic verse that appears in *The Seven Woods* and *Green Helmet* volumes. Ellmann points to Yeats's relationship with Maud Gonne, especially his frustration in failing to win her love and his bitterness after her marriage to MacBride in 1903.[3] Parkinson, on the other hand, stresses Yeats's deep involvement in the affairs of the Irish National Theatre and the Abbey as the chief reason for the changes in the style and mood of Yeats's poetry in the 1900s.[4] Ellmann and Parkinson, of course, are both right in their judgments. Yeats's decision to get more salt into his verse was certainly brought about by the bitter loss of Maud Gonne, but the craftsmanship needed to create a more direct voice and diction for a dramatic lyric came to Yeats primarily through his experience in the theatre.

Some Early Plays

Yeats began writing *The Countess Cathleen* several years before he began his plans for a national theatre and nearly a decade before the verse play was first performed in Dublin in 1899. The play was revised five times by Yeats, and, even though he worked to improve its dialogue and construction, he regarded *The Countess Cathleen* as no more than "a piece of tapestry," lacking conflict and a true climax: "The Countess sells her soul, but she is not transformed."[5] Placed chronologically, the play belongs to the period of Yeats's early verse and, to judge it by Yeats's later standards, it has little athletic joy.

Yeats's revisions of the play, however, do reflect his chief opinions during the transitional period of his early Abbey years. The story of the countess is a simple one, though controversial enough to arouse Catholic Dublin at the time of its first performance. Deeply distressed by the famine and deceived by two demons into believing that she has lost her fortune and with it her chance to help the peasants, the countess decides to sell her soul for five hundred thousand crowns and for the release of the souls already given to the demons in exchange for food. Though she dies of a broken heart shortly after distributing the money, her soul enters heaven because

> The Light of Lights
> Looks always on the motive, not the deed,
> The Shadow of Shadows on the deed alone.[6]

The most significant change brought about by Yeats's revisions, which included eliminating archaisms, adding scenes, reducing the number of characters, and redoing the ending by bringing the countess on stage to die, is the expanded role given to the poet Aleel. In scene 3 of the revised version, Aleel causes the only real conflict in the countess's soul when he pleads with her to come away with him to Danaan land until the evil days are over. While stirred by the appeal, she resists the temptation of the heart, preferring to join the poet's love, her love for the peasants, and her faith in God into a final and, for Leonard E. Nathan, far too conventional vision of sacrifice, healing, and eternal peace.[7]

The Land of Heart's Desire, first performed in London in 1894, also belongs to Yeats's early period of dream-burdened writing. In the same letter to AE in which he called for more athletic joy, Yeats wrote that the popularity of The Land of Heart's Desire came from its weaknesses, its "exaggeration of sentiment and sentimental beauty which I have come to think unmanly."[8] Mary Bruin, the play's heroine, falls victim to the lure of fairyland so pervasive in Yeats's early verse. Her death releases her from mortal hopes and fears but, unlike the death of the countess, brings about no final vision. Instead, The Land of Heart's Desire becomes a dramatic representation of that vague yearning for a dreaming peace and wisdom that Yeats wanted to purge from his writing after The Wind Among the Reeds. While there is a brief moment of emotional conflict when Shawn, Mary's husband, holds her in his arms and reminds her of their passionate life together, the play clearly belongs to the land of heart's desire:

> Where nobody gets old and crafty and wise,
> Where nobody gets old and godly and grave,
> Where nobody gets old and bitter of tongue,
> And where kind tongues bring no captivity.. . .
>
> (CPl, 70)

Cathleen Ni Houlihan and The Pot of Broth, though both written in what Yeats called "the English of people who think in Irish,"[9] stand as the extremes of Yeats's early dramatic art. In Cathleen Ni Houlihan, first performed in 1902, Yeats gave his Dublin audience his purest national vision. In later years, he wondered "Did that play of mine send out / Certain men the English shot," so effective was the production with Maud Gonne in the title role. The call in *Cathleen Ni Houlihan* is to certain death, a common fate for Yeats's early heroes and heroines, but death this time is no escape but a sacrifice for Ireland's freedom. The play takes place at Killala in the West of Ireland during the French landing in support of the 1798 Rebellion led by Wolfe Tone. Michael Gillane, about to enter into a prosperous marriage, hears Cathleen Ni Houlihan's "hope of getting my beautiful fields back again" and "of putting the strangers out of my house," and decides to dedicate himself to Ireland instead of pursuing his own ambitions. Though she appears throughout the play as an old woman plagued by troubles, Cathleen Ni Houlihan is imaginatively transformed by the famous last words of the play. When Peter Gillane, Michael's father, asks his youngest son if he saw "an old woman going down the path," he is told, "I did not, but I saw a young girl, and she had the walk of a queen."

The Pot of Broth, another of Yeats's popular successes, was excluded from the 1908 collected edition, but later returned because "it was the first comedy in dialect, of our movement, and gave Mr. William Fay his first opportunity as a comedian."[10] Yeats, however, also acknowledged that the dialect of the play was so much Lady Gregory's doing he once recommended that she include *The Pot of Broth* with her own work. The comedy is a lively piece about a tramp who outwits a shrewish woman by convincing her that his magic stone will transform a pot of hot water into a pot of broth. The tramp has a touch of the poet about him and sings about Jack the Journeyman, later to appear as a companion of Crazy Jane, but the play itself never strays beyond the boundaries of light comedy.

The King's Threshold has more than a touch of the poet about it. First performed in 1903, the play expresses Yeats's strong belief in the ancient rights of the poet. After being ordered by King Guaire to give up his seat at the great council, Seanchan the poet refuses to eat or drink and sits at the king's threshold to wait for death. Seanchan's sacred role as defender of the arts is defined in a series of scenes in which pupils, public officials, relatives, sweetheart, and finally King Guaire himself try to persuade the poet to give up his death vigil. No appeal, however, changes the poet's mind and, at

the play's end, he dies in the swoon of tragic joy, knowing that
"Dead faces laugh." Yeats's revisions of *The King's Threshold*
sharpened the conflict between the poet and the material world,
and, in 1922, he greatly reinforced Seanchan's determination to up-
hold the nobility of the arts by adding the tragic ending. The
changes, however, do little to create any real conflict or doubt in
Seanchan's own mind. He never really wavers in his faith in
poetry's right mastery over what the martyrs call the world:

> And I would have all know that when all falls
> In ruin, poetry calls out in joy
> Being the scattering hand, the bursting pod,
> The victim's joy among the holy flame,
> God's laughter at the shattering of the world.
>
> (*CPl*, 114)

In *The Shadowy Waters*, the conflict between art and life provides the background once again for the hero-poet to act out his
faith in the imagination even as his vision leads him to his own
death. Disdaining Aibric's appeal to live like other men, Forgael
forsakes his pirate craft and guides his ship after the flight of the
man-headed birds—the souls of men killed in battle. Even when
Dectora, a queen of great beauty, is captured, Forgael refuses to
accept her mortal love as his fate. While the crew decides to sail
home in Dectora's ship, she decides to stay with Forgael. Her decision, symbolized by the act of spreading her flaming hair over the
poet—an act frequently urged by the personae of *The Wind Among
the Reeds*—liberates both lovers from common reality and grants
them an immortality known only by the spirits of the dead and
the inspired poet:

> And knitted mesh to mesh, we grow immortal;
> And that old harp awakens of itself
> To cry aloud to the grey birds, and dreams,
> That have had dreams for father, live in us.
>
> (*CPl*, 167)

Critics have found *The Shadowy Waters* one of the most intriguing of Yeats's early plays because of its many stages of revision, including its transformation from dramatic poem to verse play, its autobiographical features, and its affinities with *The Wind Among the Reeds*. Yeats claimed that he worked on *The Shadowy Waters* for fifteen years before it was first published in 1900. After it was performed, first by accident in 1904 by the Irish National Theatre Society—he had given the play to the company as an exercise in speaking blank verse—then by consent in 1905 for an International Theosophical Congress in London, Yeats further revised *The Shadowy Waters* for publication in 1906. In 1907 he finally split the work into a Dramatic Poem and an Acting Version that was performed at the Abbey on December 8, 1906.

Yeats's revisions of the play changed "it greatly, getting rid of needless symbols, making the people answer each other, and making the groundwork simple and intelligible,"[11] but, even in its final form, it still clearly reflects Yeats's chief interests in the 1890s. Forgael's madness is the same imaginative frenzy that appears in King Goll, Aengus, Hanrahan, and several other personae in Yeats's early poetry:

> Yet sometimes there's a torch inside my head
> That makes all clear, but when the light is gone
> I have but images, analogies,
> The mystic bread, the sacramental wine,
> The red rose where two shafts of the cross,
> Body and soul, waking and sleep, death, life,
> Whatever meaning ancient allegorists
> Have settled on, are mixed into one joy.
>
> (*CPl*, 152)

Forgael's quest for beauty in the form of an "Ever-living woman" parallels Yeats's own quest for ideal love and beauty. Just as Forgael first refuses Dectora's love because she casts a mortal shadow, bewitches her with Druid song into believing that he is golden-armed Iollan, and finally accepts an eternal life with his beloved, Yeats had pursued Maud Gonne with Druid spells, briefly became involved with Olivia Shakespear, and finally returned to a spiritual marriage with Maud Gonne. Both imagined poet and real poet had to shake off the attraction of a real lover to remain committed to a love so pure that only spiritual consummation seemed possible.

As for the success of Yeats's revisions, critical opinions range from the position summarized and supported by Nathan that Yeats troubled *The Shadowy Waters* with his constant changes to the more positive position, expressed by Parkinson, that Yeats's alterations sharpened and unified his vision.[12] Both views, however, taking into account Yeats's effort to strengthen the roles of the sailors and Aibric and to clarify the roles of Forgael and Dectora, see the revisions as part of Yeats's effort to energize his art through dramatic conflict and eliminate at least some of the shadow through a more realistic diction. Yet even with these changes *The Shadowy Waters* still remains a tribute to Villiers de l'Isle Adam's *Axel* and an echo of its hero's declaration that "as for living, our servants will do that for us."

Yeats wrote several other plays during the first turbulent decade of his involvement in the Irish dramatic movement. He collaborated with George Moore on *Diarmuid and Grania*, which was performed in Dublin in 1901, and hastily wrote *Where There Is Nothing* for publication in 1902 to keep Moore from using the plot. The latter play was eventually remade, with the help of Lady Gregory, into *The Unicorn from the Stars*. Yeats also wrote two prose plays: *The Fool and the Wise Man*, which was performed in 1903 as *The Hour-Glass*, and *The Golden Helmet*, first performed in 1908. The latter was redone in verse and performed as *The Green Helmet* in 1910, while *The Hour-Glass* was later made into a verse and prose version for a production in 1912.

Dissatisfied with this group of plays, Yeats was much happier with his two verse tragedies, *Deirdre* and *On Baile's Strand*, from this period. *Deirdre*, first performed at the Abbey in 1906, is Yeats's version of perhaps the best known of all Irish legends—the flight of the young lovers Deirdre and Naisi from the wrath of King Conchubar and his terrible revenge upon them. Yeats's play begins at the moment when Deirdre and Naisi return to Ireland because

Fergus has brought word to them of Conchubar's pardon. Through the course of the play, it becomes clear that Fergus has been deceived and that Conchubar has set a deadly trap for the lovers. His plot to kill Naisi is successful, but his desire to reclaim Deirdre as his queen is forever frustrated when Deirdre slays herself after discovering Naisi's body.

While Yeats's lovers share a great tradition with tragic lovers ranging from Helen and Paris to Tristan and Isolde, the play's success is entirely dependent upon Yeats's controlled dramatization of Deirdre's gradual discovery of the hopelessness of her situation and her decision to act out her own tragic end rather than give herself to Conchubar. Though critics have disagreed on the level of achievement in *Deirdre*, Peter Ure has effectively traced the tragic pattern in Deirdre's recognition of the signs of approaching doom, her futile struggle to prevent the death of her lover, and her noble and austere act of choosing a fitting role when she realizes that her love has ended tragically.[13] Refusing to become Conchubar's queen, she accepts death in a manner fitting the lofty character of a tragedy, but only after she has expressed the passionate intensity of someone willing to risk all for love:

> O' singing women, set it down in a book,
> That love is all we need, even though it is
> But the last drops we gather up like this;
> And though the drops are all we have known of life,
> For we have been most friendless—praise us for it,
> And praise the double sunset, for naught's lacking
> But a good end to the long, cloudy day.

> (*CPl*, 190–91)

On Baile's Strand, first performed on the opening night of the Abbey in 1904, is one of Yeats's finest verse plays. The first of five Cuchulain plays written by Yeats, it is also a striking dramatization of the conflict of forces Yeats would later call the antithetical or subjective and the primary or objective. Heroic, rebellious, passionate, Cuchulain has the self-sustaining energy of the subjective per-

sonality. On the other hand, King Conchubar, reasonable, con-
ciliatory, compromising, has the overriding concern for external
order reflective of the objective mind. The play, primarily in its
1906 revised form,[14] focuses on the debate between Cuchulain and
Conchubar and the tragic results of Cuchulain's decision to go
against his own nature and take an oath of obedience to Conchubar:

> It's time the years put water in my blood
> And drowned the wildness of it, for all's changed,
> But that unchanged.—I'll take what oath you will:
> The moon, the sun, the water, light, or air,
> I do not care how binding.

> (CPl, 261)

Once the oath is taken, a strange young man appears to challenge
Cuchulain to mortal combat. Though he does not know that the
challenger is his son, Cuchulain instinctively likes the youth and
offers him his arm in friendship rather than battle. Conchubar,
however, by insisting that oath-bound Cuchulain defend the state's
honor, forces Cuchulain to accept the challenge. Resisting the impulse to strike out at Conchubar and believing himself momentarily
bewitched by something in the air, Cuchulain fights and defeats
the young man. When he learns that he has slain his own son, he
plunges into the sea and, distracted by grief and madness, dies fighting the waves.[15]

The strength of *On Baile's Strand* lies in Yeats's skill in weaving
the pattern of Cuchulain's tragedy within the verbal clash between
Cuchulain and Conchubar. The construction of the subplot in-
volving the Blind Man and Fool, while functioning as a source of
information about the true identity of the young man and the dark
reason behind his challenge, also enriches the play's design by using
lowly characters as ironic counterpoints to Conchubar's blind reason
and Cuchulain's foolish pride. The resultant tragedy, a subversion
of the heroic will rather than an extension of it, has far more human
and dramatic conflict than any of Yeats's early plays. In his essays
for *Samhain, Beltaine*, and *The Arrow*, occasional publications of

the Irish dramatic movement, Yeats was fond of quoting Sainte-Beuve, that nothing is immortal except style. Yeats, however, had discovered through the experiences of writing plays that style was the artistic expression of a living speech aroused and heightened by the conflict of ideas and passion.[16] *On Baile's Strand* is the best example of that discovery among Yeats's early plays.

In the Seven Woods (1904)

Approached as a book, *In the Seven Woods* represents no radical change in Yeats's verse writing. The persona of "The Withering of the Boughs" still knows "of the leafy paths that the witches take" and "where the Danaan kind / Wind and unwind their dances." The poet-lover still dreams of ideal beauty in the form of a Brangwen, Guinevere, Niamh, Laban, or Fand, and Quiet now walks the bee-loud paths of the Seven Woods of Lady Gregory's estate instead of the bee-loud glade of Innisfree. Yet Yeats in a note for the 1903 Dun Emer Press edition of *In the Seven Woods* hoped that the experience of rewriting *On Baile's Strand* would bring "a less dream-burdened will into my verses."[17]

While Yeats's comment is more relevant to the revisions of his verse in the 1908 collected edition, it still points to some important changes in style and mood that had already found their way into the *Seven Woods* poems. Unterecker, noting that Yeats tied his expressed desire for less shadow and more substance in his verse to his recently completed work on a play, sees the changes in the pared-down imagery, "the matter-of-fact language and the comparatively uninvolved syntax of the *Seven Woods* volume."[18] Parkinson, while acknowledging that the *Seven Woods* combines several lyrics "in the rhapsodic mood of the early verse," believes any change to be more a matter of mood than style: "The early poems had expressed world-weariness; in the 1903 volume Yeats expressed a certain fairy-world-weariness."[19]

While the more physical diction and syntax in the *Seven Woods* are an extension of Yeats's efforts to create a living speech in his plays, the more realistic mood reflects Yeats's disappointment in his

relationship with Maud Gonne during the period just before and
after her marriage to John MacBride. The first three poems in the
Seven Woods, all written before the marriage, explore the emotional
ordeal of the frustrated lover. "In the Seven Woods" opens the
volume with a troubled vision of "Tara uprooted" and the sounds
of "crying about the streets," but the heart can still put away "the
old bitterness" when calmed by the harmonious sounds of the Seven
Woods and the imagination can still summon the apocalyptic image
of the "Great Archer, / Who but awaits His hour to shoot." The
desire for either spiritual apocalypse or sexual fulfillment hinted at
in the last lines of "In the Seven Woods," however, is quickly
checked by the imagery of "The Arrow." The visionary arrow of
the opening lyric is now reduced to "this arrow, / Made out of a
wild thought," which is nothing more than the lover's attempt to
find some comfort in knowing that because of the passing years no
man may look upon his beloved and see the delicate and noble
beauty he preserves in his memory. Yet the lover gives himself away,
reveals his frustration and unhappiness, by confessing that "yet for
a reason / I could weep that old is out of season."

"The Folly of Being Comforted" completes the opening sequence
by mocking the small comfort of "The Arrow." The lover has been
told by "One that is ever kind" that time is on his side now that his
"well-beloved's hair has threads of grey" and that a little more
patience will bring what seems impossible. The lover's heart, however, rejecting advice compatible with the mood of withdrawal in
Crossways, *The Rose*, and *The Wind Among the Reeds*, cries out
against what is now "a crumb of comfort." It knows that her "great
nobleness" defies time, which can do no more than remake her
beauty: "O heart! O heart! if she'd but turn her head, / You'd know
the folly of being comforted" (*CP*, 76).

"Old Memory" and "Never Give All the Heart," written after
Maud Gonne's marriage, were added to the *Seven Woods* poems in
1905 and now occupy the position held by *The Old Age of Queen
Maeve* and *Baile and Aillinn* in the 1903 volume. *The Old Age of
Queen Maeve* and *Baile and Aillinn* reinforce the theme of frus-
trated and now aging love with the double image of ancient Maeve

helping love-crossed Aengus to carry off his beloved to the Land
of the Young and of Aengus, desirous of granting Baile and Aillinn
eternal love, deceiving the mortal lovers into believing "of the other's
death, so that their hearts were broken and they died." "Old Memory" and "Never Give All the Heart," however, add a new dimen-
sion to the *Seven Woods* by introducing the now rejected and bitter
lover. In "Old Memory," the rejected lover wants to send an arrow-
like thought to his lost beloved to remind her that her beauty was
half created by the image "he kneaded in the dough / Through the
long years of youth." This thought, however, is so bitter because all
work has "come to naught" that he refuses to say more for fear that
his song will become too harsh for other lovers. "Never Give All the
Heart," its advice to lovers embodied in its title, validates that advice with the bitter confession of the concluding couplet: "He that
made this knows all the cost, / For he gave all his heart and lost"
(CP, 77).

While "The Withering of the Boughs" and its imagery of
Danaan land brings the volume back, perhaps because of the bitterness of the last two poems, to the old theme of the lover's dream
knowledge that he can control the elements, the wide gap between
dream and reality is completely revealed in "Adam's Curse," regarded by many critics as the key poem in the transitional period
of Yeats's career. Written shortly before Maud Gonne's marriage,
"Adam's Curse," in a formal but direct conversational style, briefly
takes up the subjects of poetry, beauty, and love. Speaking first, the
poet tells his companions, his beloved and her close friend, that
writing poetry is hard labor, but "if it does not seem a moment's
thought, / Our stitching and unstitching has been naught." His
beloved's friend, that "beautiful mild woman," responds that
women also know they "must labour to be beautiful." Skillfully
combining the two subjects, the poet closes the conversation by ob-
serving that love, now thought an idle trade, was once a learned
art. His last thought, reserved for his beloved's ear, is that he strove
to love her in "the old high way of love," but now he and she have
become "As weary-hearted as that hollow moon."

Distinctive because of its heightened form of conversation, a

common strategy in future Yeats poems, "Adam's Curse" also introduces a physical imagery and diction alien to Yeats's earlier verse.
No longer written by invisible hands, poetry now becomes as much
a craft as an art. Common acts, scrubbing a kitchen pavement and
breaking stones, and ordinary character types, paupers, bankers,
schoolmasters, and clergymen, appear for the first time as elements
of a Yeats lyric. The result is a more direct, what Yeats described
as a more masculine and energetic poem, wavering only in its concluding image of a time-worn moon that Ellmann sees as a brief
retreat "to the techniques of *The Wind Among the Reeds*."[20]
Weary-hearted or not, the poet and his beloved are real enough in
"Adam's Curse" and the language and attitude physical and direct
enough to anticipate the stronger emotions and rhythms of the
Green Helmet poems and the greater force of *Responsibilities*.

While "Adam's Curse" marks out the future direction of Yeats's
art, the rest of the *Seven Woods* poems return to the world of fading dream and bitter loss. "Red Hanrahan's Song About Ireland"
offers up the eternal image of Cathleen Ni Houlihan as refuge
from the winds of change, but in "The Old Men Admiring Themselves in the Water" the reflected image of old age provokes thought
of a beauty that "drifts away / Like the waters." "Under the
Moon," even with its evocation of a mythic landscape and legendary beauties, also offers little comfort because to dream of a
woman's beauty "Even in an old story, is a burden not to be borne."
In "The Ragged Wood" and "O Do Not Love Too Long," both
added to the *Seven Woods* in 1908, the lover's dream that "none
had ever loved but you and I" is pricked by the later discovery that,
having loved too long, he, in a pun on Dowson's Cynara poem, has
grown out of fashion.

The *Seven Woods* volume closes on an unexpectedly positive
note with its celebration in "The Players Ask for a Blessing on the
Psalteries and on Themselves" of the "proud and careless" music
that survives the mortal hands of the players and its vision in "The
Happy Townland" of a world of perfect bliss "That is the world's
bane." As the last two poems, they also achieve a balance with "In
the Seven Woods" and "Red Hanrahan's Song About Ireland," the

first and middle poems in the volume, by offering the sounds of calm and harmony and the imagery of eternal hope and peace as relief from love's frustrations and bitterness. Most of the *Seven Woods* poems, however, offer no escape from the ravages of time and change and no relief from the conflict between dream and reality.

In his note separating the lyrics from *On Baile's Strand* in the 1903 volume, Yeats wrote that he had "made some of these poems walking about among the Seven Woods, before the big wind of nineteen hundred and three blew down so many trees, and troubled the wild creatures, and changed the look of things."[21] The poems he wrote also have that changed look about them, reflect what had been troubling his own heart and imagination at the time of the big wind. Not yet master of the stronger emotions and more masculine diction and rhythm that appear in the *Seven Woods*, Yeats, at least, had now taken his first, tentative steps toward a less decorative and dainty-footed art. While the initial effort widened the gap between dream and reality, it also moved Yeats closer to a poetry of personality, a celebration of "our delight in the whole man—blood, imagination, intellect, running together."[22]

From the *Green Helmet* and Other Poems (1910)

Though representing a decade of work, the poems in the *Seven Woods* and the *Green Helmet* volumes still number less than those in *The Wind Among the Reeds*. There is an obvious slowing down in the pace of Yeats's lyrical writing during the 1900s, partly because of the distractions of the theatre but also a result of the self-criticism leading to the conclusion that the poetry of the 1890s, "full of decorative landscape and of still life," lacked the energy and clear vision "of those who have become the joy that is themselves."[23] While the *Seven Woods* and the *Green Helmet* fall short of the joyous achievement of the poet in control of himself and his craft, the volumes, taken together, mark the shift from the dream-burdened songs of the 1890s to the modern poetry of responsibility and self-sustaining energy and vision.

The *Green Helmet* volume has even more of the pared-down look first seen in the *Seven Woods*. The poet-persona now identifies his enemies, can convert his bitterness into anger against those who have opposed him, and can also, for the first time, clearly perceive a way of life compatible with his desire for Unity of Being. Faced with the aftermath of Maud Gonne's marriage and growing problems at the Abbey, Yeats now sought a poetry of personal utterance: "I will write poetry as full of my own thought as if it were a letter to a friend, and I will write these poems in simple words, never using a phrase I could not use in prose. I will make them the absolute speech of a man."[24] What he achieves in the *Green Helmet* is a poet's song with enough salt in it to curse "every knave and dolt" but with enough insight to know that the poet's true gift is "a written speech / Wrought of high laughter, loveliness and ease."

The *Green Helmet* opens with "His Dream," a strange, puzzling lyric in the manner of the verse of *The Wind Among the Reeds*. Yeats's explanatory note that, like "The Cap and Bells," the poem was made out of a dream, hardly makes "His Dream" less disappointing as the first expression of a volume supposedly moving the poet toward a more direct speech and a clearer vision. Bloom, however, offers an explication that justifies the key position of "His Dream."[25] He sees the gaudy death ship as a symbol of Yeats's early poetry and the shrouded figure as an image of Maud Gonne as the poet's evasive beloved. The poem, then, becomes a confession, appropriately in the language and imagery of the early verse, that the poet, hiding his real emotions, sang in his youth to escape life and sought dignity in "the sweet name of Death."

The next poem, "A Woman Homer Sung," written in Yeats's new style, supports Bloom's reading of "His Dream." The poet now admits that in his youth he "shook with hate and fear" when others came near his beloved. Now "being grey," he dreams not of death but that he has brought his craft "to such a pitch" that it can shadow in a glass "What thing her body was." Denied an age when life and letters seemed "an heroic dream," his only hope of creating the proper image to capture the "fiery blood" and sweet nobility of a woman comparable to Homer's Helen is to bring a matching passion and pride to his verse instead of singing in the sarcophagus art of "His Dream." "A Woman Homer Sung" also begins a sequence of Maud Gonne lyrics that faces the poet's personal difficulties with his beloved, now very much a real woman, while occasionally judging her actions from the detached perspective of a more heroic age. In "Words," originally titled "Consolation," the poet even goes so far as to suggest that his best work, "done to make it plain" to his beloved, has been in vain and offers the ambivalent thought that had she understood he "might have thrown poor words away / And been content to live."

The possibility that the beloved is to blame for the poet's personal and public ordeal becomes the subject of "No Second Troy," the best known poem in the *Green Helmet* volume. Through the strategy of four rhetorical questions, the persona both blames and absolves the beloved for making him miserable and stirring up the passions of the mob. The first question names the crimes she has committed and leaves little doubt that her political activity has been wasted on ignorant and cowardly men. The second question, shifting the poem's focus, draws attention to her "nobleness made simple as a fire" and "beauty like a tightened bow." Since her nature, projected in the imagery of the huntress, has been refined by a singleness of purpose the third question asks the obvious: "Why, what could she have done, being what she is?" The last question, which, as Ellmann points out, "fairly explodes" because the identification of the beloved with Helen has been withheld until this point,[26] draws the bow and lets fly the accusation that the age, not his Helen, has failed to act heroically: "Was there another Troy for her to burn?" The irony of the last line is that, while shifting the blame for his misery to the age, it also hints that the persona, revealed once again as the poet, has failed to write with the courage expressed in his beloved's actions, has not captured in verse her simple nobility and taut beauty. In other words, not only was there no Troy for her to burn, there has been no Homer to write about her, only a poor, dreaming poet seeking to sail with her to fairyland.

Now that the beloved has been absolved, "Reconciliation" is

possible. While "Some may have blamed" her because she left the poet, thereby taking away those precious "verses that could move them," he can throw the decorative trappings of his art into the pit now that she has returned to him. Reconciliation, however, is not that easy, for since she has been gone the poet's "barren thoughts have chilled me to the bone." In "King and No King," the poet, seeing no tale of "Old Romance" in the loss and return of his beloved, actually lists those things now impossible because his beloved once betrayed him:

> The hourly kindness, the day's common speech,
> The habitual content of each with each
> When neither soul nor body has been crossed.
>
> (CP, 90)

"Peace" returns the poet both to Homer's Helen and the theme of reconciliation. By comparing his beloved once again to Helen, he can describe those oxymoronic qualities, her "sternness amid charm," her "sweetness amid strength," embodied in a form that "Homer's age / Bred to be a hero's wage." While admitting that time has touched that form, the poet now knows peace is also possible because of his beloved's return. "Against Unworthy Praise," the last poem in the Maud Gonne sequence, prepares the way for a shift in subject. Knowing that all has been for a woman's sake, the poet is still not completely at peace because he half yearns for praise. Having seen that "dolt and knave" have slandered his beloved yet she "Half lion, half child, is at peace," serves only as a reminder that he has yet to achieve the same self-mastery.

This concern for self-mastery now that the beloved is at peace becomes the common theme in the next group of poems in the *Green Helmet*. In "The Fascination of What's Difficult," the poet turns to the latest cause of his misery, "the day's war with every knave and dolt, / Theatre business, management of men" and vows to set his Olympian soul free from the curse of what's merely difficult. After "A Drinking Song," written for a Lady Gregory play, and three epigrams on the wisdom that comes with time and the folly of youth and praise, the poet turns to a strategy of self-mastery destined to become a major factor in the triumph of his later poems. In the poetic dialogue of "The Mask," the lover is asked to "Put off that mask of burning gold / With emerald eyes" so that the beloved "find what's there to find, / Love or deceit." The lover, however, responds "It was the mask engaged your mind" and that it will remain in place: "What matter, so there is but fire / In you, in me?" First written for an unpublished play that Yeats eventually worked up into *The Player Queen*, "The Mask" is the first definite dramatic expression of the Daimon or antiself, a concept Henn, Ellmann and many others believe critical to a complete understanding of Yeats's verse, especially in its later and more complex forms.[27]

The function of "The Mask" in the *Green Helmet* is to set the stage for several poems closely associated with Lady Gregory and Coole Park. In "Upon a House Shaken by Land Agitation," the artifice created out of the poet's passion and imagination is replaced by the Big House and its "passion and precision." The "holy blood" of the poet finally finds peace and the poet's soul its noble image where "the lidless eye that loves the sun" and "sweet laughing eagle thoughts" are born of "the best knit to the best." Though the same enemy that defeated the poet's dream of Unity of Culture threatens the Big House as well, the poem, celebrating what Daniel A. Harris calls the "beautiful life" and illustrating the poet's "public responsibility" to that life,[28] becomes the first important expression of an ideal, described by Thomas R. Whitaker as "endless history,"[29] that spurs the poet to preserve and recreate

> The gifts that govern men, and after these
> To gradual Time's last gift, a written speech
> Wrought of high laughter, loveliness and ease.
>
> (CP, 93)

"At the Abbey Theatre," added to the *Green Helmet* in 1912 and addressed to Craoibhin Aoibhin, Gaelic for Little Pleasant Branch and the pen name of Douglas Hyde, contrasts the beautiful life at Coole Park with the daily frustration endured by Yeats and Lady

Gregory in trying to please the Abbey crowd. "These Are the Clouds," "At Galway Races," and "A Friend's Illness," however, return to the values of "what the strong has done," which, though mocked by the middle class, endure in aristocratic custom and the nobility of the soul. After the sequence of Lady Gregory and Coole Park poems, "All Things Can Tempt Me" brings the *Green Helmet* back to the clash between the poet and his chief distractions: "a woman's face, or worse— / The seeming needs of my fool-driven land." Now, however, the older poet, more accustomed to the toil of writing, rejects the "airs" of his youth and wishes the voice of romance be struck "Colder and dumber and deafer than a fish."

In "The Brown Penny," the coin withheld in "All Things Can Tempt Me" is now tossed by the young man to see if he should love. The last of the *Green Helmet* poems, "The Brown Penny," originally titled "The Young Man's Song," is as ill-fitting in style and theme as "His Dream" when placed with Yeats's transitional poems, but, like the opening lyric, it returns to the manner of the early verse to comment on what the older and wiser poet has come through and discovered now that "nothing but comes readier to hand" than his craft. Realizing the crooked path of love has brought him his new voice and understanding, Yeats, in this poem, picks the common strand of his art out of the loops of his beloved's hair and is finally willing to accept all that he has done—"One cannot begin it too soon"—as preparation for what he now will do.

Henn believes that the slight revisions of the *Green Helmet* poems and those to come in *Responsibilities* reflect Yeats's deep concern for realities "that were certainly more imminent."[30] To write about these realities, his rapidly changing relationship with Maud Gonne, the turbulent uncertainties of the Abbey and Ireland's political scene, and his growing dependence on the existence, increasingly threatened, of Coole Park, Yeats had to depart from the decorative and evasive art of the 1890s, a departure dramatized in "His Dream" and "Brown Penny." When Yeats now wrote about Maud Gonne, the Abbey, Irish politics, or life at Coole Park, he turned to the more direct, physical style he had begun developing in the *Seven Woods* poems. Having reshaped his writing by bringing more salt and energy into his verse, Yeats could now take on the task, primarily through the strategy of the mask, of making himself into more of a public poet. To do this he would have to speak in an even bolder and more barbarous tongue, but, while attacking the knaves and dolts who hurt his friends and made Ireland into a blind, bitter land, Yeats would also have to take full responsibility for his words and face enemies and private difficulties. The goal now was to achieve self-mastery and control the drama of his life rather than seek an escape through dreams and fantasy.

Chapter Four

Cold and Passionate as the Dawn: The Art of Responsibility

Now that Yeats had abandoned the decorative verse of his early years and decided "there's more enterprise / In walking naked," he moved toward a more physical and precise art. Having found strength in the dramatic lyric, he now sought complete mastery of form and content and the power to transform the new reality of his poetry into a vision of reality. To move from dreaming wisdom to visionary reality, however, Yeats had to define even more dramatically the energizing conflicts of his art and had to give a more definite shape to the traditional values that sustain the artist seeking perfection in his work. It had taken Yeats twenty-five years of verse writing, but, with the publication of *Responsibilities* in 1914 and *The Wild Swans at Coole* in 1919, he had finally begun the poetic process that would make him into a master poet.

Responsibilities (1914)

While the epigraphs to *Responsibilities* suggest, with a touch of ambivalence, that the poet of the volume has now come to terms with his past—"In dreams begins responsibility"—and is now free of its distractions "for a long time now / I have not seen the Prince of Chang in my dreams"—the note for the poems beginning with "To a Wealthy Man . . ." and ending with "To a Shade" explains why Yeats turned away from his youthful dreams of escape. Stirred by the Parnell controversy, the *Playboy* riots, and the dispute over Hugh Lane's pictures, he knows "that neither religion nor politics can of itself create minds with enough receptivity to become wise, or just and generous enough to make a nation."[1] The responsibility, then, for speaking out against "lying accusations" and "unscrupulous rhetoric" and preserving "the remnant of an old traditional culture" falls to the poet.

Before assuming a public voice, Yeats addresses a prefatory poem to the spirits of his ancestors. Asking their pardon for having no child now that he is "close on forty-nine," Yeats can offer "nothing but a book, / Nothing but that to prove your blood and mine." Summoned to hear this confession are the "Old Dublin merchant" Jervis Yeats, great-grandfather John Yeats, described as "Robert Emmet's friend," those Butler and Armstrong ancestors who fought at the Battle of the Boyne, the "Old merchant skipper" William Middleton, and especially that "silent and fierce old man," Yeats's grandfather William Pollexfen, all of whom lived according to "the wasteful virtues" that "earn the sun." While this prefatory poem was probably provoked by George Moore's attack on Yeats's aristocratic posturing, it achieves far more than justifying Yeats's identification with Ireland's heroic past. As Whitaker points out, "the deprecated 'book' makes articulate the hitherto silent gestures of soldier and skipper," while Yeats, by evoking the virtues of his ancestors, "incarnates the inheritance that he addresses."[2]

"The Grey Rock," the volume's opening poem, addresses itself to another essential part of Yeats's past, his apprenticeship as a member of the Rhymers' Club. Though the poet's tale, inspired by the legendary Goban's wine, is foreign to the Rhymers' taste, the moral is "yours because it's mine." The shared moral, that faithless men betray the gods, reflects Yeats's decision to keep faith with his heritage and his craft, those priceless things defiled by his enemies. Using a form that Unterecker praises as a brilliant interchange of "chatty and casual" talk with the spirits of the dead poets and the formal narrative of "remade" legend,[3] Yeats sets up two mythic parallels: first between the goddess betrayed by her mortal lover and the actress and intimate friend Florence Farr, her passionate dreams frustrated by her fear of marrying "some poor lout," then between the Celtic gods "full of wine and meat" and the Rhymers, especially Johnson and Dowson, cursed by "wine or women" yet keeping their faith in the "Muses' sterner laws." Rejecting the decision of Aoife's lover to sacrifice himself to "his country's need," Yeats claims his own share of Goban's wine if he, too, can keep faith, "though faith was tried, / To that rock-born, rock-wandering foot" symbolic of his newly forged art and sterner vision of reality.

Armed with inheritance and craft, Yeats turns to his enemy, now clearly the Irish middle class, in the next group of poems in *Responsibilities*. Writing with what Pound called a "new robustness" and "the tooth of satire," Yeats made his first target Lord Ardilaun, who had refused to give a second and larger subscription to the planned Dublin Municipal Gallery unless there was a popular demand for Hugh Lane's pictures. In "To a Wealthy Man . . ." Yeats contrasts the wealthy man's concern for what Paudeen and Biddy want for this "blind and ignorant town" with the detached generosity of dukes Ercole, Guidobaldo di Montefeltro, and Cosimo de Medici, great patrons of the arts discovered by Yeats in Castiglione's celebration in *The Book of the Courier* of the Renaissance courts of Ferrara and Urbino. While the poem challenges Ardilaun to "Look up in the sun's eyes and give" the "right twigs for an eagle's nest," Henn points out that its "aristocratic allusiveness could have persuaded nobody, certainly not those of 'this blind bitter land.' It is rather Yeats's own purgation of his anger, the hero finding his Renaissance—perhaps Swiftian—mask in an arrogance of defeat, an assumption of pride and race, and in power over words."[4]

In "September 1913," Yeats directs his anger against Paudeen and Biddy, those small-minded Dubliners who "add the halfpence to the pence / And prayer to shivering prayer," and accuses them of betraying the heroic vision of Ireland's great leaders: "Romantic Ireland's dead and gone,/ It's with O'Leary in the grave" (*CP*, 106). The title of the poem, however, points to the real object of Yeats's mocking attack and the fact that the poem is much more personal than it appears to be with its high-minded evocation of the spirits of Robert Emmet, Wolfe Tone, and John O'Leary. By selecting the date of the infamous Dublin lockout, Yeats can "dedi-cate" his anger to Dublin editor William Martin Murphy, a political opponent of Parnell and the leader of the 1913 lockout against James Larkin's Dublin workers. Since it was Murphy and not Ardilaun who reacted publicly to Yeats's "To a Wealthy Man . . . ," "September 1913" is obviously another salvo at those refusing to fund the Dublin Municipal Gallery. That Yeats took Murphy's criticism of humbug artists personally is clear in the concluding stanza where the poet bitterly complains that if Ireland's dead heroes could return "as they were / In all their loneliness and pain, / You'd cry, 'Some woman's yellow hair / Has maddened every mother's son.'" While the lines play upon the memory of Parnell, brought down by the Dublin crowd because of his affair with Kitty O'Shea, they also allude to Yeats's own political defeats in causes fought for the sake of his love for Maud Gonne.

"To a Friend Whose Work Has Come to Nothing," written for Lady Gregory, takes the bitterness of "September 1913" and trans-forms it into one of Yeats's early images of tragic joy. Since the poet's friend, being "honour bred," cannot compete against the shameless liar, she should accept defeat

> And like a laughing string
> Whereon mad fingers play
> Amid a place of stone
> Be secret and exult,
> Because of all things known
> That is most difficult.
>
> (*CP*, 107)

In "Paudeen," the poet, blinded earlier by his anger against "our old Paudeen in his shop," finds himself in a lonely and secret place and hears in the curlews' cries, an ominous sound in *The Wind Among the Reeds*, the "sweet crystalline cry" of the soul. While "To a Friend Whose Work Has Come to Nothing" and "Paudeen" turn away from the knavish Murphy and doltish crowd and seek an image or expression of the tragic soul, "To a Shade," "When Helen

Lived," and "On Those That Hated 'The Playboy of the Western World,' 1907" are reminders, in their brief glimpses at the betrayed spirits of Parnell, Maud-Helen, and Synge, that Murphy's "foul mouth" still rules the Dublin crowd. Parnell's passionate service, echoed in Hugh Lane's dedication, Maud Gonne's lofty beauty, and Synge's sinewy art are all betrayed by word and jest or the howlings of the mob.

Accepting defeat rather than seeking the approval of those who dragged down Parnell, ridiculed the work of Synge, Lady Gregory, and Hugh Lane, and mocked Maud Gonne's beauty, Yeats picks up the masks of beggar and hermit in the next group of poems to dramatize the split between vulgar ambition and artistic vision. In "The Three Beggars," King Guaire exposes the lie in the popular belief that those with the most desire, greed, or ambition gain the most, by offering a thousand pounds to the first beggar to sleep before the third noon. The failure of the three beggars, who keep themselves awake by shouting at each other, is in sharp contrast to the crane's wisdom, that the only way to catch a trout is to act as if "I do not seem to care." This expression of the value of detachment and self-control is, in turn, symbolized in "The Three Hermits" by the old hermit, who "Giddy with his hundredth year, / Sang unnoticed like a bird." While the religious hermit fears the afterlife because he falls asleep in the middle of his prayers and the philosophic hermit cracks the flea of reincarnation, the artist-hermit transforms human doubts and philosophical truths, through his song, into a giddy image of the soul.

This contrast between beggarly ambition and self-sustaining vision is further dramatized in "Beggar to Beggar Cried," Yeats's response to Lady Gregory's suggestion that he should marry, "Running to Paradise," and "The Hour Before Dawn." The cry of the beggar that his time has come to "grow respected" is answered by the mocking "wind-blown clamour of the barnacle-geese." The song of the hermit soul running to paradise, however, corresponds to the "wind / That nobody can buy or bind." In "The Hour Before Dawn," beggar finally meets and throttles his alter ego, the hermit, who "would rob / My life of every pleasant thought / And every comfortable thing." Though the beggar's rejection of the hermit's beery sleep is seen by MacNeice as "a defence of the waking life,"[5] the beggar's claim that "beer is only beer" makes him at best a dubious Yeatsian hero. He does represent reality, but a reality that completely denies myth. First defiling, then debunking the idea of Maeve's ancient capital at Cruachan and Goban's beer, the beggar has more affinities with the Dublin crowd than the artist now interested, after his initial state of anger, in detaching himself from common passion and vulgar ambition. The beggar's physical attack on the sleeper drunk on Goban's beer finally stands as a folk representation of the public's fear and abuse of art and culture, which has been the major theme in *Responsibilities* since "To a Wealthy Man. . . ."

Now that the poet of *Responsibilities* has confessed his past follies and accepted defeat at the hands of Murphy and his mob, he turns his back on his enemies, and, like the hermit, seeks a definite image, vision, or judgment of his soul. Beginning with "A Song from 'The Player Queen'" and its dream of a golden life, *Responsibilities* shifts briefly but perceptibly from public controversies and private betrayals to the possibility of renewed hope. In "The Realists," Yeats taunts those who think that beer is only beer by asking them what art, symbolized by the marriage in "a dragon-guarded land" of the books of men and the "Paintings of the dolphin-drawn / Sea nymphs," can "Do, but awake a hope to live / That had gone / With the dragons?" In the companion pieces "The Witch" and "The Peacock," there is a sharp division drawn between common reality and a vision of reality. To toil and grow rich is "but to lie / With a foul witch," but "His ghost will be gay" who ignores ambition and makes "a great peacock / With the pride of his eye."

"The Mountain Tomb" calls for the celebration of the eternal wisdom of Father Rosicross—Christian Rosencrux, reputed founder of the Rosicrucian Order in 1848—but it also recognizes the difficulty and futility of seeking the eternal rose in an age devoid of pride and vision. Father Rosicross, his body perfectly preserved in the tomb, still sleeps, "All wisdom shut into his onyx eyes." This

ambivalent expression of hope and disappointment carries over into
the two Iseult Gonne poems, "To a Child Dancing in the Wind"
and "Two Years Later." In the first poem, the dance of the innocent
youth sharply contrasts with the poet's bitterly earned knowledge of
the "fool's triumph" and love "lost as soon as won." In "Two Years
Later," the poet, speaking with "barbarous tongue," can only warn
in vain the child fated to "dream that all the world's a friend. /
Suffer as your mother suffered, / Be as broken in the end."

The bare mention of Iseult's mother summons forth the bitter
experience of the poet's youthful love in "A Memory of Youth,"
but with a surprising result. As if he were watching a play, the poet
witnesses in the mind's eye how "even the best of love must die, /
And had been savagely undone"; yet the cry of "a most ridiculous
little bird," that sweet, crystalline cry of the soul, can still tear the
clouds away from "Love's moon." In "Fallen Majesty," the poet's
subject shifts to the beloved's beauty now undone by time, but his
new responsibility is not to mock but to record what's gone: "a thing
once walked that seemed a burning cloud." Maud Gonne is briefly
joined by Olivia Shakespear and Lady Gregory in "Friends" as
"things" to be praised, but the poet confesses that it is the memory
of "her that took / All till my youth was gone" that causes a sweetness to flow from the heart so great it shakes the poet "from head
to foot."

Having taken all into account, his heritage and his ruined
dreams, his friends and his enemies, Yeats creates a visionary reality
in "The Cold Heaven" in search of an image of what will come
now that he has accepted his responsibilities. Ellmann has pointed
out Yeats's frequent use of ghosts in *Responsibilities*, which he sees
as "the effect of prolonged psychical research,"[6] but the persona in
"The Cold Heaven" addresses himself to his own ghostly soul. The
poem, which Ellmann and many others see as the most important
in the volume and a major breakthrough in Yeats's use of the dramatic lyric, begins with the startling vision of "the cold and rook-
delighting heaven / That seemed as though ice burned and was but
the more ice." This image of an impersonal heaven that provokes a
cold, hellish passion in the heart of the observer places the poem

dramatically between heaven and hell and drives its persona's imagination

> So wild that every casual thought of that and this
> Vanished, and left but memories, that should be out of season
> With the hot blood of youth, of love crossed long ago. . . .
>
> (CP, 123)

Temporarily free of distractions, the persona, now more closely aligned with love-crossed Yeats, takes the blame "out of all sense and reason" for what he has done and what others, especially his beloved, have done to him, but the acceptance of complete responsibility riddles his soul "with light" until "I cried and trembled and rocked to and fro." Devastated by his decision, stripped clean of common reality, and riddled through with the arrows of what Henn calls "spiritual illumination,"[7] the persona now asks the critical question, justifiable within a dramatic context that places him between heaven and hell, on the fate of his soul, whether it has been purged of past sins or is doomed to repeat them in the limbo of a similar life:

> Ah! when the ghost begins to quicken,
> Confusion of the death-bed over, is it sent
> Out naked on the roads, as the books say, and stricken
> By the injustice of the skies for punishment?
>
> (CP, 123)

The next five poems seem to argue more for freedom than repetition as the outcome of *Responsibilities*. "That the Night Come," which had appeared originally with "Friends" and "The Cold Heaven" in an expanded edition of the *Green Helmet* poems published in 1912, portrays Maud Gonne as one who, like the poet, "could not endure / The common good of life" and so lived "in storm and strife" until the liberating moment when "proud death" or "night come." "An Appointment," in turn, prefers the proud, fierce movement of the squirrel to "the tame will" and "timid brain" of the officials who appointed one of their own as curator of Dub-

lin's National Museum instead of Hugh Lane. In "The Magi" and
its companion piece, "The Dolls," the poet's dissatisfaction and the
anticipation of a new beginning find expression in the fading
vision of "the pale unsatisfied ones" still seeking "the uncontrollable
mystery" even after "Calvary's turbulence" and the parable of the
dolls raging against the birth of a "noisy and filthy thing," a defiant
and ambivalent image of the new nakedness of the poet's vision.
Finally, in "A Coat," the poet directly expresses his dissatisfaction
with the embroidered song of his youth, caught and worn by fools,
and declares, as if affirming the necessity of the ordeal of "The Cold
Heaven," that "there's more enterprise / In walking naked."

The concluding poem, functioning as epilogue, expresses Yeats's
final acceptance of the best and the worst that has happened to him.
Unterecker sees "While I, from that Reed-Throated Whisperer" as
a defense of Yeats's "psychic investigations, his pride in family, his
admiration for Lady Gregory, his love of Maud Gonne; especially,
his conviction of the importance of his own work."[8] While all these
things, especially his summer visits to Coole Park, are, in Ben
Johnson's phrase, "Beyond the fling of the dull ass's hoof," Yeats
still must take into account the bitter truth that his enemies, including jealous rivals like George Moore, will take what he has
done and make it "but a post the passing dogs defile." Ending *Responsibilities* with the startling pun upon the word passing, Yeats
flashes his ability to deal verbally with fools and knaves, just as he
leaves little doubt in the earlier lines in the poem that he has found
the proper sources to become the master of his poetic art.

The Wild Swans at Coole (1919)

One of the rituals in Yeats scholarship is to point out the folly
of Middleton Murry's judgment of *The Wild Swans at Coole* as
Yeats's "swan song," his pitiful confession of final exhaustion and
defeat in "the great quest of poetry."[9] While the volume has poems
on the bitterness and dejection caused by the passing of youth, the
loss of friends and possible loss of creative energy, *The Wild Swans
at Coole* stands as a carefully designed and varied expression of the

poetic recovery from personal disappointment and failure and the movement toward a visionary art. Deliberately excluding poems like "Easter 1916," Yeats arranged *The Wild Swans at Coole*, expanding it from twenty-nine poems in the 1917 Cuala edition to forty-six in the 1919 Macmillan volume, to reflect his slow, sometimes painful journey from the purgatorial experiences of *Responsibilities* to the vision of reality inspired by his marriage and his psychic research.

Graham Martin has traced the biographical events, Yeats's proposals to both Maud Gonne and her daughter Iseult, his marriage to Georgie Hyde-Lees, his psychic correspondence with Leo Africanus, and his wife's automatic writing, that are dramatized in *The Wild Swans at Coole* and the rich variety of styles that gives expression to these key personal and spiritual experiences.[10] Events, however, become secondary in *The Wild Swans at Coole* to the search for a new personality or mask for the poet. In essence, Yeats was now seeking, after making his quarrel with the world and accepting defeat, what in *Per Amica Silentia Lunae* he called a "revelation of reality" only possible in the poet's quarrel between himself and his "anti-self."[11] To forge that antiself, to discover "all / That I have handled least, least looked upon" had by now become the overriding issue of Yeats's art and the chief concern of *The Wild Swans at Coole*.

The volume opens with a clear and dramatic image in "The Wild Swans at Coole" of the poet suspended between a past that has wounded him emotionally—"And now my heart is sore"—and a future that offers little hope for any Wordsworthian "abundant recompense." While the twilight, autumnal setting is reminiscent of Yeats's early verse, the poem sets the scene in a crisp and sparse diction that fits the poet's barren state of mind and feeling. Rather than representing a dream of escape, the "autumn beauty" of Coole Park stands as a stark image of the fading dreams of the poet in the "nineteenth autumn" since he first made his count of the "nine-and-fifty swans."

"The Wild Swans at Coole" marks the occasion of Yeats's proposal of marriage to Maud Gonne after MacBride's death in the

Easter Rising, but Yeats accomplishes far more than a contrast of his youthful hopes and passion when he first visited Coole and the barrenness of his present mood. Bradford has shown the way Yeats achieves a brilliantly controlled vision of the swan as an independent image of power and mastery by setting the scene before introducing his persona, associating the swans with the idea of passion and conquest, and shifting what was originally the third stanza to the concluding stanza of the poem.[12] The poet's own isolation, first hinted at in the odd number assigned to the swans, now becomes, with the shift in stanza arrangement, a moment of hesitation or uncertainty, echoing the dramatic moment in "The Cold Heaven," between self-conquest or defeat. While the phrasing of the question of the last stanza seems to project the inevitable loss of poetic inspiration or power, the poem's balance and precision challenges its own conclusion. "All's changed"—but whether change will bring a terrible loss of imagination or a terrible beauty remains a subject for exploration:

> But now they drift on the still water,
> Mysterious, beautiful;
> Among what rushes will they build,
> By what lake's edge or pool
> Delight men's eyes when I awake some day
> To find they have flown away?
>
> (CP, 129–30)

"In Memory of Major Robert Gregory," Yeats's great elegy, at first seems a disappointing answer to "The Wild Swans at Coole." The possible loss of Coole Park now becomes an inevitability with the death of Lady Gregory's son. The anticipated move into Thoor Ballylee is cast in a somber mood by the summons to the ghosts of Lionel Johnson, John Synge, and George Pollexfen, "Discoverers of forgotten truth / Or mere companions of my youth." As Harris points out, the tower itself "is a tomb, mocking in massive permanence the dead who already crowd his memories; imprisoned, he must ironically rely upon its strength to protect him from the howling wind."[13] As for Yeats's ghostly companions, each one reflects some incompleteness shared by the poet. Johnson, chief among Yeats's Rhymers companions, wanted sanctity but "loved his learning better than mankind." Synge, the Abbey's great artist, "chose the living world for text," but only as he was dying. Yeats's uncle, George Pollexfen, learned the secrets of the "outrageous stars" but only at the cost of growing "sluggish and contemplative." Sharing their interests, Yeats, too, appears fated to live an isolated, bitter, and sluggish old age.

The sudden appearance of Robert Gregory's ghost seems the final blow, his death bringing a tragic finish to Yeats's dream of Unity of Culture. Marsh, however, points out that Yeats's celebration of Gregory as "soldier, scholar, horseman" transforms the elegy into "a heroic apotheosis of the human activities that make life valuable."[14] Gregory becomes a symbol of the perfect balance of the reckless courage of the active man and the passionate imagination of the artist. Though the poet, seeing Gregory's life going out like a flare, claims that his death "took all my heart for speech," the poem itself preserves Gregory's virtues and transforms them into an aesthetic goal to replace the quest for dreaming wisdom of youth and the barren anger of the middle years. "In Memory of Major Robert Gregory" signifies the end of Yeats's dream of Unity of Culture, but it also marks the beginning of a movement toward Unity of Being. Like Spenser eulogizing Sidney, Yeats writes of Gregory as a fellow artist, possessed of "secret discipline" and the knowledge of the "lovely intricacies" of craft:

> Soldier, scholar, horseman, he,
> And all he did done perfectly
> As though he had but that one trade alone.
>
> (CP, 132)

In "An Irish Airman Foresees His Death," the second of three Robert Gregory poems in *The Wild Swans at Coole*, Yeats assumes the mask of Gregory, who was killed at the Italian front when his plane crashed, and speaks directly of heroic joy. The virtues of the airman, his detachment from common loyalties and ambitions, his "lonely impulse of delight," his self-mastery and noble bearing, also suggest, as in the previous poem, the aesthetic values of a newly forged art. The only apparent difference between airman and artist is that the airman seeks the consummation of his being in a single act, while the artist seeks out an image of Unity of Being.

Denied the youthful death of the hero, Yeats turns in "Men Improve with the Years" to the image of the aging poet as a dream-worn, "weather-worn, marble triton" gazing upon the picture-book beauty of youth. The first of several Iseult Gonne poems, it contrasts age's pleasures of the mind with the passion of youth, but its attitude toward the compensations of age is at best ambivalent: "Is this my dream, or the truth? / O would that we had met / When I had my burning youth!" In "The Collar-Bone of a Hare," the contrast, less ambivalently described, is between "the old bitter world" of marriage and the Land of Youth where "the best thing is / To change my loves while dancing." The old beggar Billy Byrne in "Under the Round Tower" also rejects the conventional life and dreams of sun and moon transformed into a "golden king and silver lady" dancing and singing on tower top.

The dream of golden king and silver lady sets the stage for "Solomon to Sheba," the first marriage poem in *The Wild Swans at Coole*. Within the poem's "narrow theme of love," Yeats creates another image of Unity of Being in the marriage of Solomon's wisdom and Sheba's passion. Their tale of love narrows the world, by eliminating distractions and ambiguities, into a single thought that awaits consummation in lovemaking, an act that parallels the heroic flight and flaring death of Robert Gregory. The limitations of old age, however, reduce the poet in "The Living Beauty" to gazing on "beauty that is cast out of a mould / In bronze"; and in "A Song," the aging poet admits that exercise and persistent desire are simply not enough to keep the heart from growing old. Reduced to offering advice in "To a Young Beauty" and "To a Young Girl," Yeats recovers some of his equilibrium with the image of the poet, "at journey's end," dining with Landor and Donne and the striking memory of Maud Gonne, her "blood astir." "The Scholars" further rejects the idea of passively surrendering to old age by mocking those who "Edit and annotate the lines" written by young poets, with the image of a living Catullus. "Tom O'Roughley," in turn, defies the "logic-choppers" with its claim that "An aimless joy is a pure joy" and its fragile image of wisdom as "a butterfly / And not a gloomy bird of prey."

The vacillation between youth's passion and age's wisdom resolved only in "Solomon to Sheba," provides the dramatic situation for "Shepherd and Goatherd," the third and last Robert Gregory poem in *The Wild Swans at Coole.* Yeats wrote a fourth, "Reprisals," but did not include it in the volume because he feared its bitter tone would offend Lady Gregory. Most critics have dismissed "Shepherd and Goatherd," deliberately modeled after Spenser's *Astrophel* and Virgil's Fifth Eclogue, as too simple and artificial in its use of the pastoral elegy, but Harris has shown that the poem goes beyond convention in its dramatization of Shepherd and Goatherd as "antithetical types" who understand Gregory's nature from totally opposite perspectives and "only between them can they comprehend his fullness."[15] While the youthful shepherd mourns Gregory's death as nature's loss, the older Goatherd can sing of the supernatural path taken by Gregory's soul. The Goatherd's song, with its image of the soul as a "loaded pern" unwinding itself until "lost in trance," also sounds the first clear echo from the whirling gyres of *A Vision*, while forming its own pattern with "The Cold Heaven" by answering the question on the journey of the soul after body's death.

The Goatherd's measurement of the soul's road does not, however, bring to an end the painful journey of poetic recovery in *The Wild Swans at Coole.* In "Lines Written in Dejection," the poet, denied the magical images of the "dark leopards of the moon" and the "holy centaurs of the hills," has nothing now "but the embittered sun." No longer a child of "heroic mother moon," the poet of "The Dawn" wants to convert his bitterness into a dramatic pose or mask of passionate coldness: "I would be—for no knowledge is worth a straw— / Ignorant and wanton as the dawn." "On Woman" takes this wish another step by combining the knowledge of the poet's failure and the soul's inevitable rebirth with the hope, ex-

pressed in the desire to return in the form of "Solomon / That
Sheba led a dance," for Unity of Being. Hope becomes determination and accomplishment in "The Fisherman." Reviving the past
dream of a "freckled man" in the "grey Connemara clothes," the
poet finds strength in the image of the fisherman to write of the
"beating down of the wise / And great Art beaten down." More
than this, poetic desire—to write one poem "as cold / And passionate
as the dawn"—becomes a reality in the precision and passion of
"The Fisherman" itself.

"The Hawk" adds another image of the lonely and proud imagination to The Wild Swans at Coole, but it also dramatizes the poet's
difficulty in gaining mastery of himself and his art because of his
tendency to lapse into insincerity. The poet becomes even more distracted from his work in "Memory" by the form preserved in the
mountain grass "Where the mountain hare has lain." The likelihood that this form is Yeats's memory of Maud Gonne becomes
clear in the next group of poems on Maud Gonne as the poet's
phoenix. Like the mythic bird, Yeats's memory of Maud Gonne
now rises out of the imagination's purifying flames to assume her
original and proper role as the poet's muse. First applauded in "Her
Praise" for her work among the poor, she appears in "The People"
to admonish the poet for his bitterness against the Dublin crowd.
After "His Phoenix" contrasts her beauty, her childlike simplicity,
her pride, and her "shapely body" with present-day pretenders, "A
Thought from Propertius" claims a place for her "At Pallas Athene's
side," though it also imagines her as "fit spoil for a centaur." The
last three Maud Gonne poems—"Broken Dreams," "A Deep-Sworn
Vow," and "Presences"—accepting the beloved's physical and emotional imperfections, transforms and elevates her into a pure image
of the mind.

After the epigrammatic interlude of "The Balloon of the Mind,"
"To a Squirrel at Kyle-na-no," and "On Being Asked for a War
Poem," Yeats's only direct poetic reaction to World War I, The
Wild Swans at Coole returns to the past with "In Memory of Alfred
Pollexfen." The memory of his uncle gives Yeats the opportunity
to pay homage to his grandfather William Pollexfen and "Many a

son and daughter" buried at Sligo or "Far from the customary skies." The poem also honors the instinctive, mysterious nature of the Pollexfens by giving voice to the family superstition that a seabird's cry always follows the death of a Pollexfen.

The seven lyrics of *Upon a Dying Lady* form a vignette that transforms Mabel Beardsley Wright, the sister of Aubrey Beardsley, into another image of Unity of Being. No soldier, scholar, or horseman, Yeats's dying lady mocks death with a "distinguished grace," valor, and generosity previously associated with Coole Park. Celebrated as more of an artist than the poet honoring her, she is ranked in the company of Grania, "Achilles, Timor, Babar, Barheim, all / Who have lived in joy and laughed into the face of death." The epitome of Yeats's tragic joy, she also joins hands with other figures representing the idea of Unity of Being: the Renaissance man Gregory, Solomon and Sheba, the poet's phoenix, and the fisherman in grey Connemara clothes.

Having molded several masks of tragic joy, Yeats dramatizes his own search for Unity of Being in the last group of poems in *The Wild Swans at Coole*. The first step, represented by "Ego Dominus Tuus" is to call "to my own opposite, summon all / That I have handled least, least looked upon." In *Per Amica Silentia Lunae*, Yeats describes this "mysterious one" or "anti-self" as his Daimon or his destiny embodied in "a mask whose lineaments permit the expression of all the man most lacks, and it may be dreads, and of that only."[16] When this antiself, comparable to "a new personality," comes to the poet, it brings with it a "revelation of reality," a visionary awakening celebrated by the poets of the great tradition as "ecstasy."

The theory of the antiself in "Ego Dominus Tuus" is developed within a dramatic dialogue between Hic and Ille that takes place under Ille's "old wind-beaten tower." Hic, the objective or social self, accuses Ille of wasting his time looking for an image and advises him that he would be better off finding himself. Ille, the subjective or creative self, rejects the idea of serving the world and argues that "art / Is but a vision of reality." The debate, representing the poet's quarrel with himself, eventually focuses on Dante and

Keats, artists described by Hic as "utterly" finding themselves. Ille, however, believes that Dante and Keats found in worshipping the "most exalted lady" or singing the most "luxuriant song" what was "Most out of reach." Rejecting Hic's last argument that he study the great masters instead of tracing characters in the sand, Ille remains firm in his determination to "seek an image, not a book." Owning nothing but his "blind, stupefied" heart, he calls again to the one

> . . . who yet
> Shall walk the wet sands by the edge of the stream
> And look most like me, being indeed my double,
> And prove of all imaginable things
> The most unlike, being my anti-self,
> And, standing by these characters, disclose
> All that I seek. . . .
>
> (CP, 159)

After blessing his tower and heirs in "A Prayer on Going into My House" and cursing anyone who might harm his property, Yeats returns to his search for Unity of Being in "The Phases of the Moon." Once again, the setting is the ground surrounding the lonely tower, but the personae are now Michael Robartes and Owen Aherne, figures resurrected from Yeat's early fiction and poetry. While Aherne does little more than serve as interlocutor, Robartes, still Yeats's magus, sings the mysterious truths that Ille sought from his Daimon. That knowledge, which the poet now seeks through study and meditation, corresponds to "The Phases of the Moon" section in *A Vision*. Indeed, Yeats described "The Phases of the Moon," along with "The Double Vision of Michael Robartes" and "Michael Robartes and the Dancer," as "a text for exposition."[17]

While the poet toils after "An image of mysterious wisdom," he is mocked by Robartes for finding "Mere images." When Aherne suggests that Robartes "speak / Just truth enough" to show the poet the futility of his study, Robartes, remembering "Rosa Alchemica," refuses because Yeats wrote in the "extravagant style" of Pater that he was dead and "dead I choose to be." He does sing, but only for

Aherne's ear, "the changes of the moon," which correspond to Yeats's own theory of personality and history:

> Twenty-and-eight the phases of the moon,
> The full and the moon's dark and all the crescents,
> Twenty-and-eight, and yet but six-and-twenty
> The cradles that a man must needs be rocked in:
> For there's no human life at the full or the dark.
>
> (CP, 161)

In the moon's first quarter, the personality is all heroic instinct, but in the second quarter, especially at phase twelve, "Athene takes Achilles by the hair" and the intellect controls and shapes the body. After the twelfth phase, the personality travels through two more "cradles" before reaching the visionary phase fifteen where "All thought becomes an image and the soul / Becomes a body." After the full moon "When all is fed with light and heaven is bare," the moon descends through its final phases. The personality that had struggled to find an image of itself now serves the world until the dark of the moon when everything is reduced to chaos so that "the first thin crescent" can be "wheeled round once more." Hunchback, Saint, and Fool are the last three human phases—twenty-six through twenty-eight—and represent the final deformity of body, soul, and intellect. Robartes's song now at an end, the poem seems to dissolve itself into the first phase of the moon: "a bat rose from the hazels / And circled round him with its squeaky cry, / The light in the tower window was put out."

The last five poems in *The Wild Swans at Coole* expand the key images and ideas expressed in Robartes's song. "The Cat and the Moon" makes Maud Gonne's great black cat into a playful image of the fateful correspondence between bodily rhythms and the changes of the moon: "Does Minnaloushe know that his pupils / Will pass from change to change." In "The Saint and the Hunchback," Yeats gives dramatic life to two of Robartes's symbols for the last three human phases. While the hunchback seeks the saint's blessing and a release from his obsession, symbolized by his hump,

with the glories of the past, the saint, whose phase inevitably follows the hunchback's, can offer only patience until the deformed
body is released from bitter thoughts of past conquests and passions.
In "Two Songs of a Fool" and "Another Song of a Fool," Yeats takes
on the identity of Robartes's last human phase to voice certain
truths while hiding behind the mask of mindless irresponsibility.
The first poem, as Norman Jeffares points out, actually expresses
Yeats's concern for the harelike Iseult Gonne now that he has married George, his "speckled cat."[18] The second poem, less personal,
reveals the fool's secret knowledge of the soul's final release from
the past in its image of the "great purple butterfly" who once lived
as "a schoolmaster / With a stark, denying look."

"The Double Vision of Michael Robartes" ends *The Wild Swans
at Coole* with the whirling image of a dancing girl that Frank
Kermode describes as "a movement beyond that of life" and a representation of "a higher order of truth, of being as against becoming,
which is dead only in that it cannot change."[19] Set at Cashel in
Tipperary, near the chapel restored by the twelfth-century Mun-
ster king Cormac MacCarthy, the poem opens at the dark of the
moon, where all is "dead beyond our death" and the soul reveals
its obedience to its fate, "Knowing not evil and good." This dark
vision, however, is counterpointed by another revelation by "the
moon's light / Now at its fifteenth night." Ellmann sees this second
or double vision as representing the "powers of the mind raised to
a supernatural degree. The Sphinx is the intellect, gazing on both
known and unknown things; the Buddha is the heart gazing on
both loved and unloved things; and the dancing girl, most important of all, is primarily an image of art."[20] As the double vision
fades, Robartes or the poet, overwhelmed by an image the equal of
"Homer's Paragon," makes his moan and, in an act of homage,
kisses a stone. His final act, arranging "it in a song," corresponds
to the poem just written, a poem recognizing the poet's agony when
"caught between the pull / Of the dark moon and the full," yet
affirming his power to capture in the mind's eye an image that out-
dances life's antinomies. Supplanting the fifty-nine swans, the
image of the dancing girl ends a volume that began in a mood of

self-doubt with a moment of aesthetic triumph over the conflict and limitations of time and space, and mind and heart.

The Middle Plays

While Yeats was emerging from the cloud and foam of his early verse with new images and a new sense of responsibility, he was also looking for a way to overcome the distractions of writing for a public theatre. Jeffares points out that, as early as 1899, Yeats wanted a theatre exclusively for himself and his friends, a type of play "free from the demands of commercialism, whose words could be restored to their sovereignty over gesture and scenery, and the element of ritual in drama rediscovered."[21] Believing drama an expression of life at its most intense moment, Yeats discovered in 1913 a form perfectly suited to his ideas in the Japanese Noh plays translated by Ernest Fenollosa and brought to Yeats's attention by Ezra Pound. While under the influence of Noh drama, Yeats announced that he had "invented a form of drama, distinguished, indirect, and symbolic, and having no need of mob or Press to pay its way—an aristocratic form."[22] With the help of Gordon Craig's ideas on simplified scenery, Yeats had converted the conventions of the Noh with its emphasis on symbol, allusion, ceremony, and ritual into a dramatic form that fused verse, music, and dance into "an image of nobility and strange beauty" or what Yeats called "The Theatre's anti-self."[23]

At the Hawk's Well was the first play Yeats wrote under the influence of the Noh and one of *Four Plays for Dancers*, published in 1921. Three Musicians, their faces made up to resemble masks, open the play by calling to the mind's eye, while they unfold and fold a black cloth, "A well long choked up and dry" attended by an Old Man and the Guardian of the Well. The Old Man, who has been waiting at the well for fifty years to drink from its immortality-granting waters, is joined by a Young Man, the legendary Cuchulain. Never having waited long for anything, the Young Man is confident that the waters will appear soon, but the Guardian of the Well, assuming the symbolic form of the hawk, lures Cuchulain away from the well with her dance. The waters briefly flow but the Old Man has covered his head in fear of the hawklike figure, while the Young Man follows the challenge of the hawk's cry. The play ends with the Musicians' song proclaiming the bitterness of the revelation at the well and the sweetness of the more common life:

> O lamentable shadows,
> Obscurity of strife!
> I choose a pleasant life
> Among indolent meadows;
> Wisdom must live a bitter life.
>
> (*CPl*, 219)

Wilson has traced the similarities between *At the Hawk's Well* and the Noh, Irish legend, and the quest for the Holy Grail, but his interpretation of the play's meaning as "consummate spiritual delusion" is too extreme.[24] While the dance play does suggest that life is a preparation for something that never comes, the well's immortal waters do flow at the moment when human fear and courage express themselves most intensely. *At the Hawk's Well* offers a bitter wisdom for those who seek immortality, but it also creates within its stylized patterns an image of tragic joy. Cuchulain fails to win his immortality in his mortal life, but, by pursuing the eternal cry of adventure, his immortality is assured in the legends sung after "men heap his burial-mound / And all the history ends."[25]

The Only Jealousy of Emer appears to be something of a sequel to *At the Hawk's Well*. Revised over the years and converted into a prose version called *Fighting the Waves*, the play concentrates on the moment when Cuchulain lies between life and death after having "fought the deathless sea." Beside Cuchulain are Emer, his wife, and Eithne Inguba, his mistress, both of whom try to win him back to life. Bricriu, the "Maker of Discord," takes the shape of Cuchulain, however, and challenges Emer with the vision of Cuchulain's Ghost being taken to the Country-under-Water by Fand, the same Woman of the Sidhe who had lured Cuchulain from the immortal well. Told by Bricriu that she must renounce

her love for Cuchulain as the price for his return to life, Emer decides at the last moment to accept this bitter choice and return
Cuchulain, ironically, to the arms of his mistress.

In his elaborate notes to the play, Yeats wrote that he had filled
The Only Jealousy of Emer with "those little known convictions"
about the cycle of the soul that he had described in "The Phases
of the Moon."[26] Taking the lure, Yeats critics have examined the
play in the light of Yeats's system and concentrated primarily on
Cuchulain as a tragic figure of heroic phase twelve caught between
the pull of phases fifteen and one, represented by Fand and Bricriu.
Nathan and Ure, however, see the play as an intense expression
of Emer's fate as the loving and responsible wife who, in choosing
to deny her own nature, finds her own tragic identity.[27] As Emer's
tragedy, *The Only Jealousy of Emer* is more counterpoint than
sequel to *At the Hawk's Well* because it dramatizes the moment
when a personality just the opposite of Cuchulain's finds its own
heroic fulfillment. In its final form, *The Only Jealousy of Emer*
elevates its heroine to the same tragic stature as the heroine of
Yeats's *Deirdre*.

Generally regarded as the purest of Yeats's Noh plays, especially
in its imitation of the spirit play *Nishikigi*, *The Dreaming of the
Bones* is an expression of Yeats's belief in the soul's dreaming back
through the most passionate moments of its past life. After the
Musicians' song sets the play's isolated scene and atmosphere, a
Young Man, praying in Irish, appears and is joined almost immediately by a Stranger and a Young Girl, both wearing heroic masks.
The strange couple, seeming to know that the Young Man has
fought at the Dublin Post Office, help him in his flight from the
English, but as they do, they also draw him into a conversation about
the dreaming bones of the accursed dead. After describing the terrible fate of ghostly lovers whose "lips can never meet" because of
their "memory of a crime," the Stranger and the Young Girl reveal
themselves as Diarmuid and Dervorgilla, the Irish lovers responsible
for bringing English invaders to Ireland in the twelfth century.
Told that the lovers can escape their curse only if "one of their race
forgave at last," the Young Man, sorely tempted, refuses to forgive

them and leaves them to the agony of their dance of unfulfilled passion:

> For though we have neither coal, nor iron ore,
> To make us wealthy and corrupt the air,
> Our country, if that crime were uncommitted,
> Had been most beautiful. . . .
>
>   (CPl, 443)

Yeats critics have gone into their own agony of trance in discussing *The Dreaming of the Bones.* Diversity of opinions range from Helen Vendler's argument that the Young Man is refusing the experience of Irish history to David R. Clark's judgment that the Young Man, being the consequence of the crime of Diarmuid and Dervorgilla, cannot forgive the lovers.[28] No matter what the view of the Young Man's refusal, the play itself is an intense, imaginative vision of the moment when the personae of Ireland's past and present meet, recognize each other, but fail to reach an understanding or reconciliation. *The Dreaming of the Bones* may well announce the coming of a new age in the crowing cock of March—denial is another possibility—but the force of this play, which Yeats feared was too incendiary for a Dublin audience, is in its expression of Ireland's great tragedy, its centuries of oppression, betrayal, and remorse.

Calvary, the last of the *Four Plays for Dancers,* has been something of a muddle for Yeats critics. Never performed during Yeats's lifetime, the play dramatizes Christ's dreaming back through his Passion, a journey of the soul that repeats itself every Good Friday. During His dream, Christ encounters a bitter Lazarus, a defiant Judas, and three Roman soldiers indifferent to the gift of salvation. Only after Lazarus says that he prefers death's solitude to Christ's message of love, after Judas taunts Him with his hope that "if a man betrays a God / He is the stronger of the two," and after the soldiers rebuke Him for not being "The God of dice," does Christ cry out "My Father, why hast Thou forsaken Me?"

Calvary has been a disturbing play because of the disparity be-

tween the traditional concept of the Savior and Yeats's dramatization, which has its affinity with Gautier's declaration in his preface to *Mademoiselle de Maupin* that Christ had not died for him and Wilde's "The Doer of Good," a story about a Christ bitterly condemned by those who have suffered because of his miracles. The play is further complicated by the Yeatsian bias in favor of the self-delighting as opposed to the self-serving personality. While there have been efforts to identify Christ with the indifferent Heron, symbol of the subjective personality, the play attempts no such identification—the Musicians sing "God has not died for the white heron" and later "God has not appeared to the birds." Yeats's Christ represents the extreme manifestation of the objective personality—"I do my Father's will"—challenged by a Lazarus angry that he has been forced to accept Christ's salvation, by a Judas defiant in his belief that he made the choice to betray Christ, and by the Roman soldiers who dance only to the God of chance. *Calvary*, as Yeats's cryptic notes suggest, is more a dance of choice and chance than a Noh version of the greatest story ever told.

The Cat and the Moon, which Yeats intended for *Four Plays for Dancers* "but did not do so as it was in a different mood,"[29] is another treatment of the Yeatsian subjective and objective personalities. A Blind Beggar and a Lame Beggar journey to the holy well of St. Colman to ask the saint for a miracle restoring them to wholeness. When the saint, speaking through the voice of one of the Musicians, offers the choice of a blessing or a cure, the Blind Beggar takes his sight and the Lame Beggar the blessing. The play ends when the saint climbs upon the Lame Beggar's back and forces him to perform a miracle by dancing. While the Musicians sing the verses of Minnaloushe, *The Cat and the Moon* acts out in a more comical form than Yeats's other dance plays, the basic division of personalities and the search of each extreme for a return to unity. The Blind Beggar, knowing enough of lonely wisdom, wants the vision to see the real world; the Lame Beggar, having seen enough of this world, prefers a blessed vision. Neither, however, gets the best or the worst of the bargain, for when the Lame Beggar says that his companion has lost his soul by refusing the blessing, the

saint responds with the ambivalent "Maybe so." The more likely
conclusion is that both beggars have made the right choice in seeking their opposite and have an equal chance of dancing the miracle
of completeness.

Yeats wrote or drastically revised several other plays during this
period that, while not modeled after the Noh, show Yeats's interest
in the mask of the hero and a more precise form of dramatic art.
The Green Helmet, borrowing much of its plot from the Irish
Feast of Bricriu and the English *Sir Gawain and the Green Knight*,
was written as heroic farce and as a possible introduction to *On
Baile's Strand*. Praised by John Rees Moore for its narrative gusto
and satirical bite,[30] the play gives Cuchulain the unusual role of
peacemaker, but he still emerges at the end as the epitome of the
Yeatsian hero. Cuchulain meets the first challenge of the Red Man
by taking the green helmet, offered to the bravest warrior, and sharing a drink from it with his companions. When the Red Man returns and demands the head of a warrior as his due, Cuchulain
willingly offers his own; but the Red Man, instead, places the green
helmet on Cuchulain's head, crowning him champion:

> And I choose the laughing lip
> That shall not turn from laughing, whatever rise or
> fall;
> The heart that grows no bitterer although betrayed
> by all;
> The hand that loves to scatter; the life like a
> gambler's throw.
>
> (*CPl*, 243)

The Hour-Glass, based on "The Priest's Soul," a folk story preserved by Lady Wilde, is the closest Yeats ever came to writing a
morality play. Yeats's revisions, begun in 1912 and continued off
and on until the play's publication in prose and prose-verse versions
in 1922, were prompted by his fear that he had created a coward
in the Wise Man and had made the play's moral too blatant. He
became especially distressed when he heard that a music-hall singer
had been converted by the play. In its final version, *The Hour-Glass*

dramatizes the spiritual ordeal of a foolish Wise Man who denies the invisible country by teaching that there is no God. After an angel appears and tells the Wise Man, given only an hour to live, that he will be consigned to Hell unless he finds someone who still believes in God, the Wise Man tries, in vain, to convince his students and his family that the invisible country exists. At the play's end, however, the Wise Man can refuse the Fool's belief in God because he has found in himself the believer he seeks: "I see it all: / We perish into God and sink away / Into reality—the rest's a dream." This revised ending, perceived by Henn as a dramatization of the spiritual terror to come in "The Second Coming" and *Supernatural Songs*,[31] raises the Wise Man from moral coward to spiritual hero and brings *The Hour-Glass* more into line with Yeats's middle plays.

The Unicorn from the Stars is an adaptation of *Where There Is Nothing* and still expresses the mood and ideas of the earlier play. Yeats had hoped to achieve, with the help of Lady Gregory, who practically rewrote the play into dialect, a play linking "ancient frenzies and hereditary wisdom; a yoking of antiquities; a Marriage of Heaven and Hell."[32] Martin Hearne, Yeats's visionary hero in the play, awakens from a dream of unicorns trampling grapes with the conviction that he will soon receive a command from the Unicorn from the Stars. Believing that a beggar's cry of "Destruction on us all" is his command, he leads the rabble, who mistake him for a patriot-outlaw, against the Big Houses until he falls into another trance. This time when he awakens, Martin Hearne knows that his "business is not reformation but revelation," but he is killed in a struggle with the Constables. His final vision of Heaven as "continual battle," however, is central to Yeats's own theory of art, and his earlier vision of the Apocalyptic Unicorn, which Giorgio Melchiori identifies as a major image from Yeats's esoteric beliefs, is a revelation of Yeats's increasing anticipation of the violence and ruin that would precede "a Second Coming, a new dispensation."[33]

The Player Queen, the last play from this period, began as a verse tragedy in 1908 and, by the time it was published in 1922, had been converted into a farce. Yeats changed the play because of its theme, "the finding or not finding of what I have called the Antithetical Self; and because passion and not thought makes tragedy, what I made had neither simplicity nor life."[34] The play does heavily rely on the idea that the annunciation of a new cycle of history begins with the coupling of mystical beast and human victim, an idea first explored in an early story, "The Adoration of the Magi," and later given lyric expression in "Leda and the Swan," but its chief virtue lies in its farcical treatment of ideas critical to *A Vision*, while it validates the reality of those ideas.[35] Septimus, sounding very much like Yeats when he curses popular poets and "this uncharitable town," suffers from his love for a beautiful woman and goes about proclaiming "a New Dispensation" of the Unicorn. He is made only too human, however, by his drunkenness, hypocrisy, and incompetence. Dectora and the Queen, while personifying Yeats's theory of the mask, are also humanized, the former by her ruthlessness and cunning, the latter by her timidity and lack of grace. When Dectora takes the throne, however, she acts out the triumph of her Daimon or antiself, while the event in itself brings about the new age prophesied by Septimus and the Old Beggar.

While the dance play became Yeats's most significant dramatic achievement during this period, *The Player Queen* represents his increasing effort to join passion and vision into a traditional and precise art form. Having accepted his responsibilities, he could now seek out that right mastery that had eluded him through bouts of frustration and bitterness. His future verse would have a tone of self-assurance and his new images would seem self-delighting, self-sustaining, even though his vision, at times, would grow darker. The lonely swan at Coole Park was about to become a golden bird singing to the lords and ladies of Byzantium.

Chapter Five

The Artifice of Eternity: A Poet's Vision

At the beginning of his career and through all the years of vacillation, Yeats saw himself as an Irish poet. When he dreamed of escape from a world full of sorrow, his vision took the shape of Danaan land or the lake isle of Innisfree. When he cursed fate, it was because romantic Ireland was dead and gone, and he had wasted so much energy on his fool-driven land. And when he expressed the pain of loneliness and the possible loss of creativity, his vision took the shape of wild swans at Coole Park. Even when he turned to the remote form of the Noh play because of his frustration with the Abbey crowd, he turned to Irish legend, to Cuchulain and Emer, Diarmuid and Dervorgilla, for substance.

During the period of Yeats's greatest achievement, while he completed the first edition of *A Vision* and wrote the powerful verse of *The Tower*, he expressed the drama of his life and art as much as ever in Irish imagery. As rough beast slouched toward Bethlehem, the violence Yeats saw as the annunciation of a new age had became a reality in the terrible beauty of the Easter Rising and the terror of revolution and civil war. While Yeats explored the mysteries of interpenetrating gyres and the twenty-eight incarnations of the moon, he found an image for his most complex and violent thought in his ancient tower at Ballylee. His holy city of the imagination was Byzantium, but his poems were written for the people of Burke and Grattan, for young, upstanding men, kin to Yeats's fisherman. The cause of great bitterness and pain, Ireland was still

the source of his most intense pride and the measure of his greatest
vision.

Michael Robartes and the Dancer (1921)

Michael Robartes and the Dancer serves as a bridge between *The
Wild Swans at Coole* and *The Tower*. Its political poems could
have been included in *The Wild Swans at Coole*, but were deliberately withheld because they did not fit into the retrospective pattern of the earlier volume. Its supernatural or visionary poems,
especially "Michael Robartes and the Dancer," offer a further poetic
expression of Yeats's work on *A Vision*. Yeats actually feared that he
had forsaken Goethe's advice, had put too much philosophy in
Michael Robartes and the Dancer, and made some of the poems too
difficult: "It is hard for a writer, who has spent much labour upon
his style, to remember that thought, which seems to him natural
and logical like that style, may be unintelligible to others."[1]

Michael Robartes and the Dancer has attracted its own share of
attention but mostly because of "Easter 1916" and "The Second
Coming." Bloom believes that "this would be a justly neglected
book" but for the fame of two poems, and Rajan judges it "as a
brief and not very memorable volume."[2] Donald Davie, however,
finds several poems that make up an interesting commentary on
"the matter of woman's role in society," and Unterecker, as perceptive as usual, discovers in *Michael Robartes and the Dancer* the first
vivid expression of Yeats's "themes of personal joy set against a
background of irrational destructive violence, until driving himself
into postures of prophetic ecstasy, he finally looks on life's tragic
scene with gay eyes."[3]

The first four poems are similar, except for their greater emphasis
on bodily knowledge, to the final visionary poems of *The Wild
Swans at Coole*. "Michael Robartes and the Dancer," linked to the
previous volume by its title and Yeats's note naming it as part of
his text for exposition, humanizes Robartes and the dancing girl,
identified by Henn as Iseult Gonne,[4] in a dramatic dialogue between He and She. Using the imagery of "The Phases of the

Moon," He advises She to reject abstract thought and seek knowledge in "that beating breast, / That vigorous thigh, that dreaming eye." Preferring a sinewy thought comparable to Paul Veronese's "imagined bodies" and Michael Angelo's art, He argues, within a viewpoint basic to *A Vision*, that blessedness is to be found in an image of the body, an idea, as She notes, not compatible with conventional thought.

"Solomon and the Witch," another marriage-bed poem, proves Robartes's argument. Another of Yeats's magus figures, Solomon equates the ecstasy of sexual orgasm with the visionary moment that announces the coming of a new age. He tells Sheba their lovemaking was strong enough to be "worth a crow" by the cockerel that "crowed out eternity" and "Thought to have crowed it in again," but either "too strong" or "not strong enough" to end time. Noticing "the moon is wilder every minute," Sheba wants to "try again," a desire that playfully hints that lovemaking with its frenzy and consummate unity of opposites is an experience at least approaching the perfection of Yeats's phase fifteen.

Yeats wrote an elaborate note to "An Image from a Past Life" in which he explained, using the ruse of Aherne and Robartes once again, that dream images are often "from the state immediately preceding our birth" and "from the Spiritus Mundi—that is to say, from a general storehouse of images which have ceased to be a property of any personality or spirit."[5] Thus an image of a lover from a past life may haunt one's dreams "till the last drop of emotion is exhausted," and that image, called the Over Shadower, may easily pass from one mind to another. In "An Image from a Past Life," She, now a mask for George Yeats, has seen the fearful image of "A sweetheart from another life" floating in the stream of He's mind. He tries to comfort She with the thought that the image makes him fonder, but She recognizes the image as a rival threatening the marriage-bed. While the poem serves as another Robartes text for exposition, it also has a personal side because of the likelihood that this image from a past life is Maud Gonne. She's fear carries over into "Under Saturn," a companion piece to "An Image from a Past Life," and forces He to unveil himself as Yeats and the

disturbing image as more personal than visionary. While now identifying the image as the lost love of his youth, the poet's major concern is to express his gratitude to his wife for "the wisdom that you
brought, / The comfort that you made" and remind her that his
ancestry, which she now shares, is a stronger bond to the past than
a memory of lost love.

Having explored the mysteries of the marriage-bed and expressed
his loyalty to his wife, Yeats moves on to the political event that
both inspired his return to Ireland and disturbed, with its after-
shocks, his new life. In "Easter 1916," Yeats gains a depth of statement and vision far beyond the bitter polemics of "September
1913." While honoring the sacrifice of those who died in the Rising, "Easter 1916" also raises several profound questions about the
character, motivation, and necessity of the act itself. The poem
opens with a dramatic portrait of the casual political scene before
a single act of heroism changed everything into "A terrible beauty."
The next stanza names the dramatis personae, Constance (Gore-
Booth) Markiewicz, Padraic Pearse, Thomas MacDonagh, and
even that "drunken, vainglorious lout" John MacBride, and transforms their memory into the powerful image of the stone that
troubles "the living stream." In the last stanza, however, the same
stone becomes a symbol of the harsh realities following the Rising.
The poem now raises the possibility that "Too long a sacrifice /　Can
make a stone of the heart," and asks if the deaths were really necessary and if "excess of love" bewildered them "till they died." These
important questions posed, "Easter 1916" returns to its public
theme, the transformation of Ireland's martyrs into an image of
tragic joy:

> I write it out in a verse—
> MacDonagh and MacBride
> And Connolly and Pearse
> Now and in time to be,
> Wherever green is worn,
> Are changed, changed utterly:
> A terrible beauty is born.
>
> (CP, 179–80)

The next four poems move the poet toward a more personal judgment of the Rising by responding to the questions raised in "Easter 1916." "Sixteen Dead Men" dismisses the possibility that England may keep its promise of home-rule after "Germany's overcome" with the weighty image of "MacDonagh's bony thumb." In "The Rose Tree," the question on the necessity of sacrifice is answered again in a dramatic conversation between Pearse and James Connolly. A symbol now of Ireland's national vision, the rose tree has been withered by "a breath of politic words" and can be revived only by the blood of martyrs. "On a Political Prisoner" also responds to a question in "Easter 1916," that too long a sacrifice can change the heart into a stone, but its answer appears to be yes, at least in the case of Con Markiewicz. Though her internment has brought patience, caught in the image of the gull eating "its bit" from her fingers, Yeats's political prisoner, once clean and sweet like the "rock-bred, sea-borne bird," has allowed her mind to become "a bitter, an abstract thing." The reason behind Yeats's harsh judgment of a woman he had admired so much during his youthful visits to Lissadell becomes clear in "The Leaders of the Crowd." In his last political poem in this sequence, Yeats returns to his familiar role of railing against Dubliners who mistake the gutter for Helicon and calumny for song. In other words, not knowing that "Truth flourishes where the student's lamp has shone," the mob will never appreciate the poet's gift to his country. Where fanaticism is admired, the artist's lonely sacrifice is ignored or ridiculed.

"Towards Break of Day," taking its cue from the student's lamp, returns to the theme of poetic wisdom. The poem records an actual dream Yeats and his wife shared in 1919 during a stay at a hotel in County Wicklow. While the phenomenon of lovers halving a dream is clear enough, the dream imagery of a Sligo waterfall and Arthur's "marvellous stag" comes from too much of a private experience. "Demon and Beast" presents similar problems, but Yeats does identify the crafty demon as hatred and the loud beast as desire. Only by perning in a gyre between hatred and desire can the poet finally win his freedom and gain "Right mastery of natural things." Using the portraits in the Dublin National Gallery and the monastic reveries of St. Anthony as proof that mastery is possible, the poem, something of a precursor to "Byzantium," offers a symbolic glimpse at the process by which artist and saint reach a state of vision.

Visionary process leads to the shocking vision of the rough beast with "lion body and the head of a man" that appears in "The Second Coming," one of Yeats's most memorable and provocative poems. The first stanza, reinforced by a title strongly suggestive of the hope of Christ's Second Coming and the terror of the approaching beast of the Apocalypse, prepares for the moment of revelation with the gyring image of falcon and falconer and the detached description of the collapse of civilization. The opening image, set up by the repetition of turning, creates a sense of foreboding; the falcon, a bird associated with nobility but also a bird of prey, is out of control, "cannot hear the falconer." The next lines, relying upon the passive voice, state the obvious:

> Things fall apart; the centre cannot hold;
> Mere anarchy is loosed upon the world,
> The blood-dimmed tide is loosed, and everywhere
> The ceremony of innocence is drowned;
> The best lack all conviction, while the worst
> Are full of passionate intensity.
>
> (CP, 184–85)

The repetition of surely keys the second stanza, making its revelation as inevitable as the uncontrolled destruction preceding it. Hardly are the anticipatory words spoken, when a "vast image out of Spiritus Mundi," Yeats's "general storehouse of images," appears in the mind's eye. A sphinxlike figure emerges, its shape and movement symbolic of the demon of intellectual hatred—"A gaze blank and pitiless"—and the beast of passionate energy— "moving its slow thighs." While the indignant desert birds reel or gyre above it, Yeats's demon beast, vexed to nightmare during its twenty centuries of stony sleep by Christ's rocking cradle, now "Slouches towards Bethlehem to be born," its birth to begin an age the exact and terrifying antithesis to the Christian age coming to an end.

"The Second Coming" has inspired a flood of critical comments, ranging from the harsh judgment, shared by Spender and Mac-Neice, that the poem prophesies "with a certain relish" the coming of Fascism to the more positive view, shared by Ellmann, Tindall, and many others, that the poem is more prophetic than political in its dramatization of what Yeats, in discussing his own poem, called the growing "cruelty of governments."[6] While the poem has been judged politically, Jon Stallworthy has shown that Yeats deliberately removed all topical allusions to politics and war from his early drafts to make the focus and range of the poem wider and to avoid the sort of partisanship insisted upon by Spender and MacNeice.[7] He eliminated references to the Great War and the Russian Revolution and the absence of Burke or Pitt in contemporary politics, thereby ending his early intention of setting up a correspondence in the poem between the fall of the Russian aristocracy and the failure of the modern age to champion the order and nobility of mind Yeats associated with the eighteenth century. Yeats, however, retained or added a more general diction, "anarchy," "innocence," "the best," "the worst," to create fewer distractions and place the meaning of the poem in the visionary and more generally acceptable pattern of cyclical history.

Another problem for critics is the close association between the imagery of "The Second Coming" and the central ideas of *A Vision*. Gyres whirl and cradles rock in both poem and philosophical system, while Yeats's rough beast dramatizes the moment, expounded upon in *A Vision*, when an antithetical age begets itself upon a primary age. Ellmann and others, however, have argued convincingly that the poem stands on its own prophetic authority.[8] Grounded in the increasing violence of the contemporary world and Yeats's own system of violently changing phases and ages, "The Second Coming" contains a stark, powerful vision of the chaos following the collapse of traditional values and the attendant fear of the unknown.

"A Prayer for My Daughter," "A Meditation in Time of War," and "To Be Carved on a Stone at Thoor Ballylee" close out *Michael Robartes and the Dancer* with quiet affirmations of faith in the face of the approaching horror. While the latter two poems are brief statements of Yeats's belief in the Platonic One and his commitment to his ancestry and his work, "A Prayer for My Daughter" offers one of Yeats's most heartfelt expressions of his love and respect for the custom and ceremony he had for so long associated with Coole Park, but which he now transfers to the future life he desires for his daughter. Harris praises the poem as "the emotional sequel, not simply the theoretical complement, to 'In Memory of Major Robert Gregory'" and sees its celebration of the "aesthetic innocence of the soul's self-created beauty" as a counterpoint to the historical catastrophe prophesied in "The Second Coming."[9]

Using the same ottava rima stanza of the Gregory elegy, Yeats opens "A Prayer for My Daughter" with the persona, troubled by a howling storm, pacing the floor of his tower and struggling in prayer against "the great gloom" in his mind. Having worked himself into a state of "excited reverie," he imagines

> That the future years had come,
> Dancing to a frenzied drum,
> Out of the murderous innocence of the sea.

> (CP, 185)

In defiance of the terrifying spectre of the future and his own despair, he offers up his prayer, a combination of criticism for those who think "beauty a sufficient end" and praise for a beauty tempered by "natural kindness" and a "heart-revealing intimacy." For his daughter to gain and preserve this beauty, she must acquire a learned courtesy, a merriment associated with the linnet's song, and a sense of tradition, symbolized by Daphne's "green laurel / Rooted in one dear perpetual place." Understanding the value of ceremony and custom, she can drive out hatred from her heart, recover the soul's "radical innocence," and merit a bridegroom who will bring her to "a house / Where all's accustomed, ceremonious." That the poet's art can achieve this same beauty is strongly hinted at within the imagery and dramatic structure of "A Prayer for My Daughter." The search for Unity of Being, projected here in a prayer for the future, was about to take the form of a journey to the holy city of Byzantium.

A Vision (1925, 1937)

A Vision, Yeats's revelation of his perplexing philosophical system based on interpenetrating gyres and the phases of the moon, was first published two years before the masterful poems of *The Tower*. A constant labor since his marriage in 1917, the first edition of *A Vision* appeared in early 1926, even though it was dated 1925. While Yeats's system was developed from the numerous copybooks filled with his wife's automatic writing, he kept his wife's role a secret for the 1925 publication. Instead, he identified his sources as the *Speculum Angelorum et Hominum* written by Giraldus, a sixteenth-century philosopher, *The History of the Soul Between the Sun and the Moon* by Kusta ben Luka, a Christian philosopher at the court of Caliph Harun Al-Rashid, the doctrines of an Arabian tribe called the Judwalis, and the speculations of Michael Robartes. Yeats's introduction, however, was pure fantasy in which he resurrected Robartes and Aherne from his early writings and invented the Judwalis, Kusta ben Luka, and Giraldus—the portrait of Giraldus, drawn by Edmund Dulac for the edition's frontispiece, was copied from a picture of Yeats's own face.

In the revised second edition of *A Vision* published in 1937, Yeats amended his earlier introduction and, as "Stories of Michael Robartes and His Friends," relegated it to a secondary position after "A Packet for Ezra Pound." In his new introduction, Yeats confesses that he had invented the whole business of Giraldus, the Judwalis, and Robartes's Arabian adventures because his wife did not want her role in his work to be known, but now he willingly admits that *A Vision* was inspired by an unknown writer who communicated with him through his wife's automatic writing or words spoken while she was asleep or in a trance. Taking his theme from *Per Amica Silentia Lunae*, Yeats's communicator "built up an elaborate classification of men" based on the distinction between "the perfection that is from a man's combat with himself and that which is from a combat with circumstance."[10] By November, 1917, Yeats had been given the outline of his system, "an exposition of the twenty-eight typical incarnations or phases and to the movements of their *Four Faculties*, and then on December 6th a cone or gyre had been drawn and related to the soul's judgment after death; and then just as I was about to discover that incarnations and judgment alike implied cones or gyres, one within the other, turning in opposite directions, two such cones were drawn and related neither to judgment nor to incarnations but to European history."[11]

What had been given as outline by late 1917, Yeats developed into four major essays for the first edition of *A Vision* and expanded to five for its 1937 publication. The revised edition, after its introductory materials, opens with "The Great Wheel," which is a reprinting of "What the Caliph Partly Learned" with only the title changed. "The Completed Symbol," the second essay, is, as Morton Seiden points out, "an entirely new essay . . . based on those pages in 'What the Caliph Refused to Learn' in which Yeats originally explained his geometrical symbolism."[12] It is followed by "The Soul in Judgment," a rewriting of "The Gates of Pluto," and "The Great Year of the Ancients," a long expansion "of the Platonic Year and primitive nature myth, all too briefly touched on in 'What the Caliph Refused to Learn.' "[13] The last essay, "Dove or Swan," remains unchanged except for omission of Yeats's doomsday prophecy. In its place, Yeats added "The End of the Cycle," his expression of disappointment that his final understanding remains so incomplete.

"The Great Wheel" is the most critical essay in *A Vision* because of its revelation of the book's principal symbol and its detailed discussion of the wheel and its twenty-eight incarnations. The critical symbol for Yeats's system is the gyre or, because the symbol's movement represents the struggle between the contraries of the antithetical and the primary, the double cone. As the antithetical, which "is emotional and aesthetic," gains in strength, its gyre expands while the primary gyre contracts. When the primary, which is "reasonable and moral," takes control, its gyre expands, thereby forcing the antithetical gyre to contract. The energy of Yeats's system, then, is generated by the constant vacillation between the "inner world of desire and imagination" and things external to the mind. The gyre, according to Yeats, must expand or contract according to whether mind grows in objectivity or subjectivity.[14]

Yeats adds a measure of flexibility and complexity to his system by introducing the Four Faculties, which move back and forth on the double cone in paired opposition. Representing the antithetical, Will and Mask oppose each other as what the mind is and what it most seeks to become. The primary's Creative Mind and Body of Fate, in turn, represent what the mind knows from the past lives of others and the events imposed upon the mind from without. These opposed pairs whirl in opposite directions while pulling each other back and forth, thereby creating another movement to go along with the expansion and contraction of the primary and antithetical. All this whirling and pulling gives Yeats four dimensions of human experience to balance between his objective and subjective contraries.

The discussion of the Great Wheel takes up the largest portion of *A Vision* and is by far its best known essay. By Yeats's definition, the "wheel is every completed movement of thought or life, twenty-eight incarnations, a single incarnation, a single judgment or act of thought."[15] Of these twenty-eight incarnations or phases of the moon, phases one and fifteen, equated with the dark and the full moon, are the most significant. At phase fifteen, described as the "phase of complete beauty," the human mind finds the perfect image of itself, while at phase one, the mind returns to "complete plasticity." Phases one and fifteen, however, are nonhuman, so the most critical human phases are eight and twenty-two, where the direct conflict between the antithetical and primary takes place. At phase eight, the mind finds its own strength, takes on a personality as it moves toward the fullness of phase fifteen. At phase twenty-two, the mind finds its strength broken and loses its personality as it slips toward the darkness and oblivion of phase one.

Beginning with phase two, Yeats gives an elaborate explanation for each of the twenty-eight incarnations and describes the function of the Four Faculties in each phase. The early primary phases are characterized by the slow, tentative development of individuality. Phase two is the beginning of energy, phase three ambition, while phases four and five represent the mind growing reflective of bodily instinct, then of nature's rhythm. In phase six, the "vague, half-civilized man," exemplified by Walt Whitman, appears and celebrates impulse and instinct. The mind delights in action as history in phase seven until it moves into phase eight's struggle between individuality and race that individuality must always win. In phase nine, the mind grows in self-confidence and begins its climb to perfection of thought and image. Phases ten and eleven are the incarnations of the Image Breaker, who, like Parnell, pursues a personal code of conduct and the Image Burner or Consumer, excited by his solitary belief in God. As the emphasis shifts from the instinctive to the intellectual, phase twelve, the phase of the Nietzschean hero, takes hold and the mind for the first time overcomes the body. In phase thirteen, Yeats's antithetical home for the Decadents, the personality enters its most subjective phase and the mind delights in "expression for expression's sake." Keats and many beautiful women —Helen and Maud Gonne certainly—exemplify the penultimate phase fourteen where all thought disappears into an image and "the greatest human beauty becomes possible."[16]

Yeats offers no description of phase fifteen because it represents complete beauty. All thought now becomes an image that "the soul will permanently inhabit," while the soul itself undergoes "a vision, where evil reveals itself in its final meaning."[17] Once the vision ends, the mind moves through the antithetical phases leading to the inevitable conflict of phase twenty-two that the primary is fated to win. While phase sixteen belongs to the Blakean hero who delights in "images of concentrated force," phase seventeen, Yeats's self-designated phase, offers the best opportunity for Unity of Being. In phase seventeen, exemplified by Dante and Shelley as well as Yeats, the Will still seeks out images rather than ideas and finds its true mask in the simplicity and energy of phase three. In phases eighteen through twenty-one, the mind turns to ideas more than images and expression becomes fragmentary (Wilde), dramatic (Shakespeare), and finally self-analytical (Shaw). In phase twenty-two, the direct conflict between contraries begins again, but this time the primary gains control.

In the primary phase twenty-three, exemplified by Synge, the mind turns to the external world and best expresses itself in technical mastery. Lady Gregory appears in phase twenty-four to represent the submission to a code of conduct formed completely from tradition, and another old friend, George Russell, turns up in phase twenty-five to exemplify the surrender to some organized belief or order. In phases twenty-six, twenty-seven, and twenty-eight, the incarnations of Hunchback, Saint, and Fool, the mind goes through an exhaustion of all forms of belief, renounces all forms of knowledge, and finally becomes aimless in thought and movement. Finally, the mind collapses into the complete plasticity of phase one. Mind and body become nothing more than "the instruments of supernatural manifestation, the final link between the living and more powerful beings"—that is, until they enter a new life and move once again through the phases of the moon.[18]

Books 2 and 3 of *A Vision* discuss the soul's supernatural journey before it returns to the phases of human experience. "The Completed Symbol" introduces the Four Principles, the spiritual correspondents to Yeats's Four Faculties, and unveils the Thirteenth Cone and the Great Year. The Four Principles, revealing reality but creating nothing, define the spiritual state between death and life. Corresponding to Will and Mask, Husk and Passionate Body represent the human body and its desires, but as symbol rather than substance. Spirit and Celestial Body, spiritual equivalent to Creative Mind and Body of Fate, symbolize the soul's release from its past life and its discovery of all its past reincarnations and those to come. While the Four Principles define the spiritual contraries that generate the soul between lives, Yeats's Thirteenth Cone, described as a phaseless sphere, offers a possible escape from a deterministic system. If the soul gains completeness, it is lifted out of time and reaches its ultimate stasis or rest in the Thirteenth Cone. Otherwise, it returns to the Great Wheel, which takes some two thousand years for completion, while twelve such wheels complete the cycle of a Great Year. Thus the soul's journey through phases and wheels corresponds in time to the development of human thought and personality and the movement of vast historical cycles.

"The Soul in Judgment" takes up the six states between death and birth that Yeats had already discussed to a lesser extent in "Swedenborg, Mediums, and the Desolate Places." In the first state, called the Vision of the Blood Kindred, the soul experiences a vision of all those bound to it in its past life. Next, it must undergo the Meditation or Dreaming Back in which the soul returns to past events in their order of intensity and again in their chronological order until it is emotionally exhausted. Once the chronological journey, called the Return, is completed, the soul passes through the Shiftings, where it is stripped of all memory, purified of all contraries, for its entry into the Marriage or Beatitude, Yeats's name for a spiritual state of equilibrium. In the next state, Purification, the soul, now completely free of the past, "becomes self-shaping, self-moving."[19] Finally, it enters the sixth and final state, the Foreknowledge, where it has a vision of its rebirth into another life.

Having described the soul's passage between death and life, Yeats returns to the Great Wheel and its phases in the last two books of A Vision, but broadens his phases into historical phenomena. In "The Great Year of the Ancients," Yeats discusses the Platonic Year of 36,000 years as the ideal or symbolic correspondent to his wheel and argues for a correspondence between the movement of the stars and the phases of human thought and personality. His discussion also sets the stage for a final consideration of a more compelling correspondence between the phases of the moon and the movement of history. In "Dove and Swan," Yeats selects the figure of 2,000 years for one complete movement of the wheel, which, in turn, contains two cycles of one thousand years each. He, then, describes the period from 2,000 B.C. to 1 A.D. as a complete cycle, pagan or antithetical in nature, and the present Christian or primary age, fated to end in 2,000 A.D., as another complete cycle.

In the last part of "Dove or Swan," Yeats divides the Christian age into two more cycles and shows how certain periods of history of the past 2,000 years correspond to the phases of the moon. Thus the equivalent of phase fifteen for the first thousand years is the period of the Byzantine Empire, while the collapse of Charlemagne's First Empire and the approach of the Dark Ages closes out the cycle. The second wheel within a wheel reached its phase fifteen at the time of the Renaissance, and, at the time of the writing of *A Vision*, had slipped into phase twenty-two. Yeats could now claim that an individual of one phase could very well be living out of phase historically. Indeed, the system of *A Vision* shows that antithetical Yeats had to endure the ignominy of living in a primary cycle. There was no second Troy for poet and beloved.

Yeats's surprising disappointment, expressed in his conclusion, that his dream of drawing himself into his symbol and finding the ultimate answer had never come true, has been echoed over the years by those who have tried to understand the relationship between *A Vision* and Yeats's late poetry and plays. Most critics fall short of Frank Kermode's eloquent praise of *A Vision* as "a palace of art," but Seiden and Vendler have offered the most extensive arguments for its relevance, claiming that Yeats became a major artist because of "his reliance on *A Vision*" and that the book "exists to provide a 'systematic' background against which Yeats's poetry and plays must be read to acquire their proper resonance."[20] In a more tempered study, Henn views *A Vision* as a commentary on the relationship between the poet's understanding, distorted or accurate, of history and myth and the symbolic value of his art.[21] The most balanced judgment of *A Vision*, however, belongs to Northrop Frye. who believes that the book "increased Yeats's awareness of and power to control his own creative process" and "emphasized certain forward intellectual developments for him, such as the poetic relevance of history and philosophy."[22] By also warning that *A Vision* is at best "a fragmentary and often misleading guide" to Yeats's poetry, Frye offers the often bewildered reader his own consoling view of *A Vision* as "an infernal nuisance that he can't pretend doesn't exist."[23]

A Tower (1928)

When *A Tower* was published in early 1928, Yeats wrote to Lady

Gregory that he was astonished "by its bitterness." Two months later, he repeated his astonishment to Olivia Shakespear, but added that the "bitterness gave the book its power and it is the best book I have written."[24] Critics have generally agreed with Yeats's claim for both the book's greatness and its bitterness and have attempted to identify the source of Yeats's bitter passion at a time when he was experiencing his greatest success as an artist. While Ellmann traces some of the bitterness to the death of Yeats's father, he, like most critics, believes that Yeats was most disturbed by advancing old age and the violence of the Irish civil war during the period in which he wrote the *Tower* poems.[25] While seeing himself as a "tattered coat upon a stick" and his body as a caricature of his passionate imagination, he witnessed from his tower the "dragon-ridden" days and the nights of terror and murder.

The focal point of *The Tower* is the fourteenth-century Norman castle Yeats had purchased in 1917 and renamed Thoor Ballylee. Harris believes that Yeats's renovation of his tower was a "symbolic reconstruction" of his life and art, "an ancient symbol built anew in Yeats's mind."[26] In a parallel view, John Holloway contends the power and richness of the *Tower* poems lies not in their concreteness but in their ritual making and "solemnized calling-up by the poet to people the world of his imagination."[27] It is this symbolic and ritual art, intensified by the poet's rage against old age and his bitterness at the civil war violence, that critics have judged as the essential achievement of Yeats's most honored book. Yeats's earlier desire to write a poetry of passion and precision had finally become a reality.

The Tower opens with Yeats's most famous celebration of the powers of the creative imagination and the reality of the human soul. In "Sailing to Byzantium," the poet leaves behind "Those dying generations" of young lovers caught in the "sensual music" of life's cycle and sails to "the holy city of Byzantium." Knowing that the young ignore "Monuments of unageing intellect" and recognizing himself in his old age as "a paltry thing, / A tattered coat upon a stick," the poet seeks out the city described by Yeats as the one place he would choose if granted a month in Antiquity: "in early

Byzantium, maybe never before or since in recorded history, religious, aesthetic and practical life were one."[28]

After the poet's appeal for the release of his soul so that it can attend "singing school" and study "Monuments of its own magnificence," "Sailing to Byzantium" follows the poet to his holy city where, still "fastened to a dying animal," it can petition its singing-masters to "Come from the holy fire, perne in a gyre" and gather it "Into the artifice of eternity." The last stanza, keying on the idea of a self-created immortality, projects an image of the poet's soul, free of its dying body and passionate heart, as a golden bird, "a form as Grecian goldsmiths make." Now self-sustaining, a master symbol of its own soul, the golden bird's song, both lyrical and visionary, is fit to keep "a drowsy Emperor awake" but profound enough to reveal "To lords and ladies of Byzantium / Of what is past, or passing, or to come."

"Sailing to Byzantium" has been thoroughly examined both in manuscript and in its final ottava rima form. Jeffares, Bradford, and Stallworthy have written excellent studies of the way in which Yeats shifted the emphasis in his early drafts on the physical aspects of Byzantium to a Byzantium more symbolic of artistic and spiritual perfection.[29] There have also been many searches for the sources of Yeats's symbols in the poem, though most have concentrated on Yeats's fascination with Byzantine art and the identity of Yeats's golden bird. D. J. Gordon and Ian Fletcher, Frederick L. Gwynn, and Giorgio Melchiori have pointed out Yeats's interest in the Byzantine revival of the 1890s, his visit to Ravenna in 1907, and his renewed interest in Byzantium generated by his readings in Gibbon and the Cambridge Medieval History.[30] Also noted has been Yeats's visit to Stockholm, on the occasion of his Nobel Prize, where he saw in the decorative dome of the new town hall an art that "carries the mind backward to Byzantium."[31] As for Yeats's golden bird, it has been variously identified as an echo of the nightingale of either Keats, Shelley, or Hans Christian Andersen, but Stallworthy wisely advises that Yeats deliberately "does not specify the nature of his golden bird, and we should resist the temptation to do so for him."[32]

The thread linking the numerous explications of "Sailing to

Byzantium" pernes from the common view that the poem celebrates the power of the human imagination to create images of eternity. Reflecting the judgment of many commentators, Melchiori sees Yeats's Byzantium as "an ideal image of unity of being, whether as an absolute state, or as a final achievement beyond human life."[33] Unterecker, with a similar view, finds an aesthetic balance in "Sailing to Byzantium" that allows Yeats to "sing of flesh yet be freed from its limitations."[34] Even MacNeice, who found *The Tower* "frigid, unsympathetic" on first reading, recognizes the opening poem's great theme, its "supernatural sanction" of art's supremacy.[35] Henn, however, offers the most basic summary of the intention and achievement of "Sailing to Byzantium" and the Byzantium poem that was to be written four years later: "They are great rhetorical poems of a traditional kind, which lament the passing of youth, virility, strength, and which seek to establish by symbols which are part traditional, part personal, an imagined defense against Time's decay."[36]

Harris believes that the next three poems in *The Tower* "constitute an extended, oblique analysis of the imagination" celebrated in "Sailing to Byzantium," but that by reversing the order of composition of "Nineteen Hundred and Nineteen," "Meditations in Time of Civil War," and "The Tower," Yeats also reversed the chronicle of his "gradual recovery of constructive imaginative power, his increasing consciousness of his tower's strength and his territory's fertility" to imply that his personal and poetic achievements could not avail against "inexorable historical violence and corrosive knowledge of guilt."[37] "The Tower" opens with the poet still tied to "Decrepit age," thereby making Byzantium seem more dream than reality. Never had the poet "more / Excited, passionate, fantastical / Imagination," but his age compels him to turn away from art:

> Choose Plato and Plotinus for a friend
> Until imagination, ear and eye,
> Can be content with argument and deal
> In abstract things; or be derided by
> A sort of battered kettle at the heel.

>   (CP, 192)

Pacing the battlement of the tower, the poet resists the bitter reality of old age by sending "imagination forth" to "call / Images and memories" from Ballylee's past. First Mrs. French appears as a proof of the power and authority of the imagination. Her wish to have an insolent farmer's ears clipped was taken literally by a servant so devoted that he believed in the divinity—Yeats puns the word divine—of his lady's words. Next the tale is remembered from *The Celtic Twilight* of a man drowned in the bog of Cloone because he was bewitched by the blind poet Raftery's song of Mary Hynes. That song, like those of another blind poet Homer, contains a beauty that fuses all of life's contraries into "One inextricable beam" capable of driving men mad.

The poet's declaration that to triumph he "must make men mad" prompts the memory of Hanrahan, created by Yeats in his youth as an image of his own maddening visions and frustrations. While other images, the "ancient bankrupt master," the rough Norman warriors, the nobility and peasants who have passed Ballylee's door, are called from the Great Memory to be asked if they, too, raged against old age, it is Hanrahan, that "Old lecher with a love on every wind," who most stirs the poet's mind and heart and provokes the rhetorical question: "Does the imagination dwell the most / Upon a woman won or a woman lost?" This question, its answer obvious to Yeats, drives the poet to confess his past follies and failures and forces the imagination, at last, to face the last great labyrinth, the poet's own mortality.

In the last section of "The Tower," the poet willingly accepts his mortality, yet still insists on the power of the word and the imagination by writing his will. He leaves his tower and art to "upstanding men"—the pun has been noted by a number of commentators—who appear as kin of Yeats's fisherman in grey Connemara clothes. These young fishermen are to inherit the poet's pride in his Anglo-Irish heritage, its brilliance, richness, and fertility, and his song, now fading out in the image of the swan floating upon the "Last reach of glittering stream." Prepared for death, the poet now declares his faith:

> I mock Plotinus' thought
> And cry in Plato's teeth,
> Death and life were not
> Till man made up the whole,
> Made lock, stock and barrel
> Out of his bitter soul,
> Aye, sun and moon and star, all,
> And further add to that
> That, being dead, we rise,
> Dream and so create
> Translunar Paradise.
>
> (CP, 196)

The poet, then, can accept death because he believes that the imagination, which can create reality, can also create its own eternity. With this faith, the poet makes his peace, content to study monuments of ancient culture and his own images and "memories of love." The act of preparing the soul for its passage between lives, comparable to the mother bird warming her wild nest, now becomes the poet's chief responsibility, assuming so much importance that it will blot out decay, delirium, decrepitude, and the death of friends. Having left his "faith and pride / To young upstanding men," all that remains for the poet is to enter his self-created Translunar Paradise.[38]

In "Meditations in Time of Civil War," the imagination is severely tested. Order, harmony, and grace collapse in the whirlwind of civil war violence. The madness of "The Tower" is now made monstrous by vengeful hatred. Divided into seven sections, the poem begins with "Ancestral Houses" and its image of Georgian elegance where "Life overflows without ambitious pains." The repetition of "Mere dreams, mere dreams," however, shakes the poet, who must now consider the possibility that the "abounding glittering jet" of tradition has dried up, leaving the "marvellous empty sea-shell," Yeats's symbol for the ancestral house now threatened by civil war. Since the Big House stands as the creative product of "violent bitter" men seeking their opposite in sweetness and gentleness, the poet must also wonder if present hatred and violence, having no creative outlet, will destroy the artifact most magnified and blessed by mankind.

The next five sections juxtapose the conflict of war with the conflict essential to the imagination. "My House" claims an "acre of stony ground," the tower and its winding stair, where the bitter man-at-arms, Ballylee's founder, lived in isolation and the poet now creates, "To exalt a lonely mind, / Befitting emblems of adversity." In "My Table," the poet turns to the ancient Japanese sword given to Yeats by an admirer as an emblem of changeless art and proof that "only an aching heart / Conceives a changeless work of art." The magnificent sword, however, is an image of war as well as art and summons to the poet's mind another disturbing vision of tradition and culture threatened by violence. "My Descendants" takes up another grim possibility for the future, that the inheritors of tower, sword, and art may, through "natural declension of the soul," lose these proud possessions. Should this declension happen, the poet prefers that his tower, also emblematic of his friendship with Lady Gregory and his love for George Yeats, become a "roofless ruin" fit home only for the deterministic owl reeling in the circle of the Primum Mobile.

In "The Road at My Door," the poet finally turns to the present reality of his life at the tower. The Republican Irregular and Free State Lieutenant bring the civil war to the poet's door and, with their reckless youth, mock the poet's isolation and old age, driving him deeper into his dreams of the snows of yesteryear. Stricken by what is past, passing, and to come, the poet, in "The Stare's Nest by My Window," appeals to the regenerative bees to "Come build in the empty house of the stare." While the senseless violence around him gives the poet's cry its urgency, the poet's own culpability in the violence, his creation of art out of conflict, increases the intensity of the plea, transforming it into a desolate cry of horror at "house burned" and "dead young soldier in his blood."

In the final stanza, "I See Phantoms of Hatred and of the Heart's Fullness and of the Coming Emptiness," the poet climbs the tower-top and sees a terrifying vision, for which he, like the persona of "The Cold Heaven," must accept responsibility. "Monstrous familiar images swim to the mind's eye"—a "rage-driven, rage tormented" mob crying for vengeance for Jacques Molay, burned at the stake in the fourteenth century for witchcraft, magical unicorns bearing beautiful ladies on their back, and brazen hawks whose clanging wings "have put out the moon." Wondering for a moment if he should have proved himself in action, the poet, his vision faded, accepts his lot, knows that only the "half-read wisdom of daemonic images, / Suffice the ageing man as once the growing boy." Those images, even half-read, of rage and beauty, fullness and emptiness, reveal the kinship of creativity and violence, yet grant the poet no power to alter one grain of the past, present, or future. The destruction of the ancestral house, that marvellous container of the past, becomes as inevitable as the poet's death.

In "Nineteen Hundred and Nineteen," the poet faces the most terrible of all realities, his knowledge that the artifacts of eternity are also vulnerable to violence. The poem opens with the poet's recognition that "Many ingenious lovely things are gone," including the figures, overlaid with ivory and gold, created by Phidias, the Athenian sculptor. "Many pretty toys" of the poet's youth are also gone, especially the commonly held belief that the world was getting better and that there would never be another war. Now the days are dragon-ridden. The English soldiers who fought in World War I have been sent to Ireland to put down the rebellion after England broke its promise of home rule. Now, as the hated Black and Tans, these soldiers, turned mad by violence, "leave the mother, murdered at her door, / To crawl in her own blood, and go scot-free." Faced with this reality, the poet admits that no "master-work of intellect or hand" can stand, and that he must be content with his knowledge that "triumph would / But break upon his ghostly solitude."

After recalling "a dragon of air," an illusion once created by the American dancer Loie Fuller and her troupe with ribbons of cloth, and seeing it now as a symbol of the violent and terrifying dance of history, the poet turns to a self-created image, the solitary swan leaping into the desolate heaven, as a possible symbol of his soul's destiny. Free of any hope of triumph, unable to stop the destruction of what his labor has won, the poet can mock the great, the wise, and the good, and even mock the Mocker. As frenzied in his imagination as the murderer soaked in blood, he plunges into creative madness, garlands violence, summons Herodias's daughters, who eternally demand death as the price for their dance, and finally envisions "That insolent fiend Robert Artisson," the fourteenth-century incubus of the witch Dame Alice Kyteler. These final images justify Bloom's claim that the poem's great theme is "the abyss in Yeats himself."[39] This confrontation of the abyss, which is forced by the poet's terrible knowledge that Byzantium must always fall to barbarism, produces the most violent imagery of Yeats's art and his most bitter truth—that the triumph of art over life exists only in the poet's soul, that the artifacts of his soul, like great cultures and civilizations, are not only vulnerable to violence, but because they are engendered out of conflict, share the responsibility for their own destruction.

After the remarkable achievement of "Sailing to Byzantium," "The Tower," "Meditations in Time of Civil War," and "Nineteen Hundred and Nineteen," *The Tower* offers something of a poetic interlude before resuming its brilliant intensity with "Leda and the Swan" and "Among School Children." Unterecker points out that "The Wheel," "Youth and Age," and "The New Faces," while on old age and death, have little of the "early horror" of *The Tower*.[40] "The Wheel" suggests that the search for an antiself, the theme of "Ego Dominus Tuus," is but a "longing for the tomb." In similar fashion, "Youth and Age" contends that the rage of youth and the "flattering tongue" of age but speed "the parting guest," presumably the poet's soul. "The New Faces," in turn, mocks those who will take the place of Lady Gregory and Yeats with the wisdom that "night can outbalance day" and that the "living seem more shadowy" than the souls of the dead.

While "A Prayer for My Son" appeals to a "strong ghost" to ward off any physical threat to an innocent child, its chief function, with its closing image of the Christ child protected by human love, is to prepare for the coming of the strange god in "Two Songs from a Play," "Fragments," and "Leda and the Swan." "Two Songs from a Play" envisions Athene's act of bearing away the heart of Dion-

ysus, torn into pieces by the Titans, to Zeus, who swallows it and
after engenders a new birth of Dionysus upon Semele. Taken from
Yeats's *The Resurrection*, which draws a striking parallel between
the death of Dionysus and Christ, the two songs celebrate the
resurrected god, symbolic of the beginning of a new age, though, as
Ellmann points out, the celebration is grudging because one age is
always replaced by its opposite.[41] Yeats also offers some human re-
sistance by claiming that, while all must pass away to be born
again, man's "own resinous heart" can make a ritual drama with
itself as victim and resurrected hero. This daring assertion is mocked
in "Fragments" with the image of primary Locke, hated by Blake
and Yeats for his empiricism, giving birth to the spinning-jenny,
symbol for the industrial revolution. The poem, however, mocks the
mockery of a modern world without myth by claiming the source
of its truth was ancient Nineveh, speaking through "a medium's
mouth."

The truths of "Two Songs from a Play" and "Fragments," drawing attention to the cyclical patterns of history and myth, prepare
the ground for "Leda and the Swan," Yeats's great sonnet. Yeats
originally saw the poem as a political statement, but, as he wrote,
"bird and lady took such possession of the scene that all politics
went out of it."[42] One of Yeats's most derivative poems, "Leda and
the Swan" went through several versions before it reached the
form Rajan describes as "one of the most unimprovable . . . ever
written." While Winters and Bloom have expressed their unhappiness with the poem's historical theme, most critics share Rajan's admiration for Yeats's brilliant decision to select the traditional sonnet
form for such a challenging and violent subject.[43]

Yeats's major strategy in "Leda and the Swan" is to focus on the
human perception of an act beyond human understanding, then
expand the poem's perspective to the historical and mythic. The
sonnet begins with a strong sense of the terror of the rape by describing it from within Leda's experience:

> A sudden blow: the great wings beating still
> Above the staggering girl, her thighs caressed

> By the dark webs, her nape caught in his bill,
> He holds her helpless breast upon his breast.
>
> (CP, 211)

The second stanza completes the first part of the sonnet by asking two rhetorical questions that draw attention to Leda's helplessness, thereby expanding the perspective, even while the rape is taking place, to a more detached, but still human level:

> How can those terrified vague fingers push
> The feathered glory from her loosening thighs?
> And how can body, laid in that white rush,
> But feel the strange heart beating where it lies?
>
> (CP, 211–12)

The concluding sestet begins at the moment of ejaculation, and, after completed act, reveals the historical and mythic significance of the rape, that it "engenders" a new, antithetical age, that out of Leda's eggs will come the twins Helen and Clytemnestra and Castor and Pollux, thereby also assuring "The broken wall, the burning roof and tower / And Agamemnon dead." After this revelation, the sonnet ends by posing the question of whether Leda "put on" Zeus's "knowledge with his power," whether this act, briefly joining the divine and human, merely serves the gods or also brings divine insight to their human victim or instrument. While this last question is relevant to the automatic writing that conceived *A Vision*, its more important function is to suggest a dramatic image of the *Tower* poet, stripped in his earlier poems of any hope that his work will survive, pondering the question of whether or not he has at least gained wisdom from his long, turbulent service to art.

"On a Picture of a Black Centaur by Edmund Dulac," having the disadvantage of appearing between "Leda and the Swan" and "Among School Children," is best illustrated by Yeats's comment "that all art should be a centaur finding in the popular lore its strong back and legs."[44] The poet admits that he has tried that "horseplay," studied ancient lore and "gathered old mummy wheat." Now he brings "full-flavoured wine" out of a deeper faith symbolized by the sleeping Ephesian martyrs and his beloved, whom he must protect against those "horrible green parrots," mocking images of his own rage.

"Among School Children," justly celebrated for its concluding riddle of the dancer and the dance, represents the poet's answer to his own challenge to an imagination powerless to stay the poet's mortality or prevent the destruction of its own artifacts or even reveal whether the poet's images contain eternal truths or merely his own madness. The occasion of the poem is a visit to a progressive convent school made by Yeats during his term in the Irish Senate. The poet, however, quickly drops the pose of "A sixty-year-old smiling public man" and enters a daydream of Maud Gonne's "Ledaean body" and the youthful sympathy, imaged in Plato's parable in *The Symposium* of the origin of the sexes, that united poet and beloved like "the yolk and white of the one shell."[45]

This dream of youth is suddenly transformed into a brilliant vision of Maud Gonne as a living child, a daughter of the swan, but the vision is mocked by the image of Maud in old age with hollow of cheek that could have been fashioned by Quattrocento. While this abrupt shift brings Yeats back again to his present role as "a comfortable kind of old scarecrow," the contrast of youth and age brings the poem to its major concern, that life never fulfills its promises or dreams. Indeed, the poet wonders if the mother would think her son "compensation for the pang of his birth" if she could see him in his tottering old age. He also reminds himself that even ghostly Plato, solider Aristotle, and golden-thighed Pythagoras became "Old clothes upon old sticks to scare a bird."[46]

All that remains, then, are images preserved by mother and nun, images dreamed out of passion, piety, or affection, of Presences "that all heavenly glory symbolize— / O self-born mockers of man's enterprise." These Presences now inspire the poem's most compelling question: if "Labour is blossoming or dancing" only where body, beauty, and wisdom are not bruised by desire, drudgery, and despair, what then is the nature of a life and art won out of a long, creative struggle? Is the chestnut tree its leaf, blossom, or bole, and

"How can we know the dancer from the dance?" At last, Yeats finds his justification for art but with typically Yeatsian ambivalence. It is not the artifact but the imaginative process that gives art its distinctiveness and its corresponding image of the eternally dancing Presences. Old age, like youth, is but an image created by the imagination which creates its own life and, as "The Tower" defiantly declares, its own death and eternity.

The remaining poems, with the exception of "All Soul's Night," fall short of the high level of achievement in *The Tower*. "Colonus' Praise," from Yeats's translation of Sophocles's *Oedipus at Colonus*, appears after "Among School Children," because, as Unterecker points out, its imagery of dancing ladies and "grey-leaved olive-trees" parallels Yeats's more celebrated dancer and chestnut tree.[47] The mention of "Semele's lad," in turn, anticipates "Wisdom," which, with its playful treatment of the birth of Christ—"King Abundance got Him on / Innocence"—and a Christian age created by artist's imagery and ritual, is something of a counterpoint to the difficult "Two Songs from a Play." Taken together, "Colonus' Praise" and "Wisdom" become a dying echo of Yeats's major concerns about history and the imagination in *The Tower*. Beginning with "The Hero, the Girl, and the Fool," the emphasis shifts to more personal matters, especially Yeats's emotional state just before and after his marriage.

While it has some symbolic drapery from *A Vision*, "The Hero, the Girl, and the Fool" offers Yeats's conclusion that he and Iseult Gonne were fascinated, during their brief flirtation, with the masks they created for each other, for "only God has loved us for ourselves." "Owen Aherne and His Dancers," advancing Yeats to the early days of his marriage, takes up Yeats's fear that he had not been persistent enough in persuading Iseult to marry him. The poet's heart, however, laughs out that the "young child" should mate one of her own wild kind, while the poet, in turn, now fearful that the "woman at my side" would suffer if she knew his thoughts, takes his own comfort in knowing that his chosen mate is no caged bird.

Thoughts on love complicated by youth and age wind inevitably to the memories of *A Man Young and Old*, a sequence of eleven poems on Yeats's past relationships with Maud Gonne and Olivia Shakespear. "First Love" and "Human Dignity" take up the theme, so common in Yeats's early verse, that lunar Maud Gonne was indifferent to the poet's love and ignorant of his great sacrifices for her. Unwilling, in his pride, to cry out his "heart's agony" to his beloved, the poet is caught in his sea of sorrow in "The Mermaid" by Olivia Shakespear, who, forgetting the vulnerability of her lover, plunges down with him into the depths of passion. In "The Death of the Hare" and "The Empty Cup," Yeats takes up the end of his affair with his "Diana Vernon" and confesses that his own distraction and his fear of drinking too fully from the cup were to blame in spite of his crazed thirst.

"His Memories" marks the transition from youth to old age with the comforting memory, seized upon by Ellmann as evidence of a brief sexual relationship between Yeats and Maud Gonne, that the young man did lie with beauty, did hear the cry of passion from the lips of Helen.[48] In "The Friends of His Youth," the old poet, with cracked voice and potbelly, changes Helen and Paris into old Madge and Peter, both driven mad by love or pride. Undaunted by age or madness, however, the lovers still pursue, in "Summer and Spring," the passion that now mocks their bodies. In "The Secrets of the Old," they actually taunt youth,

> For none alive to-day
> Can know the stories that we know
> Or say the things we say.

> (CP, 222)

In "His Wildness" the aging poet, now finished with life's passion, bids his soul to climb "Amid the cloudy wrack." Knowing the ancients were right in saying "Never to have lived is best," he offers in "From 'Oedipus at Colonus,'" the Sophoclean second best, "a gay goodnight," and turns his face toward death as the sequence comes to an end.

"The Three Monuments" mocks the practice of converting the

dead, whom the poet may soon join, into monuments by pointing out that the Dublin monuments of Nelson—since destroyed—O'Connell, and Parnell are mockeries of the stiff passion of each man. While the poem playfully anticipates the spirits of the dead in "All Soul's Night," Yeats had placed "The Gift of Harun Al-Rashid" after "The Three Monuments" in the first edition of *The Tower* and had wanted the long poem, which celebrates the miraculous event of the early days of his marriage, restored to its original position for his definitive edition. "The Gift of Harun Al-Rashid" is a thinly veiled narrative of Yeats's discovery of his wife's automatic writing in Kusta ben Luka's wonderment at the unconscious power of his young bride to trace out the images of the "Self-born, high-born and solitary truths" the poet-philosopher has sought through long and difficult years of study. Beyond its autobiographical function, the poem also offers a paean to Yeats's wife in the love and faith that Kusta ben Luka soon develops for his bride.

"All Soul's Night" completes *The Tower* with a gathering of midnight spirits for the unwinding of a mummy truth after a long period of meditation. After preparing a glass of muscatel for the ghostly company to drink from the wine-breath, the poet summons dead friends who most shared his obsession with the spirit world. William Thomas Horton is the first called because he loved a woman with such a frenzy of "platonic love" that he made a divine image of her in his mind.[49] Next comes Florence Emery, a past intimate of soul and body, admired for linking body and soul so closely that after finding wrinkles on her face, she went to Ceylon, out of sight of her admirers, where she taught until her death in 1917. Last called is MacGregor Mathers, the probable model for Michael Robartes, who became estranged from Yeats because he had turned "half a lunatic, half knave" in his efforts to gain control of the Golden Dawn.[50] Forgiven now by half-blind Yeats though still not forgiving, Mathers is acceptable company because his madness came from meditation on unknown things. These companions for the soul are summoned to receive a truth anticipated but never given by poem's end. The only truth that closes *The Tower* is that made out of the marvellous images of art and imagination that first appeared in "Sailing to Byzantium" and, after several shattering challenges, were restored as process rather than artifact in "Among School Children."

The Winding Stair and Other Poems (1933)

What Yeats wound so tightly in *The Tower*, he unwinds in *The Winding Stair*, which is made up of twenty-eight individual poems as well as the twenty-five verses from *Words for Music Perhaps* and the eleven, written before the publication of *The Tower*, of *A Woman Young and Old*. The view of *The Winding Stair* as a counterpoint, what Parkinson calls a "reaction to *The Tower*," is well supported by Yeats's introduction to the 1933 edition.[51] Many of the poems were written after a period of long illness: "Then in the spring of 1929 life returned to me as an impression of the uncontrollable energy and daring of the great creators. . . . Then ill again, I warmed myself back into life with *Byzantium* and *Veronica's Napkin*, looking for a theme that might befit my years."[52]

While Yeats stressed the energy, joy, and warmth he felt as he wrote the *Winding Stair* poems, Denis Donoghue observes that "*The Winding Stair*, a book misleadingly titled, is a storm of antinomies, the cry of their occasions."[53] Indeed, the opening poem, "In Memory of Eva Gore-Booth and Con Markiewicz," has the same bitterness of the *Tower* poems. After contrasting the romantic image of the youthful, aristocratic Gore-Booth sisters at Lissadell with the stark image of the sisters withered by age and politics, the poet declares the folly of political strife, "The innocent and the beautiful / Have no enemy but time."[54] Knowing this much, the poet bids himself to strike a match, its flame symbolic of both life and the destruction of the Big House, so that he can blow it out, accept the recent deaths of Eva Gore-Booth and Con Markiewicz and the loss of "the great gazebo," symbolic, according to Stallworthy and Torchiana, of the dreams for Ireland shared in youth by Yeats and "Two girls in silk kimonos, both / Beautiful, one a gazelle."[55]

"Death," written in reaction to the assassination of Kevin O'Higgins, by its very title seems an extension of the bitterness of *The Tower*, but it actually functions as a preface, with its proud claim that "Man has created death," to the debate between Self and Soul that begins the passionate affirmation of life's contraries character-istic of *The Winding Stair*. In "A Dialogue of Self and Soul," Self, long past its prime, is summoned by Soul to the ancient winding stair so that it can be delivered "from the crime of death and birth." Instead, Self, offering Sato's ancient sword and tattered, embroi-dered cover as emblems of the day's antimonies "against the tower / Emblematical of the night," claims the chance to return to life's phases, "to commit the crimes once more." Resisting Soul's double vision of perfection and oblivion, Self declares its willingness to accept once more all that life offers:

> The ignominy of boyhood; the distress
> Of boyhood changing into man;
> The unfinished man and his pain
> Brought face to face with his own clumsiness;
> The finished man among his enemies?
>
> (CP, 231–32)

Content to live it all again, Self is willing to endure every blind action, and even fall another time into "the most fecund ditch of all," the passionate love of a "proud woman not kindred of his soul." Measuring the lot and forgiving itself the lot, Self casts out bitter-ness and remorse and feels such a sweetness flowing through its breast that Soul and Self join hands, for "We must laugh and we must sing, / We are blest by everything, / Everything we look upon is blest."

Harris points out that Self, contrary to the views of Ellmann and Unterecker, never identifies itself as a poet, but he does link "A Dialogue of Self and Soul" with Yeats's other great poems on art by recognizing that Self rejects the "mystical experience which denies art. The poet, because he takes his images from the sensuous world, cannot leave it without sacrificing his vocation; he must submit his soul to its chaos."[56] The full implication of this plunge into chaos becomes the subject of "Blood and the Moon." The title represents the poem's ordeal, that to bless the tower, like the present age "Half dead at the top," is to accept the best and the worst that it symbolizes for the imagination. Reinforced by ancient images of towers and claiming Swift, Goldsmith, Berkeley, and Burke as fellow spirits, the poet takes on the task of transforming the tower into a complete symbol of the moon's unclouded purity and the blood shed by "Soldier, assassin, and executioner." To accomplish this seemingly impossible act of joining eternal wisdom, the property of the dead, and blood-stained power, a property of the living, he offers the imagery of the suspended butterfly seeming to "cling upon the moonlit skies" and the unstained visage of the moon emerging from a cloud as proof that the imagination not the artifact is the key to blessedness. Evading neither Self nor Soul, the imagination alone joins the living and the dead, accepts while purifying blood-stained history, celebrates while humanizing eternity.

In the next several poems, Yeats forges a variety of images from mythology, history, and the material world as further proof that the imagination can both celebrate and create life's dance between extremes. "Oil and Blood" starts the procession with the shocking juxtaposition of the miraculous oil that exuded from the body of St. Theresa with the blood on the lips and shrouds of vampires. While representing the extremes of Christian holiness and Satanic horror, saintly oil and vampire blood also feed the imagination, which, in the act of joining contraries, discovers that the images, though radically opposed, confirm the supernatural. In "Veronica's Napkin" and "Symbols," Yeats again creates contraries only to discover a perfect balance between them. The Heavenly Circuit of Plotinus and the constellation named after Berenice's Hair affirm the existence of universals that are equally evident in the image of Christ's face imprinted on Veronica's Veil. The blind hermit ringing the tower bell, the fool carrying the ancestral sword in its embroidered cover, in turn, are offered up as evidence that "Beauty and fool together laid," that art, like religion, discovers faith and images in extremes.

The attention shifts in "Spilt Milk," "The Nineteenth Century and After," and "Statistics" from discovering contraries to searching for imagery suitable for the materialistic age in which the poet finds himself. Knowing that art must "thin out / Like milk spilt on a stone," that "the great song return no more," that a statistical diagram must replace the Platonic image of "God's fire upon the wave," the poet simply delights in what remains: "the rattle of pebbles on the shore / Under the receding wave." In "Three Movements," the poet offers little more than a fishy parable of the literary imagination left "gasping on the strand" by time's receding wave. While "The Seven Sages" does mention Burke, Goldsmith, Berkeley, and Swift, the poem returns to Yeats's intellectual ancestors only as a contrast to contemporary Whiggery, "A levelling, rancorous, rational sort of mind." Finally, in "The Crazed Moon" the imagination, blinded for the moment by a moon staggering toward oblivion but remembering the newly risen moon in her virginal pride, feels itself ready, once again, to "rend what comes in reach."

What comes in reach, however, is a subject fit for the imagination. In "Coole Park, 1929" and "Coole Park and Ballylee, 1931," the poet finds his familiar theme of a threatened Anglo-Irish culture. In the first poem, the poet, meditating upon the image of "an aged woman and her house," recalls the swallowlike youths, Douglas Hyde, Yeats himself "ruffled in a manly pose," John Synge, and Lady Gregory's nephews, John Shawe-Taylor and Hugh Lane, who found abundance, inspiration, and pride at Coole Park.[57] The voice of "Coole Park, 1929," however, belongs to the older poet who knows that Lady Gregory's death will mean the destruction of Coole Park, which had been sold to the Irish government in 1927. Indeed, the last two stanzas commemorate Lady Gregory as the compass point for the poet's imagination and offers the poem, which anticipates the time when Coole Park will be a "shapeless mound," as "A moment's memory to that laurelled head."

In "Coole Park and Ballylee, 1931," the poet extends the imagination to his tower once again, thereby joining his destiny to the fading history of Coole Park. The opening stanza, expressing what Harris sees as Yeats's "myth of a unity of culture in the West of

Ireland," traces the waters of the Cloone River from Thoor Ballylee through its underground drop into "Raftery's 'cellar'" to its final rest at Coole Park's lake. Since the stanza ends by asking "What's water but the generated soul," the river signifies the poetic soul's immersion in folk history and the Anglo-Irish tradition. The next stanza, however, reveals the poet's dilemma, that he now stands under a wintry sun, and, unlike the autumnal poet of "The Wild Swans at Coole," knows that his soul has reached the end of its mortal journey. The suddenly mounting swan, then, rather than symbolic of the poet's fear of losing his imaginative power, becomes an emblem of the soul's liberation, so lovely and "arrogantly pure" in itself that the poet questions whether he has the words to describe its magnificence: "It can be murdered with a spot of ink."

The suspended moment ends, and the poet returns to Coole Park as a "spot" worthy of the poet's imagination. A place "more dear than life," it contrasts sharply with the present age's shifting values. Knowing what the loss of Coole Park will mean to the imagination, the poet declares his allegiance even in the face of a dark future in which the poet and his tradition are no more:

> We were the last romantics—chose for theme
> Traditional sanctity and loveliness;
> Whatever's written in what poets name
> The book of the people; whatever most can bless
> The mind of man or elevate a rhyme. . . .
>
> (CP, 240)

Unterecker sees "For Anne Gregory," a reworking of "The Hero, the Girl, and the Fool," as the last of the "meditative, personal poems that dominate the first part of The Winding Stair."[58] In this sense, "Swift's Epitaph" also sounds the final note in the poet's concern for the loss of the Anglo-Irish tradition. In both poems, the subjects are released, Lady Gregory's granddaughter from the beauty of her golden hair and Swift from his savage heart, into God's love and care. Turning to the soul's flight to God, Yeats wonders in "At Algeciras—a Meditation Upon Death" if the poet who sought approval when young by finding pretty shells can find imaginative confidence to respond to the Great Questioner. "The Choice," as Unterecker points out, was removed as the penultimate stanza of what was then called "Coole Park and Ballylee, 1932" and deliberately inserted between two poems that were originally entitled "Meditation Upon Death."[59] Its function now is to declare the poet's choice of his work rather than his life as his response, even at the risk of a "heavenly mansion," to the Great Questioner. "Mohini Chatterjee," commemorating Yeats's meeting with the Brahmin theosophist in the 1880s, adds a measure of confidence to that choice by grounding it in a belief in reincarnation and in the artist's ability to create in song his own heavenly mansion where "Men dance on deathless feet."

"Byzantium," usually discussed as a companion piece to "Sailing to Byzantium," though it was written four years later, takes up the actual process by which the artist creates his images and, in a bold stroke by Yeats, compares the creative process to the soul's journey after death.[60] Some Yeats commentators, like Ellmann, Vendler, and Finneran, have seen "Byzantium" as, in Finneran's words, "a description of how art is created."[61] Others, including Wilson, Brooks, and Henn, have emphasized the poem as, in Brooks's words, "a symbol of the heaven of man's imagination."[62] That "Byzantium" is finally about both art and the soul or, as G. S. Fraser observes, about "life, death, and art,"[63] is clear from the difficulty critics have in separating Byzantium as a heavenly city from Byzantium as imaginative process no matter what their view. This great poem, which Yeats claimed had warmed him back into life, continues the speculation on art and the imagination Yeats had begun in "Sailing to Byzantium." It is a sequel, however, to the entire body of poems in *The Tower* that unwound the artifact of eternity and discovered the self-sustaining, self-delighting dance of the imagination.

"Byzantium" opens as the "unpurged images of day recede." The great cathedral gong sounds its disdain for mere human complexities. Freed from unpurged images, the poet, in a state of suspension or trance, experiences a vision, sees "image, man or shade." Realizing, however, that he is beyond common experience, he knows what he sees is more shade than man and "more image than a shade." The poet bases his hierarchy on the knowledge that "Hades' bobbin bound in mummy-cloth / May unwind the winding path." In other words, the soul, liberated from life, must travel back through its past life, live events over again, until it finds or perhaps becomes an image that breathless mouths—breathing mouths in an early manuscript—may summon. This miracle by which the poet encounters an image of the soul is hailed as the superhuman: "I call it death-in-life and life-in-death."

The echo of Heraclitus's belief that God and man live each other's death leads the poet, in the company of the soul's image, to a vision of the miracle of art. As "Miracle, bird or golden handiwork" art joins the natural and supernatural—Yeats's answer to Sturge Moore's complaint that the golden bird of "Sailing to Byzantium" was still a part of nature—and can "scorn aloud," being changeless, "Common bird or petal / And all complexities of mire or blood." This miracle is made in a creative process comparable to purgatorial "flames begotten of flame" that rid "blood-begotten spirits" of "complexities of fury." Yet the flames of the imagination, as Finneran points out, are "powerless to alter reality itself"[64]— being more than life they "cannot singe a sleeve."

In the last stanza, the poet, seeing spirit after spirit coming to Byzantium "Astraddle on the dolphin's mire and blood," praises those golden smithies who break human complexities by creating images—"Marbles of the dancing floor"—out of "That dolphin-torn, that gong-tormented sea." In other words, the poet celebrates the imagination's power to create images out of common experience that, through the miracle of art, renew the miracle of eternity. Yet, the imagination, which changes nothing, also prepares the soul for its return to life, for both soul and imagination must plunge into life again and again until perfection is achieved or tragic joy expressed in a vision of reality that is in itself a state of perfection.

Yeats follows the joy and warmth of "Byzantium" with a vision of the "terror of all terrors" in "The Mother of God," when common mind suddenly is made aware of the miracle of "The Heavens in my womb." In "Vacillation" Yeats turns to a major consideration of the contraries that, while shocking to common humanity, challenge and inspire the imagination. Yeats opens the poem with the familiar strategy of the rhetorical question. If the destruction of antimonies is called death by the body and remorse by the heart, "What is joy?" The next seven stanzas search for an answer in the images or moments of tragic joy in which Yeats discovered, however briefly, a pure moment of feeling or thought.[65] First a tree out of the *Mabinogion* appears, half fire and half green, upon which the worshipper, experiencing what Ellmann calls "the ecstatic state of non-grief, which may be called joy,"[66] hangs an image of Attis. In the next stanza, Yeats briefly focuses on life's ambitions as a reminder that "from the fortieth winter" the poet should measure his work by men who "come / Proud, open-eyed and laughing to the tomb." Stanza four follows the poet's chronology to his fiftieth year and records a moment, also described in "Anima Mundi," of pure blessedness, when even the body blazed with radiance.

In the next two stanzas, the poem grows darker as the poet remembers a different time when soul and body were weighed down by responsibility and had to take comfort from images of lord, conqueror, and common man, all joined by the refrain, " 'Let all things pass away.' " Approaching complete darkness, the Heart, resisting the Soul's advice to seek out the salvation of Isaiah's coal, turns back to life, preferring Homer's theme of original sin to any salvation that excludes the imagination or life's contraries. Heart's decision is the reason the poet must part company with Von Hügel, even though they share a belief in miracle. While relief is possible if he "become a Christian man," the poet stands with Homer "and his unchristened heart" and chooses Samson's riddle, which reveals to the knower the sweet unity possible in contraries, as a model for his art.[67]

Now that the celebration of the blood-sodden, unchristened heart has begun, the next five poems prepare for the frenzy of passion in *Words for Music Perhaps.* "Quarrel in Old Age," playing upon the honeycomb at the end of "Vacillation," asks what had happened to Maud Gonne's sweetness after fanatics "Put her in a rage." No remorse drips here, however, for the poet knows that as long as wheels turn "that lonely thing / That shone before these eyes" still lives. In "The Results of Thought," the poet claims that he can actually summon youthful images of dear friends and restore their "wholesome strength" in spite of their aging bodies. After dutifully thanking his communicators in "Gratitude to the Unknown Instructors" for all this wisdom, the poet, born in a land of "Great hatred, little room," celebrates his own fanatic heart in "Remorse for Intemperate Speech" and "Stream and Sun at Glendalough" and his kinship with those "Self born, born anew."

In *Words for Music Perhaps*, the poet, warmed into life, now bubbles over with passion. Yeats wrote to Olivia Shakespear that the poems were fed by sexual abstinence—"I was ill and yet full of desire."[68] Crazy Jane, modeled after an old woman from Gort, appears in the first seven poems of the series. Having composed most of the poems before "Vacillation," Yeats wrote to Olivia Shakespear that he had begun "Vacillation" "to shake off 'Crazy Jane.'"[69] He told George Yeats that he "wanted to exorcise that slut, Crazy Jane, whose language has become unendurable."[70] Yet he also approved of her poems, which he saw as "all emotion and all impersonal" and "the opposite of my recent work and all praise of joyous life."[71]

The Crazy Jane poems have provoked some passionate critical reactions. Bloom calls them Yeats's mad songs, Henn sees them as "images of desire," and Rajan as symbols of "heroic inviolability."[72] The opening poem, "Crazy Jane and the Bishop," clearly establishes the madness, passion, and defiance of Yeats's most bizarre persona. Crazy Jane calls down curses on the hunchbacked bishop and finds the thought of sexual intercourse with the ghost of her Jack the Journeyman far more appealing than religious intercourse with the bishop. Reprimanded in "Crazy Jane Reproved" for preferring, like Europa, God's handiwork to God, she merely sings her "Fol de rol, fol de rol." In "Crazy Jane on the Day of Judgment," Yeats allows Crazy Jane to make her own reproof to those who foolishly argue that the soul is all: "Love is all / Unsatisfied / That cannot take the whole / Body and soul."

"Crazy Jane and Jack the Journeyman," described by Parkinson as "one of Yeats's greatest triumphs,"[73] gives Crazy Jane an instinctive knowledge of what happens to the soul after death. She would rather walk the road at night in search of Jack than come alone to God. This commitment to a passion capable of driving dead lovers to intercourse instead of a heavenly mansion is reaffirmed in "Crazy Jane on God," a poem Ellmann sees as a celebration of passion as "a guarantee of permanence,"[74] and especially "Crazy Jane Talks with the Bishop" with its argument that "nothing can be sole or whole / That has not been rent." The last poem in the sequence "Crazy Jane Grown Old Looks at the Dancers" uses the provocative image of the murderous dancers to express Crazy Jane's desire for reincarnation to have "the limbs to try / Such a dance as there was danced."

Crazy Jane's desire to dance her youthful passion once again is responded to in several poems sung by young lovers fearful of the transitory nature of love and the haunting specter of old age. In "Girl's Song," the singer, yearning for her young lover but suddenly confronted by an old man, fretfully wonders, "Saw I an old man young / Or young man old?" Yet, when her lover, in "Young Man's Song," expresses a similar fear that his love will change into a "withered crone," he is scolded by his heart for forgetting that love's image was created before time began. "Her Anxiety" challenges the heart, claiming that love, at every touch, alters into some lesser thing, but "His Confidence" responds to the challenge with its own claim that eternal love leaps out of even the worst betrayal the heart endures. While "Love's Loneliness" is sung by both lovers, "Her Dream" and "His Bargain" resume the debate and finally resolve it with the image of Berenice's hair as a dream symbol of the lovers' pledge to love with a passion that defies time even as it is consumed by it.

The determination of young lovers notwithstanding, "Three Things" brings back the problem of old age and death. Its three things are the pleasures an old woman seeks to reclaim from death: the joy of nursing her child, of giving pleasure to her man, and, most memorable, her own pleasure in lovemaking. These last two are combined in "Lullaby," which celebrates the physical comfort of love experienced by immortal lovers ranging from Paris to the "holy bird" now protected by Leda's care. Passion's afterthought receives the most poignant treatment in "After Long Silence," Yeats's tribute to Olivia Shakespear. The poem draws the curtain on unfriendly night so that aged lovers can "descant and yet again descant / Upon the supreme theme of Art and Song," for "Bodily decrepitude is wisdom; young / We loved each other and were ignorant."

"Mad as the Mist and Snow" sings of another advantage of the poet in his old age. Not only can he, in his wisdom, bolt the shutter against the foul winter wind, he can also, like Homer and Cicero, match the wintry blast with the madness of his own imagination. "Those Dancing Days Are Gone," the first line of its refrain borrowed from Pound's *Cantos*, sings madly that the curse of bodily decrepitude and death of friends is bearable because the poet still carries about the emphatic images of his youth, "the sun in a golden cup, / The moon in a silver bag." In " 'I am of Ireland,' " based on a fourteenth-century dance song repeated to Yeats by Frank O'Connor, a voice from the past, actually the voice of Cathleen Ni Houlihan, calls to the poet to take up the dance again, but Unity of Culture now seems far less possible than Unity of Being as "time runs on, runs on." In "The Dancer at Cruachan and Cro-Patrick," the idea of Unity of Being is expressed by the saintly dancer's belief that "One that is perfect or at peace" exists among "birds or beasts or men."

The next three poems introduce Tom the Lunatic, a suitable companion for Crazy Jane, as the unlikely spokesman for the idea of a permanent form behind the mutability of life. In "Tom the Lunatic," he sings that each living thing "Stands in God's unchanging eye / In all the vigour of its blood" and, in "Tom at Cruachan," that the world was begat by the "stallion Eternity" on the "mare of Time." "Old Tom Again" completes the cycle by declaring that "Things out of Perfection sail" to enter, once again, the flux of generation. In "The Delphic Oracle Upon Plotinus," the closing poem of *Words for Music Perhaps*, Yeats drops the mask of Tom to become the more imposing Oracle, so that he can offer a final vision, borrowed from Porphyry's *Life*, of great Plotinus swimming the seas to return, after his death, to the Golden Race and the company of Plato and Pythagoras. As Wilson points out, "Yeats ends all his song-cycles with a classical text in paraphrase that will bear out his main arguments in the cycle as a whole and he does so here: the heaven so much desired by Plotinus is also that desired by Jack the Journeyman and Crazy Jane."[75] In *Words for Music Perhaps*, youth dances with age, sinner with saint, until both are transformed into Unity of Being or find the place, outside of time, for perfect consummation.

A Woman Young and Old, its poems actually written before *The Tower*, brings *The Winding Stair* to its end. Its eleven poems, by repeating the number, structure, and theme of the poems in *A Man Young and Old*, gives Yeats a final opportunity, according to Unterecker, "to make the refutation of *The Tower* and its parallel series . . . obvious to his readers."[76] "Father and Child," inspired by a remark made by Yeats's daughter, opens *A Woman Young and Old* with an image of the young woman leaving the innocent and conventional world of her childhood for an attractive, dangerous life symbolized by her young man with beautiful hair and eyes "Cold as the March wind." In "Before the World Was Made," the young woman seeks an image in the mirror of her face before the world was made, and reveals in her thoughts a coldness to match that of her ideal lover. Cold thoughts become reality in "A First Confession" as the young woman is drawn into an intimate relationship her "better self disowns." As she withholds her better self, she betrays her young man, who gives all for love.

"Her Triumph" brings a dramatic change to *A Woman Young and Old*. Fancying love a casual affair, a matter of doing the "dragon's will," she encounters her "pagan Perseus," who releases in her a sexual frenzy that shocks both lovers. In "Consolation" calm follows passion and brings with it the knowledge that intense feeling is possible only in those most devoutly aware of the soul. "Chosen" also selects stillness as its theme. Seeing her lover's rest like the diurnal path of the sun that will rise again at daybreak, the young woman compares the peace and feeling of completeness after lovemaking to the perfect moment when the "Zodiac is changed into a sphere." This insight, which Wilson sees as Neo-platonic wisdom, makes love's torment a desirable fate because a "fleeting vision of reality" is "made possible by love; then for a moment, the lovers' souls seem to be back at their starting-point. . . . the spiritual and material worlds intersect and the imperfect is transformed into the perfect."[77]

After such knowledge, "Parting" seems inevitable as the lovers return to the daylight world, but the woman, now grown older, resists her lover's announcement of the dawn by offering her "dark declivities," once again, to "love's play." Defiance turns to bitterness in "Her Vision in the Wood" as love's play is replaced by the ritual drama surrounding the death of Adonis. That the death of the fertility god marks the end of youth and the beginning of old age is made clear in the woman's self-inflicted wound and her terrible knowledge that what passes before her—"That thing all blood and mire"—is "no fabulous symbol there / But my heart's victim and its torturer." In "A Last Confession," the old woman remembers her early loves, but escapes some of her bitterness of age by anticipating the intercourse of soul with soul. "Meeting" draws the series to its penultimate moment as lovers meet in old age and hate what each other sees. All that remains, then, is for "From the 'Antigone'" to close out the series and this great book with the old woman, now a tragic heroine, descending "into the loveless dust." And it is not too difficult to imagine Yeats, having climbed and descended *The Winding Stair*, awaiting the same fate, now that he had lived and recorded all extremities of thought and feeling and come to the end of his life and work.

Chapter Six

At Stroke of Midnight God Shall Win: Last Poems and Plays

In his last years, Yeats did not sustain the brilliance of *The Tower* and *The Winding Stair*, but the high quality of his poems and plays are proof that his poetic gift remained until his death. Knowing he would soon descend into the loveless dust, he persisted in his old man's frenzy in spite of serious illness and the difficulty of his craft. While admitting that his lust and rage made him seem like a fool to some, his last work shows that frenzy produced more than anger and sexual excitement. Irish politics and tradition, the poet's craft and its sources, death and immortality, and the dance of tragic joy, all play an essential role, along with a wild sexuality, in his poems and plays. Yeats believed that, like Timon, Lear, and Blake, he had to rage against life even in the face of death by remaking himself and forcing truth to obey his call. If granted this final frenzy, he could pierce the clouds, shake the dead in their shrouds, even accept life's last defeat knowing that to the end he possessed an old man's eagle mind.

A Full Moon in March (1935)

The poems of *A Full Moon in March* represent the creative problems Yeats experienced in the period after Lady Gregory's death and his determination to pull out the bolt once more for his imagination. He was never satisfied with this book and wrote to Dorothy

Wellesley that "it is a fragment of the past I had to get rid of."[1]
The poems, however, helped Yeats to overcome a brief period of
barrenness and free his imagination for its last flight.

The first six poems reflect Yeats's struggle for poetic expression.
Actually composed from lecture notes, "Parnell's Funeral" opens *A
Full Moon in March* with a harsh political statement made dramatic
through the imagery of ritual sacrifice. Parnell's death and the
popular belief that a star fell when his body was lowered into the
grave serve as a reminder to Yeats of the ritual killing of a beautiful
youth—"image of a star laid low"—by the Great Mother, who cuts
out his heart after piercing it with an arrow. This myth, based on a
dream discussed in *Autobiographies*, aligns Parnell's death with the
deaths of Apollo and Dionysus and turns a political event into the
moment of historical and mythic crisis when an age reverses itself.
Having raised Parnell from political victim to sacrificial god, Yeats
turns his attention to the Dublin mob that dragged down its leader,
the poets who rhymed the lie that Ireland was the better for the act,
and the Irish leaders who failed to commit themselves, by eating
Parnell's heart, to their leader's vision. He accuses citizen, poet, and
politician of not having the strong blood and bitter wisdom to bring
about the new age demanded by Parnell's death.

Political frustration is also the key to "Three Songs to the Same
Tune," written by Yeats as a marching song for O'Duffy's Blue
Shirts, the Fascist group Yeats briefly supported. While Yeats later
remade the songs, increasing their extravagance and obscurity so
they could not be marched to, they appear in *A Full Moon in
March* as a celebration of "a good strong cause" and "good strong
blows" and an appeal for a blood sacrifice to make Ireland worthy
of its martyrs. The songs end with a plea for soldiers to accept their
natural leaders and for those leaders to assume their natural authority.

Yeats's "Alternative Song for the Severed Head in 'The King of
the Great Clock Tower'" follows Yeats's marching songs with a roll
call of tragic heroes from Ireland's legendary past as inspiration for
a new generation of warriors; but "Two Songs Rewritten for the
Tune's Sake" mercifully changes the subject from politic frenzy to

the passionate heart. Borrowing tunes from *The Pot of Broth* and *The Player Queen*, Yeats sings of the bold passion surviving old age and the curse of the poet who "rhymes for a beautiful lady, / He rhyming alone in his bed." "A Prayer for Old Age" praises those who think "in a marrow-bone" even if old age makes them appear foolish, while the poet of "Church and State" declares that his political songs were made from cowardly dreams—Yeats quickly became disenchanted with O'Duffy—and that he will accept a communion of bitter wine and stale bread rather than pretend the mob can be stirred to heroic passion.

The remaining twelve poems in *A Full Moon in March* make up *Supernatural Songs*, written by Yeats shortly after his Steinach operation. Described by Yeats as an early Christian hermit whose vision "echoes pre-Christian thought" coming "perhaps from Egypt,"[2] Ribh, the persona of the series, gives Yeats a saintlike mask through which he can criticize abstract religious ideas and celebrate the marriage of the natural and supernatural. Rajan sees Ribh as the perfect counterpoint to Crazy Jane because he represents "the sexuality of spirit rather than the spirituality of sex."[3]

In the opening poem, "Ribh at the Tomb of Baile and Aillinn," Ribh, with tonsured head and the cracked voice of a ninety-year-old man, appears with an open breviary that he reads by the light of the angelic intercourse of Baile and Aillinn. This radiant light shines forth on the anniversary of the lovers' death because their passion was so pure they had to perish before they could embrace. Ribh stands in a circle of supernatural light that illuminates the text that "whole is joined to whole" and that body finds its perfect consummation with soul just as soul experiences the pleasures of the body but without all the straining joy. In "Ribh Denounces Patrick," the same view holds true: "Natural and supernatural with the self-same ring are wed." Ridiculing the idea of the Trinity because it excludes the female, Ribh points to the doctrine of the Great Smaragdine Tablet, that things below are copies of things above and that sexual intercourse, while incomplete, corresponds to the act of Godhead begetting Godhead.

Anticipating that the reader will not understand "Ribh Denounces Patrick," "Ribh in Ecstasy" sings that the soul's joy is "in its own cause or ground" rather than human knowledge or understanding. Accordingly, "There" offers fresh images, borrowed from ancient and personal mythology, of the perfection possible for the soul:

> There all the barrel-hoops are knit,
> There all the serpent-tails are bit,
> There all the gyres converge in one,
> There all the planets drop in the Sun.
>
> (CP, 284)

In "Ribh Considers Christian Love Insufficient," the important matter is the sexual consummation of soul and god. Rejecting the tinsel and trash of Christian love and virtue, Ribh chooses hatred as the passion needed to free the soul from "every thought of God mankind has had." Rid of passive emotions, the soul, at midnight, can surrender to its Master and enter into His perfection. "He and She" makes the soul's consummation in God into a deterministic vision. As She, the soul cannot but follow the phases of the moon to either the perfection of the full or the oblivion of the dark of the moon.

"What Magic Drum?" returns the soul to its common round by focusing on the child born of the intercourse between mortal and God. While, as Ellmann points out, the identity of this child is unknown, the visit of the mysterious and bestial father and the ominous beating of the drum give the event a "supernatural sanction."[4] "Whence Had They Come?" advances to the moment of the soul's first passion and compares its ecstasy to the spiritual and bodily passion that can beat down great civilizations. The poem's odd juxtaposition of first passion and frigid Rome is made possible because of Ribh's knowledge that the sexual act corresponds to the sacred drama that begets historical ages: "What sacred drama through her body heaved / When world-transforming Charlemagne was conceived?"

"The Four Ages of Man" further links the pattern of human

experience with historical cycles by identifying the development of the body, heart, mind, and soul with the struggle of the moon through its four quarters. Yeats made this identification even clearer in a letter to Olivia Shakespear that he sent with a first draft of the poem: "They are the four ages of individual man, but they are also the four ages of civilization."[5] The poem also moves Ribh closer to the philosophy of *A Vision*, a movement that continues in "Conjunctions," "A Needle's Eye," and "Meru," the last three *Supernatural Songs*. Yeats also explained the meaning of "Conjunctions" in a letter to Olivia Shakespear, pointing out that the conjunctions of Jupiter and Saturn and Mars and Venus correspond to the primary and antithetical personalities in his system.[6] "A Needle's Eye," echoing another key idea of *A Vision*, claims that all the contraries of life must pass through the needle's eye of God before becoming a part of the heavenly fabric.

As the last of *Supernatural Songs*, "Meru" draws together all that Ribh thought into the sonnet form and concludes that, since "man's life is thought," he

> . . . cannot cease
> Ravening through century and century,
> Ravening, raging, and uprooting that he may come
> Into the desolation of reality.
>
> (CP, 287)

His raging over, Ribh bids the great civilizations of Egypt, Greece, and Rome good-bye and joins the hermits on Mount Meru or Everest. He now descends into a wintry night without the help of God's glory and man's monuments. Described by Unterecker as a surrender to chaos, by Whitaker as an acceptance of history, by Ellmann as an illustration of man's courage to face the void, and by Bloom as the anticipation of a new dawn of the imagination,[7] Ribh's descent, for Yeats, was a symbol for the passing of civilization and the corresponding movement of the soul toward the moment when, stripped clean of illusions, it passes through the needle's eye and encounters its final vision.

Last Plays

During the 1920s, Yeats was involved in the Abbey's affairs, but he did not write plays for the Abbey as he had done in the past. While Bradford suggests a variety of reasons—Yeats's increased political activities as a senator, his work on *A Vision*, his preparation of two volumes of plays for a collected edition—he also admits that this period of inactivity is puzzling because "Yeats seems always to have found time to write what he had to write."[8] Whatever the reasons, Yeats returned to playwriting in 1925 or 1926 with his work on *The Resurrection*.[9] Though the play was first published in 1927, Yeats, thinking it too chaotic, revised it in 1930 for publication the following year. The play was published again with an introduction in *Wheels and Butterflies* in 1934, the same year it was first performed at the Abbey.

The Resurrection, resembling Yeats's earlier dance plays, is a dramatic study of Christ's resurrection from the viewpoint of the Greek, the Hebrew, and the Syrian. Proud of his intellectual heritage and embarrassed by the followers of Dionysus in the streets, the Greek believes that the soul is separate from the body and that Christ's body was a mere phantom: "We Greeks understand these things. No god has ever been buried; no god has ever suffered." Taking the opposite position, the Hebrew believes in Christ because, being "nothing more than a man," he was "the best man who ever lived."[10] While the Hebrew is badly shaken by the Syrian's news that Christ has risen from the tomb, the Greek experiences an even greater shock when, touching Christ's side, he discovers that a real heart is still beating.

While most of *The Resurrection* is taken up by the conversation between the Greek and the Hebrew, Yeats's spokesman in the play appears to be the Syrian. More than a messenger, the Syrian declares his belief in the Yeatsian idea that a new age is born in the opposite image of the age it replaces and, in turn, will perish in the birth of its antinomy.[11] The songs of the Musicians also celebrate the Heraclitean notion that Dionysus and Christ must live each other's death, die each other's life as does the appearance of the followers of Dionysus at the very moment Christ reveals himself to his disciples. Neither an acceptance nor a rejection of Christianity, *The Resurrection* gives Yeats an opportunity to create his own myth celebrating the miracle of body and soul, Christ and Dionysus.[12]

In the same year that Yeats revised *The Resurrection*, he also completed a play combining his interest in spiritualism and his study of Jonathan Swift. First performed at the Abbey in November, 1930, *The Words Upon the Window-Pane* is a dramatic expression of Yeats's belief, stated in his introduction to the play, that the eighteenth century was the "one Irish century that escaped from darkness and confusion" and his fear that modern Ireland had completely surrendered to mob rule.[13] The play opens just as a séance is to begin in an old lodging house that once belonged to friends of Swift's Stella. The setting is critical because, as Clark has shown, Yeats uses the house as a symbol of Swift's life, "having decayed like him, having the same memory cut into it."[14] Several Dickensian minor characters, representing contemporary mercantile and religious interests, turn up for the séance, but Dr. Trench, the president of the Dublin Spiritualists' Association, and John Corbet, a Cambridge student writing an essay on Swift and Stella for his doctorate, provide the necessary information about spiritualist practices and Swift's political ideas and his relationship with Stella and Vanessa. Representing adept and reluctant initiate, Trench and Corbet prepare the audience for the Swiftian influence that disrupts the séance by taking over Lulu, the medium's control, and for the revelation of Swift's spirit dreaming back through its past life, obsessed with Swift's failure to marry Vanessa or Stella and leave behind a child for the next generation.

Torchiana sees Swift's conversations with Vanessa and Stella as Yeats's warning to modern Ireland to emulate Swift's pride of intellect, expressed by the words from Stella's poem cut upon the windowpane, and avoid surrendering to a mindless passion, represented by Vanessa's demand for marriage and a child.[15] Representing Choice and Chance, Stella and Vanessa also provide Yeats with a way to dramatize the tragic conflict between Swift's savage indignation against injustice and his reluctance to risk his own humanity. Echoing the dark passages from the early *Tower* poems, Swift's words reveal his unwillingness to roll the "white ivory dice," to accept responsibility for body as well as mind: "O God, hear the prayer of Jonathan Swift, that afflicted man, and grant that he may leave to posterity nothing but his intellect that came to him from Heaven."

Swift's choice of Stella's intelligence over Vanessa's passion comforts him, leads him to believe that her words overpraising his moral nature will transform him and that she will be there to close his eyes at the end. Swift, however, because incomplete, is a poor prophet. His fate is to die alone, a filthy old man, his face covered with boils, and to dream back in his remorse of spirit through agonies of his past life. At the end of the play, Swift, something of an Irish Oedipus, knows the Sophoclean wisdom that never to have lived is best: "Perish the day on which I was born."

While *The Words Upon the Window-Pane* represents the tragic struggle of the mind against the common round of passion and history, *A Full Moon in March* and *The King of the Great Clock Tower* dramatize the irresistible attraction between the antinomy of soul and body, the supernatural and natural, and art and life.[16] *A Full Moon in March* appears before *The King of the Great Clock Tower* in *Collected Plays*, but was actually written after its counterpart. In his preface to the two plays, Yeats wrote that "In *The King of the Great Clock Tower*, there are three characters, King, Queen, and Stroller, and that is a character too many; reduced to the essentials, to Queen and Stroller, the fable should have greater intensity. I started afresh and called the new version *A Full Moon in March*."[17]

The King of the Great Clock Tower, written originally by Yeats as a prose exercise to force himself "to write lyrics for its imaginary people" during a spell of poetic inactivity opens with a song celebrating the timeless dance of Tir-nan-oge. The play, however, quickly enters the world of the Great Clock when the Stroller, wearing a "half-savage mask," appears and insists that he see the Queen he has put into his songs since being told that the King had married a woman the "most beautiful of her sex." Disappointed by the Queen's beauty, the Stroller becomes even more brazen by demanding the Queen fulfill the prophecy of Aengus—that she shall dance for him and kiss his mouth on the stroke of midnight. The enraged King orders the Stroller beheaded, but when the severed head appears before the Queen, she dances with it and fulfills the prophecy by kissing its lips.[18] The play ends with the song of the severed head, revealing the mysterious attraction of life for death, and the song of the Attendant, celebrating the eternal dance of all living things with the image of "Castle Dargin's ruin all lit."

In *A Full Moon in March*, Yeats removes the King and changes the identity of the Stroller to the Swineherd. While the first change tightens the structure of the play and places more emphasis upon the Queen, the second creates a more striking contrast between spirit and body and makes the attraction between opposites seem even more incredible. The play has obvious affinities with *The King of the Great Clock Tower*, but the focus shifts from the individual quest for an eternal image to the Blakean idea of eternity in love with the productions of time. The Swineherd appears in response to the Queen's challenge that he who "best sings his passion" shall become her King. Having no song, the insolent Swineherd is beheaded like all the others, but the Queen takes up his head and sings to it of her cruel, virgin love. In turn, the severed head sings of its own transformation because of its attraction for an image beyond its language or comprehension.

In *The Herne's Egg*, in Yeats's own words, "the strangest wildest thing I have ever written,"[19] the human mind is again drawn to the supernatural. The play's hero, King Congal of Connacht, is a comic figure, at times, but he suffers a fate more grimly tragic than Yeats's Swift. *The Herne's Egg* opens upon a scene of Edenic conflict in which Congal and King Aedh of Tara have just fought their fiftieth battle. To celebrate the new peace, Congal and his men steal the Great Herne's eggs for the feast, and provoke the anger of the priestess Attracta, who calls down a curse that the thief must become a fool and die by a fool's hand. The curse begins to take hold at the feast when Congal, served a hen's egg by mistake, kills Aedh with a table leg. Discovering that Attracta made the switch,

Congal forces her to lie with him and his men. The punishment for their crime is to be reincarnated into a lower form, but Congal must also die at the hands of a fool. Defying the Great Herne, Congal takes his own life, but at the moment of death he realizes that the prophecy is fulfilled because he has become a fool. The copulation of two donkeys at play's end reveals Congal's form when he returns in the next life.

While the sources for herne and egg have been thoroughly explored by Wilson and Melchiori,[20] Yeats's own poetry, especially "Leda and the Swan" and the Musician's song in *Calvary*, offer the most obvious clues to the meaning of *The Herne's Egg*. The conflict between Attracta, who believes in "no reality but the Great Herne," and god-defying Congal represents the chaotic end of an age of harmony. While Attracta is humanized and Congal made aware of his soul by their struggle, both characters merely act out their roles as agents of the new dispensation. The play, as many critics have observed, is an outrageous farce of Yeats's own mythology, but the play's extravagant world is still dependent on Yeats's vision of reality. Though Congal challenges the Great Herne, his reincarnation as a donkey reveals the vulnerability of the soul between lives, as *The Words Upon the Window-Pane* expresses its agony.

In *Purgatory*, Yeats's tragic hero, now the Old Man, also challenges the supernatural by committing an act to horrify the gods. Within a setting of ruined house and bare tree, the Old Man explains to his sixteen-year-old son why he has returned to his birthplace after so many years. The souls in Purgatory must relive their sins many times, and learn

> The consequence of those transgressions
> Whether upon others or upon themselves;
> Upon others, others may bring help....
>
> (*CPl*, 682)

The Old Man, then, narrates the tragic history of the house, his mother's marriage to a common groom, her death in childbirth, his father's drinking and gambling, and his murder of his father in the burning house with the same knife he now uses to cut his dinner. The reason for the Old Man's curious interest in the souls in Purgatory becomes clear when he reveals that this is the anniversary of his mother's wedding night and his own begetting, that the curse on her soul is to dream back to the pleasure and remorse of the night and the act. In a desperate act to free his mother's soul, the Old Man turns upon his son, catching him in the act of stealing money from his purse, and kills him with the same knife he used to kill his father. Murderer of his father and his son, this most terrible and tragic of Yeats's heroes believes that he has ended the family's history and purified his mother's soul. Hearing hoof-beats, however, he makes the horrifying discovery that he is

> Twice a murderer and all for nothing,
> And she must animate that dead night
> Not once but many times!

> (*CPl*, 689)

Purgatory has been admired for its taut, passionate language, what Clark describes as a combination of "actual speech rhythm and rhythmical impulse,"[21] and interpreted on the levels of aesthetics, politics, theology, and eugenics. Torchiana, taking the lead from Donald Pearce and John Heath-Stubbs, sees the play as a political criticism of modern Ireland. He notes that Yeats, in response to a brief controversy after the Abbey performance of *Purgatory*, had said the play is about a spirit who "suffers because of its share, when alive, in the destruction of an honoured house; that destruction is taking place all over Ireland to-day."[22] While Virginia Moore has described the play "as 'esoteric' as all of Yeats's plays" and Helen Vendler as "a symbol of the imagination at work,"[23] most critics have taken Yeats at his word, that *Purgatory* expresses his "conviction about this world and the next."[24] Ure offers the most sensible view that the play reveals the impossibility of human interference in "the progress of the soul from grave to cradle or from grave to beatitude."[25] The Old Man's tragic failure to free his mother's soul proves that the soul must move through its fated course. The horrible murder in *Purgatory* ends no cycle, releases no soul, only enacts a crime the Old Man will have to repeat for many lives to come.

After writing several plays in which the hero suffers the tragic defeat of those who rage against God and the judgment of the soul, Yeats turned to his favorite hero, the legendary Cuchulain, for his last play, a dramatic expression of the hero's final acceptance of his fate. *The Death of Cuchulain*, the fifth play in the Cuchulain cycle, summarizes and completes the life of Yeats's most generous, passionate, and courageous hero.[26] After a theatrical gambit in which an Old Man warns the audience they must know "the old epics and Mr. Yeats' play about them," the play begins as a bewitched Eithne Inguba tries to lure Cuchulain into a hopeless battle. When Cuchulain reads Emer's letter warning him to wait for reinforcements, the spell is broken, but Cuchulain, resisting the supernatural, believes that his mistress seeks his death so that she can take a younger lover. Declaring that he makes the truth, Cuchulain goes off to battle, thereby making the attempted deception into his own reality.

When Cuchulain reappears, he bears six mortal wounds, but insists upon dying on his feet. At this point, Aoife, the mother of Cuchulain's son, killed in combat by his own father, enters to exact the revenge denied to her for so long. Seeking Cuchulain's death, she cannot strike the final blow "for I have things / That I must ask questions on before I kill you." As she goes out, the Blind Man appears and, for a bounty of twelve pennies, cuts off Cuchulain's head. The play ends with Emer's dance of rage and adoration and the harlot's song praising the muscular, yet elusive bodies of the ancient heroes and asking those inevitable Yeatsian questions about the relationship between vision and reality:

> Are those things that men adore and loathe
> Their sole reality?
> What stood in the Post Office
> With Pearse and Connolly?

What comes out of the mountain
Where men first shed their blood?
Who thought Cuchulain till it seemed
He stood where they had stood?

(*CPl*, 704–5)

The commentary on *The Death of Cuchulain* ranges from Vendler's criticism of the play as the "most disconnected and jerky" in the Cuchulain cycle to Nathan's praise of the play's extraordinary honesty in not denying "that failure and defeat and death are human realities."[27] Yeats's own comment, that *The Death of Cuchulain* hides his private philosophy in "an old faery tale,"[28] suggests that his last play expresses his thoughts on the soul and his love of mythology in a final vision of the hero-warrior now willing to accept death, even in the most demeaning form, so that his soul can finally begin its own heroic journey. Emer's dance and the Harlot's song also reveal the power of the human heart and imagination to celebrate the virtues of the hero in a form so intensely realized that thought and feeling appear transformed into a living body. The poet, too, can die the hero's life and live the hero's death.

New Poems (1938)

Bradford has pointed out that the heading of *Last Poems* for all of the poetry after *A Full Moon in March* is not accurate because the lyrics and ballads beginning with "The Gyres" and ending with "Are You Content?" were published as *New Poems* by Cuala Press.[29] After the strain of writing the poems for *A Full Moon in March*, Yeats decided to write for his *New Poems* "all nonchalant verse."[30] *Last Poems*, according to Bradford, "can be properly applied only to those poems Yeats wrote or finished during the last year of his life, between January 1938 and January 1939, as they were published by the Cuala Press in the order Yeats intended in July of 1939."[31]

Yeats's own comment notwithstanding, *New Poems* does not open on a nonchalant note, though "The Gyres" and "Lapis Lazuli" create an atmosphere of tragic joy for some of the casual pieces to follow. In "The Gyres," Old Rocky Face, variously identified as the sphinx, the man in the moon, Shelley's Ahasuerus, and, by George Yeats, as the Delphic Oracle, is summoned to look upon a scene of nightmarish chaos that clearly corresponds to the end of an historical cycle:

> For beauty dies of beauty, worth of worth,
> And ancient lineaments are blotted out.
> Irrational streams of blood are staining earth;
> Empedocles has thrown all things about;
> Hector is dead and there's a light in Troy. . . .
>
> (CP, 291)

Yet the death of friends, political violence, the whirling gyres of conflict, and the loss of heroic vision provoke the laughter of tragic joy. Only one word, rejoice, is heard from the cavern, for while things grow coarse and whirl toward darkness, "workman, noble and saint" will spin on the "unfashionable gyre again."

"Lapis Lazuli" repeats the theme of tragic joy, but this time joy becomes the gaiety of art confronted with inevitable destruction. Edward Engelberg finds three figures of gaiety in the poem: the poets who ignore the threat of war, those who rebuild "Old civilizations put to the sword," and "the wise, who are no longer of this world, the transfigured souls of the tragic heroes, symbolized in 'Lapis Lazuli' by the carved design of the three Chinamen."[32] The carved Chinamen emerge out of a pattern of conflict between images of Elizabethan and Greek art and images of war ranging from the Battle of the Boyne to World War I. Out of the contraries of art and war, the poet learns that "All things fall and are built again, / And those that build them again are gay." With this truth, the poet creates in the mind's eye an image carved out of lapis lazuli of two Chinamen who ask for "mournful melodies," yet are gay in their ancient wisdom that all will return on that unfashionable gyre.

After the opening lyrics celebrating tragic joy, the Hokku "Imitated From the Japanese" reveals the "most astonishing thing," that the poet himself has never "danced for joy." Undaunted, Yeats creates in "Sweet Dancer" an image of Margot Ruddock as a dancing girl escaping "bitter youth" and ranting crowd within the whirling vision of her own madness.[33] In "The Three Bushes," one of Yeats's best known ballads, he shows that he can also create music for the dance in the contrapuntal rhythms of spiritual and passionate love. Begun as a project with Dorothy Wellesley, who was writing a poem on the same subject, "The Three Bushes" so caught Yeats's imagination that by the time he was finished he had also completed six attendant ballads exploring the philosophical realities of the dance between spirit and body.[34]

In "The Three Bushes," the lady tells her lover that, because he needs the proper food of love, she will creep into his bed at midnight, but he must light no candles lest she die of shame. Desiring love yet fearing to lose her chastity, the lady solves her dilemma by sending her chambermaid to her lover's bed. The ruse works, her "lover looked so gay," but it seems to work too well when chambermaid looks "half asleep all day." The lover's joy is brief, however, because after a year of riding to passion's rhythms, he is killed in a fall from his horse. When the lady hears of her lover's death, she, in turn, falls into a death swoon, for she "Loved him with her soul." The chambermaid, taking charge of the graves, plants two rose bushes so that roses and roots merge. When she dies years later, the compassionate priest who heard her confession has her buried

> Beside her lady's man,
> And set a rose-tree on her grave,
> And now none living can,
> When they have plucked a rose there,
> Know where its roots began.
>
> (CP, 296)

Yeats follows "The Three Bushes" with six ballads sung by lady, lover, and chambermaid. In the first three songs, the last two originally parts of the same poem, the lady reveals that love "hurts the soul" because it forces her to adore that which makes her "No better than a beast / Upon all fours." After confessing that her soul desires as much as adores her lover, she tells the chambermaid to prepare for their shared lover who loves the lady's soul and the chambermaid's body and "Yet keep his substance whole." The lady's last concern—"If soul may look and body touch, / Which is the more blest?"—is answered with the delightful imagery of the soul's kiss provoking a "contrapuntal serpent hiss" and the caressed thigh causing "labouring heavens sigh."

The songs of lover and chambermaid bring an end to sexual play and look to its aftermath. "The Lover's Song" sees mind, bird, "straining thighs," after finding fulfillment in opposition, all seeking some final rest. Originally intended as prayers before dawn, the chambermaid's two songs focus on the lover "sunk in rest." Seeing that her "ranger," a word that, according to Colin Meir, has the Anglo-Irish connotation of masculine virility and alarm,[35] has become "Weak as a worm," the chambermaid instinctively knows limp worm means that, body satisfied, spirit "has fled / Blind as a worm." While lover's worm shocked and repulsed Dorothy Wellesley, it is a striking final image of body's consummation and the spirit's helplessness in the face of the unknown.

After this sequence of love ballads, Yeats placed five personal lyrics that Unterecker sees as expressions of the tragic joy experienced "by Yeats and his friends."[36] Tempted by rest and quiet, the poet in "An Acre of Grass" realizes neither loose imagination nor mill of the mind "Can make the truth known." Yet even though truth never comes, the poet still seeks "an old man's frenzy" to remake himself into an image of Timon, Lear, or William Blake, "Who beat upon the wall / Till truth obeyed his call." Raging against God to the end, the poet desires "An old man's eagle mind" capable of piercing the clouds and shaking the dead.

"What Then?," described by Yeats as "a melancholy biographical poem,"[37] also expresses the idea that life is a long preparation for something that never comes. While the poem describes the major phases of Yeats's life, his youthful dreams, his years of toil and eventual success in bringing his work to perfection, its refrain, sung by Plato's ghost, taunts the poet by singing repeatedly "What Then?"[38] In "Beautiful Lofty Things," the poet, accepting the idea that he can never know the truth, displays the power of his eagle's mind to embody the truth in an image. He creates Olympian images, "O'Leary's noble head," his defiant father and a visionary Standish O'Grady, a courageous Lady Gregory and a Maud Gonne comparable to Pallas Athene, as his legacy of things "never known again." In "A Crazed Girl" and "To Dorothy Wellesley," Yeats adds two new friends to his list of Olympians. Margot Ruddock qualifies because she had wound herself in her own desperate, self-sustaining music. Also a poet, Dorothy Wellesley is granted Olympian stature because she has the restrained passion of the "sensuous silence of the night" and of the Proud Furies Yeats associates with the spirits of other passion-driven poets, which obviously include himself. The Proud Furies ascending the midnight stair to Lady Wellesley's chamber, then, are a source of inspiration for her poetry as her chamber becomes the trysting-place for poets to share their passion.

With "The Curse of Cromwell," Yeats begins a series of violent political ballads. Taking his rage out on Oliver Cromwell, "the Lenin of his day," Yeats, using the voice of the peasant poet, laments the passing of ladies and swordsmen and savagely attacks those who talk "money's rant" and mount their neighbors to get up in the world. The poet, "allied," as Daniel Hoffman points out, "by birth to the lower orders, by talent a ballad singer, and by station in the service of the vanished aristocracy,"[39] experiences the Yeatsian vision of a great house, "its windows all alight," where "swordsmen and the ladies can still keep company," but he awakes to old ruins and must sing to dogs and horses if he seeks an understanding audience.

Colin Meir sees the two Casement ballads as close "to the street ballad tradition" in their use of a "vigorous public language for what is nothing more than a public theme."[40] "Roger Casement," provoked by Yeats's reading of *The Forged Casement Diaries*, rails against the politicians and other public figures who used the forged diaries to blacken Casement, convicted and eventually executed for high treason,[41] as a degenerate, thereby blocking any chance for a reprieve. The ballad ends with a demand that "amends be made /

To this most gallant gentleman." In "The Ghost of Roger Casement," the poet, continuing his attack on England, sees the restoration of Casement's good name demanded by Casement's ghost "beating on the door."

In "The O'Rahilly," the focus shifts from public controversy to
a public personality in its celebration of one of the most flamboyant
rebels killed in the Easter Rising. Desiring to hear the clock strike
he helped to wind, the O'Rahilly meets his death at the hour of
freedom with the kind of heroic gesture so admired by Yeats:

> They that found him found upon
> The door above his head
> "Here died the O'Rahilly.
> R.I.P." writ in blood.
>
> > (CP, 306)

"Come Gather Round Me, Parnellites" combines public controversy
and public personality by dismissing the scandalous story of Parnell
with a defiant song praising Parnell as a lover of the people and his
lass, arguing that proud, upright Parnell should be celebrated for
both his passions.

The image of a passionate Parnell triggers the lustful ballad,
"The Wild Old Wicked Man," whose speaker chooses nothing
more than to sing a ballad that "can pierce the heart," to forget life's
misery for a while "Upon a woman's breast," and to die a wild and
wandering man rather than "on the straw at home." The four epigrams following "The Wild Old Wicked Man" were originally
published as "Fragments." "The Great Day" and "Parnell" mock
revolution and political change, while "What Was Lost" celebrates
the lost cause. "The Spur" offers Yeats's best known defense for
the lust and rage of his last years:

> You think it horrible that lust and rage
> Should dance attention upon my old age;
> They were not such a plague when I was young;
> What else have I to spur me into song?
>
> > (CP, 309)

"A Drunken Man's Praise of Sobriety" picks up the theme of lust and rage by offering the whirling dance as a cure for the drunkenness of those who insist upon drinking their fill of life. One such personality appears in "The Pilgrim" to declare that, after being drunkard, lecher, and penitent, too, he can challenge any sort of truth or advice about the soul with his careless song. After reckless dance and careless song, Yeats offers another ballad intended, according to Meir, "not to incite or persuade but to reveal the personality, the passion of the individual."[42] "Colonel Martin" is Yeats's version of a popular story that he saw as a reflection of the reckless grace of the Irish countryman. Having discovered, after years abroad, that his wife has become the mistress of a rich man, Colonel Martin is awarded three kegs of gold, but he has his servant throw the gold to the poor. The ballad ends on a note of pathos, however, by revealing that the servant, forgetting to keep any of the gold for himself, spends his last days picking up seaweed on the strand—a fate suggesting that Colonel Martin's gesture was more reckless than gallant.

"A Model for the Laureate" is the kind of poem Yeats claimed he "would have written had I made Laureate, which is perhaps why I was not made Laureate."[43] Written on the occasion of the abdication of Edward VIII, the poem mocks kings who keep their lovers waiting while attending affairs of state. In "The Old Stone Cross," a figure out of Ireland's heroic past mocks politicians, journalists, and actors who are ignorant of "what unearthly stuff / Rounds a mighty scene." Faced with folly and ignorance, yet still haunted by ghostly images, the poet of "The Spirit Medium" is willing to banish the arts from his life and take up "the stupidity" of digging for "root, shoot, blossom or clay" because it makes no demand. What the poet really wants becomes clear in "Those Images." Calling the banished Muses home from Moscow or Rome —the political extremes are obvious—the poet seeks images of "the lion and the virgin, / The harlot and the child"—contraries familiar to Yeats's art, especially in those poems and stories on the annunciation of a new age.

"The Municipal Gallery Revisited," its formality strangely out of place in a collection dominated by ballads of lust and politics, echoes "Those Images" because, as Arra M. Garab observes, its paintings are arranged in antithetical pairs that "create a network of tensions largely responsible for the highly charged tone manifested throughout the poem's wide and frequent oscillations."[44] In the opening stanzas, the poet describes "images of thirty years," an ambush balanced by "pilgrims at the water-side," portraits of "Casement upon trial," "Griffith staring in hysterical pride" counterpointed by Kevin O'Higgins wearing "A gentle, questioning look," and John Lavery's painting of kneeling rebels and abbot or archbishop "Blessing the Tricolour." These paintings of "an Ireland / The poets have imagined, terrible and gay" overwhelm the poet, who sinks down, "Heart-smitten with emotion."

The "heart recovering," the poet, with covered eyes, remembers other paintings in the Municipal Gallery more personal to him, yet also containing images of the heroic spirit in the face of almost certain defeat. Mancini's portrait of Lady Gregory, praised by Synge as a masterpiece, especially haunts the poet, now clearly Yeats, because its art can embody only imperfectly her greatness. Her end and the poet's own approaching death bring a final image, an echo from Yeats's Nobel speech, of Lady Gregory, Synge, and Yeats as the defenders of an art rooted in the soil—the desire in "The Spirit Medium" to "grope with a dirty hand" is now clarified. Recalling his father's portrait of Synge, Yeats, still in the midst of images of Ireland's glory, asks that future generations judge him by his glory that he "had such friends."

The question in the title of "Are You Content?" seems already answered by the assurance of "The Municipal Gallery Revisited," but the poet, faced with death, refuses to rest—"I am not content." Knowing that he has earned the right to spend his last days relaxing with good company or "Smiling at the sea"—a chilling prophecy of Pound's last years—or, like Browning's old hunter, talking with the gods, he tenaciously clings to life and, in spite of glory, defiantly sings "But I am not content."

Last Poems

Bradford has listed the order Yeats intended for his *Last Poems*:

1. Under Ben Bulben
2. Three Songs to the One Burden
3. The Black Tower
4. Cuchulain Comforted
5. Three Marching Songs
6. In Tara's Halls
7. The Statues
8. News for the Delphic Oracle
9. Long-Legged Fly
10. A Bronze Head
11. A Stick of Incense
12. Hound Voice
13. John Kinsella's Lament for Mrs. Mary Moore
14. High Talk
15. The Apparitions
16. A Nativity
17. The Man and the Echo
18. The Circus Animals' Desertion
19. Politics[45]

This proper arrangement of *Last Poems*, while for the most part the same as the order in *Collected Poems*, has some critical differences, including one, the positioning of "Under Ben Bulben" as the first rather than the last poem in the collection, that should come, in Bradford's words, as an "electric shock" to those "who have never encountered the poem anywhere but at the end of *Collected Poems* where it seemed to belong."[46] Excluded from Yeats's final arrangement are "Why Should Not Old Men be Mad?," "The Statesman's Holiday," and "Crazy Jane on the Mountain," all published in *On the Boiler*, but this decision has no effect other than to remove a degree of stridency from *Last Poems*. The major difference between Yeats's arrangement and the order in *Collected Poems* is the appearance in the former of "Under Ben Bulben," "The Black Tower," and "Cuchulain Comforted" at the beginning of the collection rather than at the end.

In its proper position, "Under Ben Bulben" becomes more overture than epitaph because the poems to follow become an extension and elaboration of its summary of Yeats's major themes.[47] Originally called "Creed" and "His Convictions," the poem opens by demand-

ing an oath to be sworn to such mysterious figures as Shelley's
Witch of Atlas and those violent horsemen and women of supernatural beauty who have floated through Yeats's poetry since *The
Wind Among the Reeds*. Oath presumably taken, Yeats reveals
what the sages, "Completeness of their passions won," know about
life and death: that a man lives and dies between the eternities
of race and soul and that he lives many times before reaching his
final rest. Using John Mitchel's " 'Send war in our time, O Lord' "
as his Evening Prayer, the poet declares that conflict drives a man
to knowledge of his work and love and inspires the artist to "fill
the cradles right" and bring mankind to "Profane perfection." After
his stirring advice to future generations of Irish poets to "Sing whatever is well made" and to select images from Ireland's folk and
aristocratic traditions, Yeats writes his own epitaph in language cold
and passionate as the dawn and addressed only to those riding to
life's conflicts:

> Cast a cold eye
> On life, on death,
> Horseman, pass by!

> > (*CP*, 344)

The refrain of "Three Songs to the One Burden" makes it clear
that the poem after "Under Ben Bulben" belongs to the world of
the "fierce horsemen" rather than the grave. It takes up the question
of what can be done to prevent the people and the poets from losing
their indomitable Irishry. Selective breeding—"Throw likely couples
into bed"—is recommended in the first song, splendid isolation,
symbolized by the reclusive life of Henry Middleton, Yeats's cousin,
in the second, and heroic rebellion and sacrifice, epitomized by the
Easter Rising, in the third, though this last, the shedding of "Ireland's blood," must occur in every generation.

"The Black Tower," the last poem written by Yeats, takes up
oath and call to action and combines them into an image of the
earthbound warriors who remain steadfast in their defense of the

tower, presumably a symbol of Ireland's history and culture. While there has been sharp disagreement on the identity of those who bribe or threaten the warriors and whether the cook is honest or deceitful, the poem's focus is on the determination of the warriors, descendants of those buried upright on the mountain, to stand firm in the winds of change and corruption that follow the breakdown of aristocratic order. Determining if those who take the place of the rightful king are Fascist, Communists, or members of the Fianna Fail is as secondary to the poem's meaning as deciding whether the cook hears the great horn or is lying.[48] The important matter in "The Black Tower" is that the warriors, shaken by threats and bribes still stand "on guard oath-bound," even in the face of worsening times, because they know, remaining faithful to their heroic vision, that the prophecy of a new order sings in the same roaring wind of change that shakes "Old bones upon the mountain."

"Cuchulain Comforted," another death poem, turns to Yeats's most famous warrior for an image of heroic completeness. Having faced challenge after challenge, Cuchulain now strides among the dead about to meet that which will complete his heroic vision. While the meaning behind Cuchulain's encounter with the cowardly Shrouds has baffled critics and generated a great deal of debate, Vendler has unwound the mummy truth of "Cuchulain Comforted" by discovering that Cuchulain is entering what in Yeats's *A Vision* is called the Shiftings, where the soul is set free from conflict by living through a life completely opposite to that which it has lived before.[49] In other words, Cuchulain, having lived heroically, now finally encounters what life has hidden from him— a horrible fear of death—and achieves an ecstasy only possible when the soul has such a complete vision of the antinomies of Good and Evil that "even the most horrible tragedy in the end can seem a figure in a dance."[50]

"Three Marching Songs," a revision of "Three Songs to the Same Tune," brings the poet back to the turmoil of Ireland's history and renews the poet's challenge to future generations to sustain the vision of Ireland's heroic dead lest "history turns into rubbish" and heroic acts are degraded into "a trouble of fools." Marching wind subsides in the next poem as the poet creates in the old man of "In Tara's Halls" an image of his own determination not to surrender Choice until the bitter end. He chooses, like the old man who lies down in his coffin and stops his breath, to remain rebellious until he wills his soul's adventure to begin.

"The Statues," the most puzzling poem in the collection, picks up the theme of "Three Marching Songs," but offers a much more elaborate vision of the relationship between art and history. Engelberg claims that "The Statues," telling no less than the story of civilization from Pythagoras to the present, "is Yeats's great parable poem, his final reconciliation between the motion and rest of reality, his vision of a past and his prophecy of a future, and his daring image of art powerful enough to save a civilization."[51] After beginning with the measurements of Pythagoras, so perfect that passion-stricken youth presses "Live lips upon a plummet-measured face," the poems move on to those "Greater than Pythagoras," the Greek artists who "put down / All Asiatic vague immensities" and were actually responsible for the victory at Salamis: "Europe was not born when Greek galleys defeated the Persian hordes at Salamis; but when the Doric studios sent out those broad-backed marble statues against the multiform, vague, expressive Asiatic sea, they gave to the sexual instinct of Europe, its goal, its fixed type."[52]

The difficult third stanza of "The Statues" seems to extend, then reverse the historical flow as an image from Yeats's victorious army of antithetical statues crosses over to the "many-headed" primary, grows round and slow, and creeps finally, like Grimalkin, to "Buddha's emptiness." In the last stanza, the poet turns the wheel once more, and claims that the Easter Rising, like Salamis, marked the moment when the antithetical began its struggle against "this filthy modern tide" and further claims that Irish art, symbolized by the statue of Cuchulain in the Dublin Post Office, inspired the Rising by creating an heroic image for Irish rebels:

> When Pearse summoned Cuchulain to his side
> What stalked through the Post Office? What intellect,
> What calculation, number, measurement, replied?
>
> (CP, 323)

After his complex vision of the gyring movement of history from ancient Greece to modern Ireland, Yeats offers a playful vision of the Immortals. Among the "golden codgers" of "News for the Delphic Oracle" are the mythical lovers, Niamh and Oisin, united once again, Pythagoras, surrounded by his choir of love, and Plotinus, salt-flakes still on his breast from his swim across the generative seas. While the Immortals enjoy the perfect rest that follows passionate or intellectual completeness, the figures of the second stanza are still active. Riding the traditional dolphins to the Land of the Immortals, they still relive their pasts, plunge into the seas, until the dolphins "pitch their burdens off." In the last stanza, the focus now definitely shifts from stasis to motion in the wild vision of nymphs and satyrs copulating in the foam, a scene that Wilson sees as the dance of the soul about to lapse again into generation.[53]

The emphasis upon vision continues in "Long-Legged Fly" with portraits of Caesar, Helen, and Michaelangelo caught in the moment when the "mind moves upon silence" like "a long-legged fly upon the stream." The poem dramatizes the revelatory moment when the heroic or artistic soul communicates with its Daimon, sees a vision or hears a song most opposite to its own nature or experience. Visionary reality persists in "A Bronze Head," but the playfulness ends abruptly in the vision of terror the poet sees behind Lawrence Campbell's bronze painted plaster cast of Maud Gonne's head. Wondering which form, Maud Gonne's youthful body or this mummy image of old age "has shown her substance right," the poet, even with the help of MacTaggart's theory that forms are composite, cannot escape the stare of "bird's round eye," which defies the idea of composite forms and taunts the poet with its secret knowledge and terror of a world not worth saving from its filth and violence.

The terrifying vision of "A Bronze Head" fades into the playful image in "A Stick of Incense" of Saint Joseph liking "the way his finger smelt" even as he marvels at the Christian miracles of Virgin womb and empty tomb. The sense of terror returns, however, in "Hound Voice," but the secret knowledge shared by Yeats's women is eased somewhat by the image of Yeats and his companions—

huntresses perhaps is the better word—united again in some far dawn to take up the hunt and sing once more the "chants of victory amid the encircling hounds." "John Kinsella's Lament for Mrs. Mary Moore" repeats this theme but in a more playful mood as the bold singer of the ballad speaks his complaint against God for taking his "old bawd," yet is sure of being with her again in an Eden he has read about in a book owned by a priest for whom he has nothing but contempt.

"High Talk" follows outrageous ballad as Yeats keeps up the contrapuntal rhythm of *Last Poems*. Claiming that processions lacking "high stilts have nothing that catches the eye" and that women and children "demand Daddy-long-legs," the poet, while admitting his stilts are not as high as his ancestors, calls himself Malachi Stilt-Jack and takes his oath to "stalk on, stalk on" after those things Unterecker describes as "the extravagant stuff that literature is."[54] In "The Apparitions," Yeats offers a more realistic description of himself in old age, sitting up half the night to talk what sounds unintelligible to others. The poet, however, needs all the metaphor he can gather to challenge the fifteen apparitions, "the worst a coat upon a coat-hanger," symbolic of "increasing Night / That opens her mystery and fright."

In "A Nativity," Yeats draws metaphorical help from the artists Delacroix and Landor and the actors Irving and Talma to create a nativity scene that gives him the opportunity to ponder the mystery and fright surrounding the death of one age and the beginning of the next. In "The Man and the Echo," however, Yeats is entirely on his own as he finally enters the night of his own death. Speaking into "a cleft that's christened Alt," the poet hears only the chilling echo of his own dying voice. He asks first whether his verse did any great harm or perhaps failed to do enough to prevent harm, but the only answer is the echo of his own words—"Lie down and die." Rebuking himself, the poet declares his faith in the images of his work as a judgment of his soul, but hears again only the chilling echo of his immediate fate—"Into the night." Finally, asking "Rocky Voice" if "we in that great night rejoice," he hears not an echo but the distracting cry of a rabbit caught by a hawk or owl. While

Vivienne Koch sees the distraction as life imposing itself upon the poet's consciousness,[55] it seems more likely that the moment of the poet's death has come now that all the questions have been asked.

"The Circus Animals' Desertion" supports the idea that the moment has come for the poet to take off the mask of tragic joy and pack away his images. In the poem, Yeats parades for the last time his major themes and images in what Bradford calls "an allegorical procession,"[56] and admits the truth behind Oisin, Cathleen, and Cuchulain, that each figure, though complete because it developed out of "pure mind," was initially created out of the frustrated desires of the poet's heart. All masks removed, what remains is the refuse of the heart:

> A mound of refuse or the sweepings of a street,
> Old kettles, old bottles, and a broken can,
> Old iron, old bones, old rags, that raving slut
> Who keeps the till. Now that my ladder's gone,
> I must lie down where all the ladders start,
> In the foul rag-and-bone shop of the heart.
>
> (CP, 336)

With "Under Ben Bulben" in its proper place, "The Circus Animals' Desertion" gives Yeats the opportunity to draw the curtain on his great career with a grim, yet truthful statement of his life and death. But Yeats refuses to end his last book on a passive note. Instead, he closes with the startling image in "Politics" of the old man still lusting for his youth, still desiring to live it all again. In *Last Poems*, Yeats, after the dance of tragic joy, grimly accepts the reality of death and is willing to descend into the foul rag-and-bone shop of the heart, but he chooses in his last poem to sing of passion and love as if to make sure that his soul, beginning its journey, will be free to join hands with the souls of dead and mythical lovers: "But O that I were young again / And held her in my arms!"

Chapter Seven

The Sages and the Singing-Master: Influences and Contributions

In "Art and Ideas," Yeats wrote that "works of art are always begotten by previous works of art, and every masterpiece becomes the Abraham of a chosen people."[1] He made a similar statement about style in "The Tragic Theatre." To create ideal forms and understandable symbols, the poet had to write in "a style that remembers many masters that it may escape contemporary suggestion."[2] Yeats's comments on the essential influence of singing-masters on the work of the poet argue strongly for a dedication to tradition, to an inherited body of literature. Yeats agreed with T. S. Eliot that the poet "is not likely to know what is to be done unless he lives in what is not merely the present, but the present moment of the past." The reader cannot properly appreciate a poet unless he understands "his relation to the dead poets and artists."[3]

Yeats's own work proves that his comments on poetry and tradition are not merely the expression of an ideal. Variously described as lyric, epic, or dramatic, thereby fitting all the categories of Joyce's early aesthetic theory, Yeats's verse, as Beum has shown, has the "coherence, classically argumentative structure, meter, rhyme, symmetry" of the traditional poet.[4] Yeats, however, while writing with a classical idea of poetry, had his own distinct view of what poets belonged to the Great Tradition. Unlike Eliot and Pound, he had a romantic vision of art and, unlike most modern poets, had a very strong sense of national identity. He also believed, contrary to the views of present day writers, that the poet possessed special power and authority, and after studying the arcane as well as the known wisdom of the past, the master poet could embody in his images the vast, mysterious realities of the universal mind.

The Last Romantic

Many of the great poets of the past found their way into Yeats's writings, and some became models for various personality types in *A Vision*. Dante, Spenser, Shakespeare, Blake, and Shelley were subjects for major essays, and all but Spenser appear in "The Great Wheel." Dante, Spenser, and Shakespeare were especially intriguing subjects for Yeats because he saw them as artists divided between their vision of reality and the demands of their age. He believed that Dante struggled between his vision of God's love, his own passionate nature, and his commitment to "a complex external law, a complex external Church."[5] In Spenser, Yeats found a balanced genius strained by public responsibilities. Spenser's art, most beautifully expressed in the sensuous beauty of his "pictures of happiness," became too consciously allegorical because he felt obliged to write about "a system of life which it was his duty to support . . . so many generations believed that he was the first Poet Laureate, the first salaried moralist among the poets."[6] Yeats discovered his image of Shakespeare in *Richard II*, where the fall of the elegant, contemplative Richard to the rough, expedient Bolinbroke represents Shakespeare's vision of a noble England fading into a vulgar, mechanical age: "The courtly and saintly ideals of the Middle Ages were fading, and the practical ideals of the modern age had begun to threaten the unuseful dome of the sky."[7] In Shakespeare, as in Spenser and Dante, Yeats saw genius divided between visionary art and contemporary politics and believed that the master dramatist succeeded in creating wonderful images of conflict and beauty as his humanity faltered and failed.

Of all the poets sharing in his Great Tradition, Shelley and

Blake emerge as the most significant for Yeats's romantic vision. He placed Blake in the most dynamic phase of *A Vision*. By making Blake the representative of phase sixteen or the Positive Man, Yeats could describe Blake's mythology or symbolism as "the overflowing and bursting of the mind" caught in a poetic frenzy, a mind capable of delighting "in certain glowing or shining images of concentrated force," yet also capable of extreme hatred.[8] He gave Shelley the compliment of placing him, along with Dante and Landor, in phase seventeen, the same phase Yeats had selected for himself. As Daimon personalities, Dante, Shelley, and Yeats represent the poets with the greatest opportunity to achieve Unity of Being. Dante, however, never able to keep out of politics, achieved Unity of Being only in his intellect, which envisioned good and evil, and his image of "the heavenly Beatrice." Shelley, while a great poet, "was not of the greatest kind" like Dante because he lacked a vision of evil and fell into mechanical invention and "vague propagandist emotion" in his longer poems.

In spite of this judgment, Yeats still regarded Shelley as the model poet. Though lapsing from time to time into writing political pamphlets and dreaming of converting the world into his ideal, Shelley had created two masterful and haunting images of poetic solitude: "a young man whose hair has grown white from the burden of his thoughts, an old man in some shell-strewn cave whom it is possible to call, when speaking to the Sultan, 'as inaccessible as God or thou.'"[9] Yeats admired the Shelleyan young man and hermit and, at different phases of his career, created similar poetic personalities in his young lovers yearning for old age and death, his mad hermits, his ancient philosopher Ribh, and Old Rocky Face.

Shelley's influence began when Yeats imagined himself in his early years as the hero of romance, as Shelley's Prince Athanase or the youth of *Alastor*. His interest in Shelley increased when Yeats changed his early image of himself as romantic hero into a vision of himself as heroic poet pursuing a vision of Intellectual Beauty. While Yeats became critical of Shelley as he matured as a poet, his interest in Shelley never faltered. George Bornstein sees Yeats's visit to Field Place, the Shelley family estate, in July, 1938, just six months before his death, as part of a "lifelong fascination" with Shelley: "As a boy he imagined himself a Shelleyan hero; as a young man he imagined himself a Shelleyan poet. With middle age he reacted violently against Shelley and asserted his poetic independence. By the end of his life, as the visit to Field Park shows, Yeats reconciled himself to Shelley with a distinct but by no means unqualified admiration."[10]

Yeats's chief criticism of Shelley, as stated in *A Vision*, was that he had no vision of evil. In other words, the conflict that Yeats saw as essential to great art was entirely lacking in Shelley's poetry. Shelley gave the world in *Prometheus Unbound*, one of Yeats's sacred books, a "mysterious song" of his simple faith in eternal peace and beauty, but, hating life, he could write only of a perfect happiness "veiled in mist, or glimmering upon water."[11] In "The Philosophy of Shelley's Poetry," Yeats wrote that Shelley had only a single "vision of a boat drifting down a broad river between high hills where there were caves and towers and following the light of one Star" and but one hope that by brooding upon his vision he "would lead his soul, distangled from unmeaning circumstance and the ebb and flow of the world, into that far household where the undying gods await all those souls that have become simple as flame, whose bodies have become quiet as an agate lamp."[12]

What Yeats found lacking in Shelley, he discovered in Blake. Like Heraclitus and Boehme before him, Blake believed that contraries were essential to life. In *The Marriage of Heaven and Hell*, he wrote: "Without Contraries is no progression. Attraction and Repulsion, Reason and Energy, Love and Hate, are necessary to Human existence." Yeats also admired Blake's complete faith in the imagination's power to divide "us from mortality by the immortality of beauty" and to link "us to each other by opening the secret doors of all hearts."[13] Blake had learned from Boehme and others that the imagination was "the first emanation of divinity" and concluded, unlike Boehme, "that the imaginative arts were therefore the greatest of Divine revelations."[14] Hazard Adams explains that Blake so completely believed in the divine authority of the imagination that he "visualized a poetic tradition (in his opinion *the true poetic* and prophetic tradition) beginning in biblical revelation and even before in Greek myth, moving to Chaucer, Spenser, Milton, Blake himself, and onward to, shall we say, Yeats or those poets who might be expected to renew the arts on Britain's shores."[15]

Yeats's serious study of Blake began with his collaboration on the three-volume edition of Blake's work published by Quaritch in 1893. Working with Edwin Ellis, Yeats attempted a detailed explanation of Blake's symbolic system or mythology. While the edition had the advantage of publishing for the first time *The Four Zoas*, Yeats and Ellis created a problem by changing certain lines to restore them to what they called the perfect sound and rhythm of the rest of the text. Yeats also tried, in his enthusiasm, to claim an Irish extraction for Blake on some rather questionable evidence. Yet, in spite of editorial indiscretions, the edition stands as a testament to Yeats's early grasp of Blake's symbolic power, his hatred of reason and materialism, and his faith in the universal mind.

Yeats's intense study of Blake, unlike his interest in Shelley, never turned critical during his career. In his essays, he praised Blake for the passionate simplicity and energy of his imagination and claimed that "Blake was the first writer of modern times to preach the indissoluble marriage of all great art with symbol."[16] In *A Vision*, he made Blake the Positive Man or the poetic personality most capable of complete self-absorption and most able to create a permanent art out of life's ceaseless conflict. Yeats believed that only in symbol did the poet of Blake's phase express the frenzy of his imagination. Because of his passion and energy, the Blakean poet created symbols that had the solidity, sharpness, and coherence of an independent reality. In other words, a poet of Blake's imagination did not merely project an ideal world, he created his own reality, concrete, self-sufficient, yet universal enough in meaning to embrace history and prophesy the future. In his last years, Yeats still sought the imaginative frenzy of Blake "Who beat upon the wall / Till Truth obeyed his call."

While Yeats found in Shelley an image of the ideal poet, he saw in Blake what Adams describes as "the heroic personality facing the wheel of history, forced to achieve some psychological balance or perish."[17] Like Blake, Yeats wanted to create his own mythology out of the circular movement of life and history to show the essential unity of body and soul and time and space. Yeats, however, as Adams has shown, had more difficulty escaping "the shell of time" and was more tragic than Blake, who had become, in Yeats's mind, the poet of liberated imaginative power, celebrating life's contraries, forging images out of an imagination so intense that poet's mind and the universal mind became one. Blake had "announced the religion of art" and "deified imaginative freedom."[18] Accepting Blake as the singing-master of his soul, Yeats dedicated himself, in spite of personal failures and the tragedies of his age, to an art that made the act of the imagination its central drama or ritual and celebrated the creations of the imagination as the artifacts of eternity.

An Irish Poet

While Yeats saw himself participating in Blake's poetic tradition, he never forgot that he was born an Irish poet. At an early moment in his career, he declared in "To Ireland in the Coming Times" that his reader should

> Know, that I would accounted be
> True brother of a company
> That sang, to sweeten Ireland's wrong,
> Ballad and story, rann and song....
>
> (CP, 49)

At the end of his life, he bestowed all that he had learned about Blakean contraries and the Great Tradition to a future generation of Irish poets. It was essential that Irish poets learn their trade by listening to singing-masters rather than current pretenders and by singing of

> ... the peasantry, and then
> Hard-riding country gentlemen,
> The holiness of monks, and after
> Porter-drinkers' randy laughter;

Sing the lords and ladies gay
That were beaten into the clay
Through seven heroic centuries. . . .

(CP, 343)

The two passages, written nearly fifty years apart, offer an un-
distorted view of Yeats's early hope for Irish art and his belief,
near the end of his career, that he had held to his youthful vision,
which he now passed on to the new generation. While the first
passage seems political because it mentions "Ireland's wrong," its
meaning has more to do with the word "sweeten." Yeats's early ambition, after coming under O'Leary's influence, was to sweeten, that
is, to improve, Ireland's cultural life. To accomplish this, he argued
for a national literature that avoided the political excesses of Young
Ireland verse. Because of Ireland's wrong, Yeats and his brother
poets had a duty to use Irish themes, but those themes should ele-
vate the people, liberating them from Ireland's real enemies: "ignorance and bigotry and fanaticism, the eternal foes of the human
race which may not be abolished in any way by Acts of Parlia-
ment."[19]

Yeats's strategy for encouraging a literature more visionary and
nationalistic than political was to draw attention to Ireland's heroic
past preserved in its myths and folklore. As Phillip L. Marcus has
demonstrated, Yeats was often openly critical of the Young Ireland-
ers for writing a political literature "of emotion and impulse un-
tempered by art and consequently even when most powerful,
blended with the flaccid and the commonplace."[20] Instead of political doggerel, Yeats wanted a literature expressing the Celtic or folk
genius that "delights in unbounded and immortal things" and
expresses its love with "a passion whose like is not in modern
literature and music and art, except where it has come by some
straight or crooked way out of ancient times."[21]

Urging friends like Katharine Tynan and George Russell to write
in the Celtic manner, Yeats also championed the cause of writers
like Samuel Ferguson, whom Yeats called "the greatest Irish poet,
because in his poems and the legends, they embody more completely

than in any man's writings, the Irish character. Its unflinching devotion to some single aim. Its passion. . . . And this faithfulness to things tragic and bitter, to thoughts that wear one's life out and scatter one's joy, the Celt has above all others."[22] It was this Celtic element that Yeats felt made the Irish poet worthy of a great cause. With the help of Lady Gregory and Standish O'Grady, Yeats gathered folk and legendary materials for his art and elevated them into the heroic ideal embodied in Oisin, Fergus, and especially Cuchulain. He was able to project a vision of Ireland free of political divisiveness even while he became embroiled in public controversies.[23] At the same time, he gave new life to Irish myth by making his own desires and frustrations a part of the lyric fabric of his Irish verse, thereby creating heroes representing Ireland and its poet.

Yeats's interest in the heroic life continued throughout his career, but he saw the dream of Unity of Culture fade away as he became entangled in bitter controversy during the years he pursued Maud Gonne and worked for an Irish National Theatre. As the mask of tragic joy took the place of the ideal of the Castle of Heroes, Yeats shifted his allegiance from the Celtic element to the Anglo-Irish tradition epitomized by Coole Park and Lady Gregory. Rather than dream of fairyland, Yeats turned to Ireland's eighteenth century and, while never losing sight of Cuchulain, found new heroes in Swift, Burke, and Berkeley.[24] Swift's savage defense of intellectual liberty, Burke's belief in the historical and organic growth and continuity of the state, Berkeley's hatred of Lockean materialism and his faith in the human perception of God rather than in God as an abstract idea gave Yeats, along with Goldsmith's delight in concrete realities, a more mature vision of Ireland free from the tyranny of middle-class opinion, popular politics, and religious hypocrisy.

Yeats's two Irelands, the legendary Ireland of his youth and the traditional Ireland of his mature years, never became realities, but did become in Yeats's mind a single image perfectly balanced in content and form. He believed that Irish legend, preserved by the peasantry, was the sourcebook for Irish poets. Torchiana points out that Yeats "continued to the end of his life to hold the folklore

and stories of the Irish peasant as his great literary material."[25] Yet
to avoid exploiting Irish myth for some personal and political end,
the poet had the responsibility for finding the proper form for his
material. Struggling against his own inclination toward dreaming
wisdom, while holding nothing but contempt for propagandists and
journalists, Yeats, in his most bitter years, found in the Anglo-Irish
tradition, most nobly expressed in the eighteenth century, his
images of human excellence. Yeats's final vision of Irish art reflected the traditional values of order, balance, and continuity even
as modern Ireland was distracted by images of violence and madness. In his most optimistic moment, Yeats wrote that poets "were
to forge in Ireland a new sword on our traditional anvil for that
great battle that must in the end re-establish the old, confident joyous world."[26] Yet even in his darkest moment, he could still write
of an Anglo-Irish pride like that "of the hour

> When the swan must fix his eye
> Upon a fading gleam,
> Float out upon a long
> Last reach of glittering stream
> And there sing his last song.

(CP, 196)

The Magus

While Yeats saw himself as a romantic poet by personality and
an Irish poet by trade, his great ambition, at times a dangerous one
for his art, was to reveal a truth in his verse that could transform
the common materials into a radiant, ever-living image, an imaginative act corresponding to the alchemist's feat of changing common
metal into gold. Believing symbols the greatest of powers, he saw
the poet as the only possible successor to the magician. In "Magic,"
Yeats declared his commitment to the philosophy and practice of
magic and his faith in the three ancient doctrines that were the
foundation of magic:

(1) That the borders of our mind are ever shifting, and that many minds can flow into one another, as it were, and create or reveal a single mind, a single energy.

(2) That the borders of our memories are as shifting, and that our memories are a part of one great memory, the memory of Nature herself.

(3) That this great mind and great memory can be evoked by symbols.[27]

Yeats also stated that the imagination of the poet was always "seeking to remake the world" because it was in touch, either consciously or unconsciously, with the patterned impulses of the great memory. He asked if there could be anything so important for his generation of poets than "to cry out that what we call romance, poetry, intellectual beauty, is the only signal that the supreme Enchanter, or some one of His councils, is speaking of what has been, and shall be again, in the consummation of time?"[28]

Yeats's interest in magic began when, as an adolescent, he daydreamed that he was one of the magical heroes of Romance. As a young man, his interest became more serious and advanced through his involvement with the Dublin Hermetic Society, his relationship with Madame Blavatsky and the Theosophical Society, and his membership in the Order of the Golden Dawn. The Hermetic Society provided Yeats with a link between art, religion, and magic. Its members proclaimed that the revelation of the poets was the closest the modern world could come to religious authority and that myth, created out of pure imagination, was literal as well as symbolic truth. Though his relationship with the Theosophical Society was strained, Yeats's conversations with Madame Blavatsky were his first encounter with what Ellmann describes as a "comprehensive cosmology,"[29] especially her professed knowledge of the boundless Eternal Principle, the universal law of conflict and change, and the evolution or reincarnation of the soul through several levels of existence until it achieved a state of permanent balance and rest.

Yeats accepted Madame Blavatsky's revelations as general principles and found support for them in his readings in philosophy and poetry, especially in Blake; but he also wanted to practice what his teachers and master poets had preached. His meeting with Mac-Gregor Mathers and his initiation into the Golden Dawn gave him his first real contact with occult rituals and orders as well as the opportunity to practice the art of magic under formal supervision. George Mills Harper writes that Yeats had advanced in three years to the fifth of ten grades necessary for adeptship, while it took him another nineteen years "to move from the sub-grade Zelator to the sub-grade Theoricus, the link with the invisible degrees." During this time, his chief work was "making and consecrating 'certain magical implement'" and studying subjects ranging from reading symbols to astral projection and the Tarot Deck.[30]

The focal point in Yeats's poetry and prose for his study of magic was Michael Robartes, who first appears in The Wind Among the Reeds and "Rosa Alchemica" as a magus possessing the occult wisdom and authority to start a new religious order.[31] Even though he is killed in "Rosa Alchemica," Robartes represents the side of Yeats that believed that symbol and ritual had the power to transform common reality into some ultimate revelation. In the 1890s, Yeats believed that he was participating in the beginning of a world-wide revolt of the spirit against the material world. The study and practice of magic was at the center of the revolt and the artists of the occult were to be the priests of the new order.

Yeats's desire to get more salt and energy into his verse seems to argue that he set aside his robe and magic wand by the 1900s, but the reappearance of Robartes in the poems for exposition and the introduction to A Vision suggests otherwise. The resurrected Robartes represents a Yeats no less involved in occult study and psychical research, but much more the sage or philosopher in his search for revelation. Walter Kelly Hood sees the early Robartes as "a Rosicrucian wearing Druid robes and speaking like Walter Pater," but the Robartes of A Vision is "an occult teacher concerned with the intricacies of a new system . . . and an aristocratic social commentator."[32]

The later Robartes represents Yeats's development from his early years in the Golden Dawn when he was so captivated by the mystical knowledge and symbol-making power of MacGregor Mathers to the years after his marriage when he could call upon Plato, Plotinus, and Porphyry or Buddhism, Brahminism, and the *Upanishads* or Nietzsche, Hegel, Whitehead, and MacTaggart. Yeats's thoughts in his later years ranged from the Neoplatonic concern with the relationship between the individual soul and the divine Soul to the modern philosophical study of time, space, and reality. He sought out mediums and attended séances, yet debated the philosophies of Bertrand Russell and G. E. Moore. Yeats's unknown writer gave him the key symbol and outline for *A Vision*, but his own study of religious, philosophical, and historical writings gave the book its sense of authority.

The richness of Yeats's thought in *A Vision* and his later poems did not eliminate the danger that he might sacrifice his art to his occult study. He was just as capable of losing himself in his system as he was in preparing symbols for the Castle of Heroes. He became so excited by his wife's automatic writing that he was willing to devote the rest of his life to deciphering her disjointed sentences. Fortunately, when he addressed his desire to his unknown writer the answer was—"we have come to give you metaphors for poetry."[33] The image of the magus with the philosopher's stone could be just as perilous as the sorcerer with his magic wand.[34]

Early in his career, Yeats chose the role of poet and in spite of the frustrations of his time and his own nature, he eventually resisted all distractions, his heroic dreams, his labors for a revival of Irish culture, and even his study of the philosophy and practice of magic, and made his art into a celebration of the imagination and the contraries essential to the creative process. His poetry was filled with the imagery of romantic vision, Irish legend, and magic ritual, but his focal point was the visionary, mythmaking magic of the imagination. The dancer could be a beautiful young girl, an Irish saint or hermit, or a wild and wicked sinner, but the movement of the dance was inseparable from its image: "O body swayed to music, O brightening glance, / How can we know the dancer from the dance?" (CP, 214).

The Modern Poet

Yeats's reputation as a singing-master is rarely challenged today, and there are many teachers, poets, and scholars who believe that Yeats is the greatest lyric poet of the modern age. Yet Yeats found his age an uncomfortable fit and preferred Byzantium to modern London or Dublin. He hated the modern obsession with materialism and viewed the products of the realism and naturalism of the theatre and the novel as nothing more than mechanical reproductions of life. In his introduction to the *Oxford Book of Modern Verse*, he wrote that art "became passive before a mechanized nature . . . when Stendhal described a masterpiece as 'a mirror dawdling down a lane.' "[35] When O'Casey arrived on the Abbey scene with his first realistic drama, Yeats wrote if "Robinson wants to produce it let him do so by all means and be damned to him. My fashion has gone out."[36]

While Yeats admired and supported many of his contemporaries, he saw a decline of passionate imagination in their work. In the first edition of *A Vision*, he placed Pound, Eliot, Joyce, and Pirandello in phase twenty-three because their art was all technical inspiration. Their major works, *The Cantos, The Waste Land, Ulysses,* and *Henry IV*, "eliminate from metaphor the poet's phantasy and substitute a strangeness discovered by historical or contemporary research." They also "break up the logical processes of thought by flooding them with associated ideas or words that seem to drift into the mind by chance."[37] In the *Oxford Book of Modern Verse*, while acknowledging Eliot's great influence upon his generation, Yeats found Eliot's style "grey, cold, dry." Finding great style but little form in Pound's work, he believed that Pound, as much as Eliot, was responsible for "the lack of form and consequent obscurity which is the main defect of Auden, Day Lewis, and their school."[38]

Yeats's reputation as a major modern poet is firmly established, but his qualifications as the central figure in modern poetry are as doubtful as his appreciation of modern art. During a time of great experimentation, he placed himself within the romantic tradition of Blake and Shelley. When many writers were becoming exiles, Yeats declared himself an Irish poet and eventually aligned himself, during a period of violent political change, with the conservative values of the Anglo-Irish tradition. While his contemporaries were expressing the modern anguish, Yeats was deeply involved in psychical research on the passage of the soul between lives. None of his individual poems stands out, in spite of Yeats's greatness, as a testament to the modern temper. Instead of *The Waste Land*, he gave the modern reader "Sailing to Byzantium" and "Byzantium." Unlike Joyce, who admired the cunning hero and created Stephen Dedalus and Ulyssean Leopold Bloom, Yeats chose the courageous hero and turned to warrior Cuchulain for his chief image of the past. Though he admired the great epics of literature, Yeats never tried anything on the scale of Pound's *Cantos* because his talent was as a lyric poet.[39] His authoritarian politics were wrong for the poets of the 1930s and for the emerging Irish nation, and his influence on Irish poets, as judged by John Montague, "has been disastrous" because his famous advice in "Under Ben Bulben" has inspired stereotypes of melancholy and roguishness rather than new images of the indomitable Irishry.[40] Parkinson notes that "when an occasional critic speaks of the modern age as the Age of Yeats, he never sounds convincing."[41]

Yet for all the evidence that Yeats's greatness has little to do with his own age, that it is the result of his lyric gift, his romantic vision of the power of the human imagination, and his respect for traditional values, Yeats is in many ways a representative modern poet, perhaps even more so than Pound and Eliot. His chief claim to modernity, in spite of his protests against much of modern life and literature, is that he participated in practically all of the important literary movements of his time. His genius as a modern poet is evident in his unwillingness to surrender his own vision to any particular movement or literary influence; yet, by the time his career was over, he faced the same public issues and private anguish that characterize the modern age.

In the 1880s and 1890s, Yeats was active in the London literary scene that produced the first modern poetic personalities, the aesthete and the decadent. He was influenced by the Pre-Raphaelite

artists, especially Rossetti, the first English *poete maudit,* and by
Pater, whose advice in *The Renaissance* to live for the poetic passion was painted golden by Wilde. Yeats shared the decadent's disdain for the moral tone of the Victorian poets and the growing
materialism of London society, and was influenced by the decadent's
declaration of the autonomy of the artist and the supremacy of art.
His secret ambition, when a member of the Rhymers' Club, was to
become a better craftsman than poets like Johnson and Dowson.
Yet Yeats could never believe Wilde's epigram that nothing suc-
ceeds like excess. Looking back on the Tragic Generation, Yeats
wrote that he had feasted with poets who "discussed life at its most
intense moment," but he could not share their desire to live the forbidden experiences explored in their art. After Wilde's death,
"everybody got down off his stilts; henceforth nobody drank ab-
sinthe with his black coffee; nobody went mad; nobody committed
suicide; nobody joined the Catholic church; or if they did I have
forgotten."[42]

While Yeats, by his nature, found it impossible to take Wilde's
advice that the only way to get rid of a temptation was to yield to it,
he was suited, by artistic temperament, to the symbolist movement,
which he discovered primarily through Symons. He had no trouble
responding to the symbolist's efforts to spiritualize literature and
he shared the movement's fascination with magic, folklore, and
visionary experience. Symbolist principles exactly corresponded to
his own dream of spiritualizing Irish art and they fed his romantic
vision of the artist, in touch with the great memory, creating a
higher form of reality. What Yeats had to struggle against was the
tendency of the symbolist poet to make his study of the soul so
private that he often lost touch with universal experience as well as
his reader. Just as dangerous as the decadent cultivation of the
personality was the symbolist tendency toward obscurity.

While it is tempting to think that Pound rode to the rescue,
saved Yeats from obscurity by bringing to his poetry the discipline
and concreteness it needed, the themes of Yeats's early poetry and
the development of his career prove otherwise. Yeats was well aware
of the dangers of obscurity, even when he was being his most

mysterious. He had also decided to write a more precise and passionate lyric a few years before meeting Pound, who, as Ellmann points out, saw Yeats's poetry as a "splendid bridge from Mallarmé and the symbolists" to "imagism and vorticism."[43] Yeats's decision to make his verse more physical actually anticipated Pound's imagist goals, which evolved into the most important movement in modern poetry just before and after World War I. Yeats's poetry, however, never became as fragmented and passive as that written by Pound and Eliot. While Prufrock measured out his life in coffee spoons and Pound's stylist took shelter "from the world's welter," Yeats's personae danced and sang to the music of life's tragic joy.

Yeats associated himself with aesthete, decadent, symbolist, and imagist, but the constant in his life and art was Ireland. While his early lyrics may have been too melancholy and his later poetry too authoritarian, he was an active participant and, at times, a moving force in the birth of a modern nation. Early in his career, he fought for a revival of interest in Ireland's heroic past and, in spite of his failure to bring about Unity of Culture, he was the main figure in establishing a national theatre. Later in his career, he became the champion of the fading Anglo-Irish tradition, especially during the time of revolutionary and civil war violence. For Conor Cruise O'Brien, Yeats was far too crafty, far more the Fascist than he should have been for a poet with such an ideal vision of Ireland;[44] but, even at his most cunning and extreme, Yeats could claim, like no other modern poet, especially the poet of the 1930s, that he had given voice to his country's aspirations, had celebrated its martyrs, and had become its most demanding critic in its first decades as a nation. And while doing all this, he did not allow his political poetry to forsake his vision of reality. Spender, who deplored Yeats's interest in a "Mussolini-type Fascism," praised Yeats as the poet who "expressed better than anyone in this century the dilemma of the man of imagination who feels bound through principles, loyalties, beliefs to support a particular kind of political action."[45] Samuel Hynes, summarizing Yeats's influence on the poets of the 1930s, judges Yeats as the first modern poet "to accept contemporary history as a subject and to respond to it *as a poet*; and this strikes me as a far more revolutionary thing to do in poetry than, say, the introduction of urban images and pylons."[46]

Yet Yeats's claim to modernity goes beyond his dramatic expression of the political realities of his age as it also goes beyond his participation in its major literary movements. He is also modern, and this may be his most compelling qualification, because he realized the importance of responsibility and commitment at a time when the world around him was falling apart and recognized the value of faith in an age stricken by the collapse of conventional or traditional beliefs. Out of the flux and uncertainty of modern life, he created a self-sustaining, self-delighting belief in the reality of the imagination and remained faithful to his vision of reality throughout his career. He was willing to take the risk that the creative struggle of the poet, even in the worst of times, was still a vital subject for art, and he explored and celebrated his subject in some of the most beautiful and powerful poems ever written on the relationship between art and life.

Yeats, however, never substituted art for life. While his poetry expressed the creative power of the imagination, it also explored the intellectual despair and emotional anguish of modern life. T. S. Eliot, at best a grudging admirer of Yeats, thought, as did Pound and Auden, that Yeats's philosophical and occult ideas were silly, but in *Little Gidding*, as Ellmann has discovered,[47] Eliot saw Yeats in his last years understanding perfectly the pain and bitterness of those who hope for so much only to discover tragically that as the years mount up life's gifts betray dream and vision again and again:

> Let me disclose the gifts reserved for age
>   To set a crown upon your lifetime's effort.
>   First, the cold friction of expiring sense
> Without enchantment, offering no promise
>   But bitter tastelessness of shadow fruit
>   As body and soul begin to fall asunder.
> Second, the conscious impotence of rage
>   At human folly, and the laceration
>   Of laughter at what ceases to amuse.

> And last, the rending pain of re-enactment
> Of all that you have done, and been; the shame
> Of motives late revealed, and the awareness
> Of things ill done and done to others' harm
> Which once you took for exercise of virtue.
> Then fools' approval stings, and honour stains.
> From wrong to wrong the exasperated spirit
> Proceeds, unless restored by that refining fire
> Where you must move in measure, like a dancer.

Eliot selects exactly the right images, the refining fire and the dancer, for what Yeats discovered as the saving grace of the human mind, the capacity of the imagination to create pure images and patterns out of life's mire and blood even during an age in which corruption and disorder are the vogue. Yeats was not as experimental as the writers who dominated modern literature because he resisted the compulsion to break up the imagery and rhythms of his art to correspond to the fragmentation of his age. His vision celebrated the tragic joy of life, but, for Yeats, tragic always modifies, never shatters or consumes joy.

If Yeats was the last Romantic, it is only because new generations of poets have lost the capacity or the nerve to create a vision of reality. If his influence on Irish poetry has been disastrous, it is only because Irish poets have not discovered the richness and complexity of his vision of Ireland. If his interest in the occult seems silly and embarrassing, it is only because his critics have failed to appreciate his quest for universal realities corresponding to the realities of the human mind. And if it has been difficult to describe the modern literary period as the Age of Yeats, it is mainly because Yeats created and sustained a vision of poetry as a gift of the ages and not a reflection of a single age. As much as any poet of tradition or modern life, he knew that life was tragic, but he also discovered that to have imagination is to be gay. With his gift for the dramatic lyric, Yeats, who claimed he never danced for joy himself, created perfect and irresistible images and rhythms for the modern age and ages to come of the tragic dancer and the joyful dance.

Notes and References

Chapter One

1. *Collected Poems* (New York, 1956), p. 242; hereafter cited as CP.
2. *The Variorum Edition of the Poems of W. B. Yeats*, ed. Peter Allt and Russell K. Alspach (New York, 1957), p. 778; hereafter cited as *VE*.
3. William M. Murphy, *Prodigal Father: The Life of John Butler Yeats* (Ithaca, N.Y.: Cornell University Press, 1978), p. 43.
4. William M. Murphy, "The Ancestry of William Butler Yeats," *Yeats Studies* 1 (1971): 19.
5. By July, 1872, there were six children in the Yeats family. Susan, nicknamed Lily, was born on August 25, 1866; Elizabeth, nicknamed Lolly, on March 11, 1868; Robert on March 27, 1870; John, nicknamed Jack, on August 29, 1871; and Jane on August 29, 1875. Robert, however, died on March 3, 1873, after a cold had developed into croup, and Jane fell ill her first year and died on June 6, 1876.
6. *Autobiographies* (London, 1955), p. 41.
7. Ibid., p. 43.
8. Ibid., p. 62.
9. Ibid., p. 64.
10. Ibid., p. 90.
11. *Uncollected Prose by W. B. Yeats*, ed. by John P. Frayne (New York, 1970), 1: 104.
12. *Memoirs*, ed. by Denis Donoghue (London, 1972), p. 40.
13. Ibid., p. 42.
14. Ibid., p. 64.
15. Ibid., p. 88.
16. *The Letters of W. B. Yeats*, ed. Allan Wade (New York: Macmillan, 1955), p. 288.
17. *Memoirs*, p. 105.
18. Lady Gregory, *Our Irish Theatre* (New York: Capricorn, 1965), pp. 8–9.

19. *W. B. Yeats 1865–1939* (London: Maunsel, 1962), p. 118.

20. *The Letters of W. B. Yeats*, p. 397.

21. See Richard Ellmann, *Yeats: The Man and the Masks* (London, 1979), pp. xxvi–xxvii.

22. *W. B. Yeats: Man and Poet* (London: Routledge, 1949), p. 175. Ellmann identifies the unmarried woman as Mabel Dickinson, but he offers no evidence to support his claim. See *Yeats: The Man and the Masks*, p. xxviii.

23. *The Letters of W. B. Yeats*, p. 614.

24. Ibid., p. 678.

25. *The Senate Speeches of W. B. Yeats*, ed. Donald R. Pearce (Bloomington: Indiana University Press, 1960), p. 99.

26. *The Letters of W. B. Yeats*, p. 737.

27. Ibid., p. 799.

28. Ibid., pp. 811–12.

29. Ibid., pp. 835–36.

30. Ibid., p. 916.

Chapter Two

1. *The Letters of W. B. Yeats*, p. 798.

2. Ibid., p. 798.

3. *Letters to W. B. Yeats*, ed. Richard J. Finneran et al. (New York: Columbia University Press, 1977), 2:551–52.

4. *The Letters of W. B. Yeats*, pp. 33, 104.

5. *W. B. Yeats: A Critical Introduction* (New York, 1965), p. 22; *Yeats* (New York: Barnes & Noble, 1963), p. 17–18; *Yeats: The Man and the Masks*, pp. 52–53.

6. *The Poetry of W. B. Yeats* (New York: Oxford University Press, 1941), p. 62.

7. *The Lonely Tower: Studies in the Poetry of W. B. Yeats* (London: Methuen, 1965), p. 112.

8. *A Reader's Guide to William Butler Yeats* (New York, 1959), p. 50.

9. *Yeats* (New York: Oxford University Press, 1970), p. 87; *Swan and Shadow: Yeats's Dialogue with History* (Chapel Hill: University of North Carolina Press, 1964), pp. 22–28.

10. *The Letters of W. B. Yeats*, p. 88.

11. *Yeats: The Man and the Masks*, p. 51; Daniel Albright, *The*

Myth Against Myth: A Study of Yeats's Imagination in Old Age (London: Oxford University Press, 1972), pp. 94–116; especially David Lynch, *Yeats: The Poetics of the Self* (Chicago: University of Chicago Press, 1979), pp. 92–123.

12. *The Letters of W. B. Yeats*, p. 111.

13. *Letters to the New Island*, ed. Horace Reynolds (Cambridge, Mass., 1934), p. 174; *Essays and Introductions* (New York, 1961), p. 49.

14. *VE*, p. 845.

15. "The Sacred Book of Arts," in *Yeats: A Collection of Critical Essays*, ed. John Unterecker (Englewood Cliffs, N.J.: Prentice-Hall, 1963), pp. 13, 18.

16. *The Identity of Yeats* (New York, 1964), p. 22.

17. Henn sees Yeats's early poetry as emotional and his progress as a poet from the emotional to the intellectual. See *The Lonely Tower*, p. 109.

18. *The Poetic Art of William Butler Yeats* (New York: Unger, 1969), p. 42.

19. *VE*, p. 842.

20. Ibid., p. 846.

21. *Yeats*, p. 106.

22. *A Reader's Guide to William Butler Yeats*, p. 75.

23. Ibid., p. 78.

24. Ibid., p. 82.

25. *W. B. Yeats: Self-Critic: A Study of His Early Verse* (Berkeley, 1951), p. 149.

26. For a detailed discussion of the sources for "The Two Trees" see F. A. C. Wilson, *Yeats's Iconography* (New York: Macmillan, 1960), pp. 247–54.

27. *Autobiographies*, p. 153.

28. Ibid., p. 153.

29. *The Identity of Yeats*, p. 63.

30. *Essays and Introductions*, p. 193.

31. *VE*, p. 800.

32. *Yeats: The Man and the Masks*, p. 159; *W. B. Yeats*, p. 37.

33. *Poetic Knowledge in the Early Yeats: A Study of "The Wind Among the Reeds"* (Charlottesville: University Press of Virginia, 1969), p. 13.

34. David Daiches thinks that the names were intended to help Yeats

more than his reader. See his essay in *The Permanence of Yeats*, ed. James Hall and Martin Steinmann (New York: Collier Books, 1950), p. 134. George Bornstein sees the personae as "three aspects of the imagination" with the emphasis on Aedh as the imagination sacrificing itself to Intellectual Beauty. See *Yeats and Shelley* (Chicago: University of Chicago Press, 1970), p. 58.

35. *VE*, p. 803.

36. *Mythologies* (New York, 1959), p. 285.

37. See the Wilson and Leavis remarks in *The Permanence of Yeats*, pp. 20, 169.

38. *The Permanence of Yeats*, p. 95.

Chapter Three

1. *The Letters of W. B. Yeats*, p. 434.

2. Ibid., pp. 434–35.

3. See, for example, *Yeats: The Man and the Masks*, pp. 162–66.

4. *W. B. Yeats: Self-Critic*, pp. 79–122. Denis Donoghue argues for Nietzsche's influence in *Yeats* (London: Fontana, 1971), pp. 54–69.

5. *Autobiographies*, p. 417.

6. *Collected Plays* (London, 1952), p. 50; hereafter cited as *CPl*.

7. *The Tragic Drama of William Butler Yeats* (New York: Columbia University Press, 1965), p. 30. See also David R. Clark, "Vision and Revision: Yeats's *The Countess Cathleen*," in *The World of W. B. Yeats*, ed. Robin Skelton and Ann Saddlemeyer (Dublin: Dolmen Press, 1965), pp. 158–76.

8. *The Letters of W. B. Yeats*, p. 434.

9. *The Variorum Edition of the Plays of W. B. Yeats*, ed. Russell K. Alspach (New York, 1966), p. 235.

10. Ibid., p. 254.

11. *The Letters of W. B. Yeats*, p. 453.

12. *The Tragic Drama of William Butler Yeats*, pp. 41–80; *W. B. Yeats: Self-Critic*, pp. 59–78.

13. *Yeats the Playwright: A Commentary on Character and Design in the Major Plays* (London: Routledge, 1963), pp. 49–58.

14. See Birgit Bjersby, *The Interpretation of the Cuchulain Legend in the Works of W. B. Yeats* (Upsala: Lundquist, 1950), pp. 76–77, for a discussion of the significant changes made in *On Baile's Strand*.

15. See Yeats's poem "Cuchulain's Fight with the Sea," in *CP*, pp. 33–36.

16. See *Explorations* (New York, 1962), pp. 108, 155.

17. *VE*, p. 814.

18. *A Reader's Guide to William Butler Yeats*, p. 97.

19. *W. B. Yeats: Self-Critic*, p. 96.

20. *Yeats: The Man and the Masks*, p. 152.

21. *VE*, p. 814.

22. *Essays and Introductions*, p. 266.

23. Ibid., p. 271.

24. See quoted manuscript of unpublished lecture given on March 9, 1910, in William Bradford, *Yeats at Work* (Carbondale: Southern Illinois University Press, 1965), p. 42.

25. *Yeats*, pp. 168–69.

26. *The Identity of Yeats*, p. 111.

27. See, for example, Henn's chapter, "The Masks—Self and Anti-Self," in *The Lonely Tower*.

28. *Yeats: Coole Parke & Ballylee* (Baltimore: Johns Hopkins University Press, 1974), p. 58.

29. *Swan and Shadow*, p. 151.

30. " 'The Green Helmet' and 'Responsibilities,' " in *An Honoured Guest: New Essays on W. B. Yeats*, ed. Denis Donoghue and J. R. Mulryne (London: Edward Arnold, 1965), p. 39.

Chapter Four

1. *VE*, p. 818.

2. *Swan and Shadow*, p. 170.

3. *A Reader's Guide to William Butler Yeats*, p. 115.

4. *An Honoured Guest*, p. 41. In the 1914 edition of *Responsibilities*, the narrative poem "The Two Kings" appeared between "The Grey Rock" and "To a Wealthy Man ...," thereby increasing the sense of aristocratic pride and allegiance at the beginning of the book.

5. *The Poetry of W. B. Yeats*, p. 113.

6. *Yeats: The Man and the Masks*, p. 201.

7. *An Honoured Guest*, p. 52.

8. *A Reader's Guide to William Butler Yeats*, p. 129.

9. *The Permanence of Yeats*, pp. 10–14.

10. *An Honoured Guest*, p. 56–60.

11. *Mythologies*, p. 331.

12. *Yeats at Work*, pp. 51–63.

13. *Yeats: Coole Park & Ballylee*, p. 129.

14. *An Honoured Guest*, p. 71.

15. *Yeats: Coole Park & Ballylee*, p. 118–21.

16. *Mythologies*, p. 335.

17. *VE*, p. 821.

18. *A Commentary on the Collected Poems of W. B. Yeats* (Stanford, 1968), p. 214.

19. *Romantic Image* (New York: Vintage, 1964), p. 91.

20. *The Identity of Yeats*, p. 255.

21. Jeffares and A. S. Knowland, *A Commentary on the Collected Plays of W. B. Yeats* (London: Macmillan, 1975), p. 81.

22. *Essays and Introductions*, p. 221. For an extended discussion of the influence of Fenollosa and Pound see Richard Taylor, *The Drama of W. B. Yeats* (New Haven: Yale University Press, 1976), pp. 34–64.

23. *Essays and Introductions*, p. 229. Also see *Yeats: The Man and the Masks*, p. 214.

24. *Yeats's Iconography*, p. 59. See *Yeats at Work*, pp. 174–216, for a study of the manuscripts of *At the Hawk's Well*.

25. Nathan in *The Tragic Drama of William Butler Yeats* sees the play as Cuchulain's "spiritual birth as a tragic hero," p. 173.

26. *Variorum Edition of the Plays*, p. 566.

27. *The Tragic Drama of William Butler Yeats*, p. 228; *Yeats the Playwright*, p. 74.

28. *Yeats's Vision and the Later Plays* (Cambridge: Harvard University Press, 1963), p. 192; *W. B. Yeats and the Theatre of Desolate Reality* (Dublin: Dolmen Press, 1965), p. 56.

29. *Variorum Edition of the Plays*, p. 805.

30. *Masks of Love and Death: Yeats as Dramatist* (Ithaca: Cornell University Press, 1971), p. 161.

31. *The Lonely Tower*, p. 281.

32. *Variorum Edition of the Plays*, p. 714.

33. *The Whole Mystery of Art: Pattern into Poetry in the Work of W. B. Yeats* (London: Routledge, 1960), pp. 50–53.

34. *Variorum Edition of the Plays*, p. 761.

35. See the summary of critical comments in *A Commentary on the Collected Plays of W. B. Yeats*, pp. 143–46.

Chapter Five

1. *VE*, p. 853.
2. *Yeats*, p. 313; *W. B. Yeats*, p. 116.
3. *An Honoured Guest*, p. 73; *A Reader's Guide to William Butler Yeats*, p. 157.
4. *The Lonely Tower*, p. 188.
5. *VE*, p. 822.
6. *The Poetry of W. B. Yeats*, p. 132; *Yeats: The Man and the Masks*, pp. 232–33; *Forces in Modern British Literature* (New York: Vintage, 1956), p. 168; *The Letters of W. B. Yeats*, p. 851.
7. *Between the Lines: Yeats's Poetry in the Making* (London: Oxford University Press, 1963), pp. 17–25.
8. *The Identity of Yeats*, pp. 257–60. See also Unterecker, *A Reader's Guide to William Butler Yeats*, p. 164 and Rajan, *W. B. Yeats*.
9. *Yeats: Coole Park & Ballylee*, pp. 137–40.
10. *A Vision* (London, 1962), pp. 8–9.
11. Ibid., p. 11.
12. *William Butler Yeats: The Poet as a Mythmaker 1865–1939* (East Lansing: Michigan State University Press, 1962), p. 109.
13. *William Butler Yeats: The Poet as a Mythmaker*, p. 110.
14. *A Vision*, p. 73.
15. Ibid., p. 81.
16. Ibid., p. 131.
17. Ibid., p. 136.
18. Ibid., p. 183.
19. Ibid., p. 233.
20. *Romantic Image*, p. 26; *The Poet as a Mythmaker*, p. 147; *Yeats's Vision and the Later Plays*, p. 5.
21. *The Lonely Tower*, p. 192.
22. "The Rising of the Moon: A Study of *A Vision*," in *An Honoured Guest*, p. 13.
23. *An Honoured Guest*, p. 14.
24. *The Letters of W. B. Yeats*, pp. 738, 742.
25. *Yeats: The Man and the Masks*, p. 240.
26. *Yeats: Coole Park & Ballylee*, p. 92–94.
27. "Style and World in *The Tower*," in *An Honoured Guest*, p. 97.
28. *A Vision*, p. 279.
29. "The Byzantium Poems of W. B. Yeats," in *William Butler*

Yeats: The Byzantium Poems, ed. Richard J. Finneran (Columbus, Ohio: Merrill, 1970), pp. 17–27; "Yeats's Byzantium Poems: A Study of Their Development," in *Yeats, A Collection of Critical Essays*, pp. 93–130; *Between the Lines*, pp. 87–136.

30. "Byzantium," in *Yeats: A Collection of Critical Essays*, pp. 131–38; "Yeats's Byzantium and Its Sources," pp. 28–40; *The Whole Mystery of Art*, p. 225.

31. *Autobiographies*, p. 554.

32. *Between the Lines*, p. 101.

33. *The Whole Mystery of Art*, p. 202.

34. *A Reader's Guide to William Butler Yeats*, p. 174.

35. *The Poetry of W. B. Yeats*, pp. 136, 139.

36. *The Lonely Tower*, p. 236.

37. *Yeats: Coole Park & Ballylee*, p. 153.

38. See *Yeats: Coole Park & Ballylee*, for a similar conclusion and for a discussion of different views of Torchiana and Whitaker on "The Tower," pp. 184–200.

39. *Yeats*, p. 356.

40. *A Reader's Guide to William Butler Yeats*, p. 184.

41. *The Identity of Yeats*, pp. 260–63.

42. *VE*, p. 828.

43. *W. B. Yeats*, p. 132; *Yeats*, p. 323.

44. See Unterecker, *A Reader's Guide to William Butler Yeats*, p. 189.

45. For a thorough study of the poem's background and allusions see Torchiana, " 'Among School Children' and the Education of the Irish Spirit," in *In Excited Reverie*, ed. A. Norman Jeffares and Kenneth Cross (London: Macmillan, 1965), pp. 123–50.

46. See Tindall on the golden thigh of Pythagoras, *The Permanence of Yeats*, p. 277.

47. *A Reader's Guide to William Butler Yeats*, p. 192.

48. *Yeats: The Man and the Masks*, pp. xxvi–xxvii.

49. See Finneran and Harper, " 'He loved strange thought': W. B. Yeats and William Thomas Horton," in *Yeats and The Occult*, ed. George Mills Harper (Toronto: Macmillan 1975), pp. 190–203. See also the Horton letters in *The Letters of W. B. Yeats* and *Letters to W. B. Yeats*, vols. 1–2.

50. See Laurence W. Fennelly, "W. B. Yeats and S. L. MacGregor Mathers," in *Yeats and the Occult*, pp. 285–306.

51. *W. B. Yeats: The Later Poetry* (Berkeley: University of California Press, 1964), p. 57.

52. *VE*, p. 831.

53. "On *The Winding Stair*," in *An Honoured Guest*, p. 107.

54. For background materials see Stallworthy, *Between the Lines*, pp. 164–76 and Donald Torchiana, *W. B. Yeats and Georgian Ireland* (Evanston, Ill.: Northwestern University Press, 1966), pp. 323–26.

55. *Between the Lines*, p. 172; *W. B. Yeats and Georgian Ireland*, p. 326.

56. *Yeats: Coole Park & Ballylee*, p. 205.

57. For background materials see Stallworthy, *Between the Lines*, pp. 178–200, Torchiana, *W. B. Yeats and Georgian Ireland*, pp. 326–29, and *Yeats: Coole Park & Ballylee*, pp. 223–44.

58. *A Reader's Guide to William Butler Yeats*, p. 213.

59. Ibid., p. 214.

60. For a discussion of the controversies surrounding the two poems see Finneran's "Introduction" in *William Butler Yeats: The Byzantium Poems*, pp. 3–5.

61. Ibid, p. 7.

62. *The Permanence of Yeats*, p. 82.

63. *The Byzantium Poems*, p. 127.

64. Ibid., p. 8.

65. For background on manuscripts and publication history see Bradford, *Yeats at Work*, pp. 128–34 and Ellmann, *The Identity of Yeats*, p. 268–74.

66. *The Identity of Yeats*, p. 273.

67. For a view that argues for a more Christian Yeats see Virginia Moore, *The Unicorn: William Butler Yeats' Search for Reality* (New York: Macmillan, 1954), pp. 403–6.

68. *The Letters of W. B. Yeats*, p. 814.

69. Ibid., p. 788.

70. See Hone, *W. B. Yeats*, p. 425.

71. *The Letters of W. B. Yeats*, p. 758.

72. *Yeats*, p. 398; *The Lonely Tower*, p. 70; *W. B. Yeats*, p. 149.

73. *W. B. Yeats: The Later Poetry*, p. 215.

74. *The Identity of Yeats*, p. 277.

75. *W. B. Yeats and Tradition* (New York: Macmillan, 1958), p. 214.

76. *A Reader's Guide to William Butler Yeats*, p. 236.

77. *W. B. Yeats and Tradition*, pp. 210–11.

Chapter Six

1. *The Letters of W. B. Yeats*, p. 843.
2. *Variorum Edition of the Plays*, p. 1311.
3. *W. B. Yeats*, p. 153.
4. *The Identity of Yeats*, p. 283.
5. *The Letters of W. B. Yeats*, p. 826.
6. Ibid., p. 828.
7. *A Reader's Guide to William Butler Yeats*, p. 253; *Swan and Shadow*, p. 117; *The Identity of Yeats*, pp. 233–34; *Yeats*, pp. 418–19.
8. *Yeats at Work*, p. 217. For a study of Yeats's theatrical career see Liam Miller, *The Noble Drama of W. B. Yeats* (Dublin: Dolmen Press, 1977).
9. Yeats's version of Sophocles's *King Oedipus* was performed at the Abbey in late 1926. He was also working on a version of Sophocles's *Oedipus at Colonus* which was performed in September, 1927.
10. Vendler, in *Yeats's Vision and the Later Plays*, sees the Greek, Hebrew, and Syrian representing "three dialectical positions," p. 179.
11. In his introduction, Yeats describes this idea as a "myth that was itself a reply to a myth." See *Explorations*, p. 392.
12. For a discussion of the Heraclitean inspiration and the manuscripts see Bradford, *Yeats at Work*, pp. 237–67.
13. *Explorations*, p. 345.
14. *W. B. Yeats and the Theatre of Desolate Reality*, p. 61.
15. *W. B. Yeats and Georgian Ireland*, p. 135.
16. The criticism of the two plays has generally followed the same lines and has reflected the various interests of Yeats in myth, philosophy, history, and art. For a summary, see Jeffares and Knowland, *A Commentary on the Collected Plays of W. B. Yeats*, pp. 246–47.
17. *Variorum Edition of the Plays*, p. 1311.
18. The scene echoes Yeats's early story "The Binding of the Hair" and Wilde's *Salome*. See *Variorum Edition of the Plays*, p. 1311.
19. *The Letters of W. B. Yeats*, p. 845.
20. *W. B. Yeats and Tradition*, pp. 94–136; *The Whole Mystery of Art*, pp. 164–99.
21. *W. B. Yeats and the Theatre of Desolate Reality*, p. 96.
22. *W. B. Yeats and Georgian Ireland*, pp. 357–65.
23. *The Unicorn*, p. 425; *Yeats's Vision and the Later Plays*, p. 198.

24. *The Letters of W. B. Yeats*, p. 913.

25. *Yeats the Playwright*, pp. 111–12.

26. For an extended study of the Cuchulain cycle see Bjersby, *The Interpretation of the Cuchulain Legend*; also see Daniel Hoffman, *Barbarous Knowledge: Myth in the Poetry of Yeats, Graves, and Muir* (New York: Oxford University Press, 1967), pp. 84–125, and Reg Skene, *The Cuchulain Plays of W. B. Yeats* (London: Macmillan, 1974).

27. *Yeats's Vision and the Later Plays*, p. 236; *The Tragic Drama of William Butler Yeats*, p. 261.

28. *The Letters of W. B. Yeats*, p. 917.

29. "Yeats's Last Poems Again," in *The Dolmen Press Yeats Centenary Papers* (Dublin: Dolmen Press, 1968), p. 259.

30. *The Letters of W. B. Yeats*, p. 904.

31. "Yeats's Last Poems Again," p. 259.

32. *The Vast Design: Patterns in W. B. Yeats's Aesthetics* (Toronto: University of Toronto Press, 1964), pp. 170–71. The poem was inspired by a piece of lapis lazuli sent to Yeats by Harry Clifton of an ascetic and his pupil climbing a mountain toward trees and a temple.

33. For Yeats's description of her tragedy see *The Letters of W. B. Yeats*, p. 856.

34. See Stallworthy's discussion of Yeats's correspondence with Dorothy Wellesley and the manuscripts of the poems in *Vision and Revision in Yeats's Last Poems* (London: Oxford University Press, 1969), pp. 80–111.

35. *The Ballads and Songs of W. B. Yeats* (London, 1974), p. 115.

36. *A Reader's Guide to William Butler Yeats*, p. 265.

37. *The Letters of W. B. Yeats*, p. 895.

38. For a discussion of Yeats's use of the refrain see *The Identity of Yeats*, pp. 201–4.

39. *Barbarous Knowledge*, p. 57.

40. *The Ballads and Songs of W. B. Yeats*, p. 118.

41. For background materials see *A Commentary on the Collected Poems of W. B. Yeats*, pp. 465–71.

42. *The Ballads and Songs of W. B. Yeats*, p. 123.

43. *The Letters on Poetry from W. B. Yeats to Dorothy Wellesley* (London: Oxford University Press, 1964), p. 141.

44. *Beyond Byzantium: The Last Phase of Yeats's Career* (DeKalb: Northern Illinois University Press, 1969), p. 74.

45. "Yeats's *Last Poems* Again," pp. 287–88.

46. Ibid., p. 261.

47. For a study of background and manuscripts see Stallworthy, *Vision and Revision in Yeats's Last Poems*, pp. 148–74.

48. For a summary of views see Harris, *Yeats: Coole Park & Bally-lee*, pp. 248–52.

49. *Yeats's Vision and the Later Plays*, p. 249.

50. The passage selected by Vendler is from the first edition of *A Vision*.

51. *The Vast Design*, p. 187.

52. *Explorations*, p. 451.

53. *W. B. Yeats and Tradition*, p. 222.

54. *A Reader's Guide to William Butler Yeats*, p. 285.

55. *W. B. Yeats: The Tragic Phase* (Baltimore: Archon Books, 1951), p. 120.

56. *Yeats at Work*, p. 165.

Chapter Seven

1. *Essays and Introductions*, p. 352.

2. Ibid., p. 243.

3. "Tradition and the Individual Talent," in *The Sacred Wood* (New York: Knopf, 1930), p. 49.

4. *The Poetic Art of William Butler Yeats*, pp. 16–17.

5. *Essays and Introductions*, p. 135. The conflict between Dante's passion and his divine vision is stressed in "Ego Dominus Tuus."

6. *Essays and Introductions*, p. 369. Also see A. G. Stock, "Yeats on Spenser," in *In Excited Reverie*, pp. 93–101.

7. *Essays and Introductions*, p. 106.

8. *A Vision*, p. 138.

9. Ibid., p. 143.

10. *Yeats and Shelley*, p. 3.

11. *Essays and Introductions*, pp. 78, 93.

12. Ibid., p. 95.

13. Ibid., p. 112.

14. Ibid., p. 112.

15. *Blake and Yeats: The Contrary Vision* (Ithaca: Cornell University Press, 1955), p. 20.

16. *Essays and Introductions*, p. 116.

17. *Blake and Yeats: The Contrary Vision*, p. 149.

18. Ibid., p. 296.

19. *Uncollected Prose by W. B. Yeats*, 1:206.

20. *Yeats and the Beginning of the Irish Renaissance* (Ithaca: Cornell University Press, 1970), p. 142.

21. *Essays and Introductions*, p. 180.

22. *Uncollected Prose by W. B. Yeats*, p. 87.

23. For a discussion of the major controversies see Marcus, *Yeats and the Beginning of the Irish Renaissance*, pp. 61–129.

24. There are individual chapters on Swift, Burke, Berkeley, and Goldsmith in Torchiana, *W. B. Yeats and Georgian Ireland*.

25. Ibid., p. 113.

26. *Essays and Introductions*, p. 249.

27. Ibid., p. 28.

28. Ibid., p. 52.

29. *Yeats: The Man and the Masks*, p. 58.

30. "From Zelator to Theoricus: Yeats's Link with the Invisible Degrees," *Yeats Studies* 1 (1971): 83–84.

31. See William O'Donnell, "Yeats as Adept and Artist: *The Speckled Bird, The Secret Rose*, and *The Wind Among the Reeds*," in *Yeats and the Occult*, pp. 55–79.

32. "Michael Robartes: Two Occult Manuscripts," in *Yeats and the Occult*, p. 217.

33. *A Vision*, p. 8.

34. See Michael J. Sidnell, "Mr. Yeats, Michael Robartes, and Their Circle," in *Yeats and the Occult*, pp. 225–54.

35. *The Oxford Book of Modern Verse* (London: Oxford University Press, 1936), p. xxvii.

36. *The Letters of Sean O'Casey 1910–1941*, ed. David Krause (New York, 1975), p. 103.

37. See appendix A in *Blake and Yeats: The Contrary Vision*, p. 297.

38. *The Oxford Book of Modern Verse*, pp. xxi, xxv.

39. Engelberg believes that Yeats's imagination was epic even if he wrote primarily as a lyric poet. See the *Vast Design*, p. 3. Donald A. Stauffer thinks Yeats devoted his art to "universal images of sculptured stillness." See *The Golden Nightingale: Essays on Some Principles of Poetry in the Lyrics of William Butler Yeats* (New York: Hafner, 1949), p. 64.

40. "Under Ben Bulben," *Shenandoah* 16 (Summer 1965): 21–22.

41. *W. B. Yeats: The Later Poetry*, p. 233.

42. *The Oxford Book of Modern Verse*, p. xi.

43. *Eminent Domain: Yeats Among Wilde, Joyce, Pound, Eliot, and Auden* (New York: Oxford University Press, 1967), p. 63.

44. "Passion and Cunning: An Essay on the Politics of W. B. Yeats," in *In Excited Reverie*, pp. 207–78.

45. "The Influence of Yeats on Later English Poets," *Tri-Quarterly* 1 (Winter 1965): 87.

46. "Yeats and the Poets of the Thirties," in *Modern Irish Literature: Essays in Honor of William York Tindall*, ed. Raymond J. Porter and James D. Brophy (New York: Iona College Press, 1972), p. 5.

47. *Eminent Domain*, pp. 94–95.

Selected Bibliography

PRIMARY SOURCES

Autobiographies. London: Macmillan, 1955.

The Collected Plays of W. B. Yeats. London: Macmillan, 1952.

The Collected Poems of W. B. Yeats. New York: Macmillan, 1956.

Essays and Introductions. New York: Macmillan, 1961.

Explorations. Selected by Mrs. W. B. Yeats. New York: Macmillan, 1962.

John Sherman and Dhoya. Edited by Richard J. Finneran. Detroit: Wayne State University Press, 1969.

Letters of W. B. Yeats, edited by Allan Wade. New York: Macmillan, 1954.

Letters to the New Island. Edited by Horace Reynolds. Cambridge: Harvard University Press, 1934.

Memoirs. Transcribed and edited by Denis Donoghue. London: Macmillan, 1972.

Mythologies. New York: Macmillan, 1959.

The Speckled Bird. Annotated and edited by William H. O'Donnell. Toronto: McClelland and Stewart, 1976.

Uncollected Prose by W. B. Yeats, 1886–1896. Edited by John P. Frayne. New York: Columbia University Press, 1970.

Uncollected Prose by W. B. Yeats, 1897–1939. Edited by John P. Frayne and Colton Johnson. New York: Columbia University Press, 1976.

The Variorum Edition of the Plays of W. B. Yeats. Edited by Russell K. Alspach. New York: Macmillan, 1966.

The Variorum Edition of the Poems of W. B. Yeats. Edited by Peter Allt and Russell K. Alspach. New York: Macmillan, 1957.

A Vision. London: Macmillan, 1962.

SECONDARY SOURCES

The bibliography of secondary sources is limited to the works most helpful to the beginning student of Yeats. Many of the more specialized works on Yeats have been quoted in the preceding chapters.

ELLMANN, RICHARD. *The Identity of Yeats*. New York: Oxford University Press, 1964. An excellent study for the beginning student, Ellmann's book traces the development of theme, symbol, style, and verse form in Yeats's work. The appendix contains individual explications of thirty-four poems by Yeats.

————. *Yeats: The Man and the Masks*. With a new preface. London: Oxford University Press, 1979. First published in 1948, Ellmann's critical biography is superior to the biographies of Hone and Jeffares and remains the standard work at least until the publication of the authorized biography of F. S. L. Lyons. Also recommended is William M. Murphy's *Prodigal Father: The Life of John Butler Yeats*. Ithaca, N.Y.: Cornell University Press, 1978.

FINNERAN, RICHARD J. "W. B. Yeats." In *Anglo-Irish Literature: A Review of Research*, edited by Richard J. Finneran. New York: Modern Language Association of America, 1976. Finneran's long and thorough essay is the starting place for the student interested in Yeats's scholarship. This superior review ranges from establishing proper texts to examining basic studies of the poetry and plays.

HENN, T. R. *The Lonely Tower: Studies in the Poetry of W. B. Yeats*. London: Methuen, 1965. Henn's critical study is probably the most widely respected book in Yeats's studies. It has excellent chapters on Yeats's Anglo-Irish background, the poetry and plays, and *A Vision*.

JEFFARES, A. NORMAN. *A Commentary on the Collected Poems of W. B. Yeats*. Stanford: Stanford University Press, 1968. While the commentary sometimes varies in length and value from poem to poem, Jeffares's book is a good starting place for the study of an individual poem by Yeats. Also valuable and more reliable is *A Commentary on the Collected Plays of W. B. Yeats* (1975) by Jeffares and A. S. Knowland.

JOCHUM, K. P. S. *W. B. Yeats: A Classified Bibliography of Criticism*. Urbana: University of Illinois Press, 1978. Jochum's book is the standard secondary bibliography in Yeats studies. For later publications the annual *MLA International Bibliography* and the annual review number of the *Journal of Modern Literature* are valuable. The standard primary bibliography is Allan Wade's *A Bibliography of the Writings of W. B. Yeats* 3rd Ed. Rev. Edited by Russell Alspach (London: Rupert Hart-Davis, 1968).

Letters to W. B. Yeats. 2 vols. Edited by Richard J. Finneran, George Mills Harper, and William M. Murphy. New York: Columbia University Press, 1977. This two-volume collection of letters to Yeats is a valuable companion to *The Letters of W. B. Yeats.* The letters on occult business are especially interesting.

PARKINSON, THOMAS. *W. B. Yeats Self-Critic: A Study of His Early Verse.* Berkeley: University of California Press, 1951. A valuable discussion of the development of Yeats's style with special emphasis on Yeats's revision of his verse and the influence of his Abbey experiences. The manuscript studies by Bradford and Stallworthy are valuable companions. See also Parkinson's *W. B. Yeats: The Later Poetry* (1964), an outstanding book on the later verse.

RAJAN, BALACHANDRA. *W. B. Yeats: A Critical Introduction.* London: Hutchinson, 1965. Rajan's book is a solid introductory study that discusses Yeats's prose and letters as well as the poetry and plays. Rajan's comments on Yeats's poetic ideas are sensible and incisive.

UNTERECKER, JOHN. *A Reader's Guide to William Butler Yeats.* New York: Noonday Press, 1959. Unterecker's book has the advantage of discussing Yeats's poems in relation to each other and their arrangement into books. His critical views are moderate and perceptive, but his discussion of *Last Poems* should be supplemented by Bradford's "Yeats's *Last Poems* Again" in *The Dolmen Press Yeats Centenary Papers* (Dublin: Dolmen Press, 1968).

Index

222

821.912
Y 41

114 257